PITT SERIES IN POLICY
AND INSTITUTIONAL STUDIES

The Budget-Maximizing Bureaucrat

Appraisals and Evidence

André Blais and Stéphane Dion, Editors

UNIVERSITY OF PITTSBURGH PRESS

Published by the University of Pittsburgh Press,
Pittsburgh, Pa., 15260
Copyright © 1991, University of Pittsburgh Press

Library of Congress Cataloging-in-Publication Data

The Budget-Maximizing Bureaucrat / André Blais and Stéphane Dion,
    editors
        p.   cm. —(Pitt series in policy and institutional studies)
    Includes bibliographical references.
    ISBN 0-8229-3679-8
    1. Bureaucracy.   2. Representative government and
    representation.
    3. Expenditures, Public.   4. Niskanen, William A., 1933–
    Bureaucracy and representative government.   I. Blais, André.
    II. Dion, Stéphane.   III. Series
    JF1501.B78   1991
    350′.001—dc20   90-29888
                                                              CIP

A CIP catalogue record for this book is available from
the British Library.

Contents

Acknowledgments

The book is the outcome of a conference held in Montreal, 14–15 April 1989. First drafts of the chapters were presented and discussed at the conference. The authors substantially revised their chapters in the subsequent months, so that the final versions benefited from the many comments and suggestions made at the conference, as well as from those of an anonymous referee.

The conference and the book would not have been possible without the collaboration of many persons and institutions. The conference was organized by the Département de science politique and the Centre de recherche et développement en économique, at the Université de Montréal. It was funded by the Social Sciences and Humanities Research Council of Canada and the Faculté des arts et des sciences at the Université de Montréal. We wish to thank all these institutions for their enthusiastic support. We also want to thank our authors for their patience in responding to (some of) our innumerable questions, comments, suggestions, and objections and the University of Pittsburgh Press referee for a conscientious review.

—André Blais, Stéphane Dion
10 August 1990

THE BUDGET-MAXIMIZING BUREAUCRAT

ANDRÉ BLAIS AND
STÉPHANE DION

Introduction

This book deals with one of the most provocative and debated
models of bureaucratic behavior. The central hypothesis to be examined is that bureaucrats attempt to maximize their budgets,
because it is in their interest to do so, and that the strategies they
adopt contribute substantially to the overall growth of the state.
The basic idea has been developed most systematically by William
Niskanen in *Bureaucracy and Representative Government* (1971).

    There is no doubt about the importance of the model in general
and of Niskanen's book in particular. In his review, Mitchell (1974)
claims that "it is the most significant work yet produced by an
economist on the role of bureaucracy," and that it should "attain
the status of a classic in the study of bureaucracy" (1775). Miller
(1977) describes it as the most rigorous extensive theory of bureaucratic behavior, and Wade (1979) considers the model to be "the
most serious and elaborated on both the positive and normative
planes. . . . A most stimulating attempt to explain expansions of
the scope of government in democratic societies" (346). Mueller's
(1989) survey of the public choice model presents the book as "the
first systematic effort to study bureaucracies within a public choice
framework" (251). McLean (1987) notes that it is "the most comprehensive . . . model of the supply of bureau goods and services"
(86). Finally, Bendor (1988) acknowledges that it "was the forerun-
ner of numerous formal models and that even today it is probably
the single most cited study" (354).

3

Niskanen's impact is in no way limited to academia. The central ideas of the model have been widely disseminated among intellectual and political circles, especially conservative ones. As a consequence, *Bureaucracy and Representative Government* has largely contributed to the belief in bureaucratic inefficiency. A testimony of that impact is the reception the author and his model got from conservative governments in the United States and Britain. Once elected, the Thatcher government assigned one of Niskanen's works (*Bureaucracy: Servant or Master? Lesson from America* 1973) as required reading for civil servants (Goodin 1982, 23). As for President Reagan, he appointed Niskanen to his Council of Economic Advisers.

The book is a typical product of an economist, replete with graphs and equations incomprehensible to the lay public as well as to the majority of public administration analysts. Yet the basic assumptions that underlie the whole argument are simple (some would say simplistic) and straightforward. According to Niskanen, the three crucial elements of a theory of supply by bureaus are their own characteristics, their relationship with the environment, and the bureaucrat's maximand—that is, what he or she attempts to maximize.

A *bureau* is defined as a nonprofit organization financed by an appropriation or grant from a sponsor. The word *bureaucrat* has two meanings: in a general sense, it includes all full-time employees of a bureau, but for the most part it refers to senior officials of a bureau, with a separate identifiable budget. The bureau's environment is dominated by its relationship with its sponsor. The bureaucrat's maximand is the total budget of the bureau. As a consequence, bureaus supply a larger-than-optimal output.

The first basic assumption of the model is therefore that bureaucrats *attempt to* maximize their budgets. They do so, the model argues, because the higher the budget, the better off the bureaucrats are—or, to use the traditional economic jargon, the higher their utility. Niskanen lists a number of variables that enter the bureaucrat's utility function (interest): salary, perquisites, reputation, power, patronage, output, ease of making changes, and ease of managing the bureau. He contends that all these variables except the last two are a positive monotonic function of the total budget.

Bureaucrats also maximize their budgets in order to survive. Niskanen asserts that the tenure of senior bureaucrats depends critically on the behavior of their employees. The latter may choose to be more or less cooperative and efficient and, as a consequence, the bureau may perform more or less efficiently. Since that performance affects the senior bureaucrat's tenure, he or she tries to obtain the employees' collaboration. In return for that collaboration, the bureaucrat will defend their interests. As their interest also lies in a larger budget, which increases opportunities for promotion and enhances job security, the senior bureaucrat has further incentive to request a larger budget.

2 - The second assumption is that bureaucrats largely *succeed* in maximizing their budgets. This is tantamount to saying that, in relationship to their sponsors, bureaucrats are most powerful. Why is it so? According to Niskanen, the relationship between the bureau and the sponsor is one of a bilateral monopoly, in which the bureau offers an output in exchange for a budget. As such, this type of situation produces indeterminate outcomes. He argues, however, that "the relative incentives and available information, under most conditions, give the bureau the overwhelming dominant monopoly power" (1971, 30).

The reasons for this asymmetry are twofold. First, the sponsor lacks the incentive to use its potential power. Since it is not profit seeking, its officers cannot "appropriate as personal income part of the difference between the budget they would be willing to grant and the budget they in fact do grant to the bureau" (ibid., 29). Politicians, for their part, are mainly concerned with their reelection, which is "only weakly related to the total net benefits generated by the organization" (ibid.). Second, even if and when it has the incentive, the sponsor is handicapped by a lack of information. Bureaucrats know much more about the production processes than sponsors, and it is thus easier for them to exploit the situation as monopoly suppliers than it is for sponsors to exploit it as monopoly buyers.

The idea that bureaus strive to grow is not new. It has been part of folk wisdom and has found its most cynical expression in the famous *Parkinson's Law and Other Studies in Administration* (1962). Such mistrust of state bureaucracy is not confined to the political right. Marx (1970) himself denounces the chase for high positions and pictures the bureaucracy in extremely negative terms. In fact, Niskanen manages to give scientific credentials to an old and widespread view. Even the idea of a budget-maximizing bureaucracy can be found in Tullock (1965) and Downs (1967). In both cases, however, the hypothesis was but one among many propositions on bureaucratic behavior. Niskanen's contribution has been to center his whole analysis around one single thesis, the budget-maximizing bureaucrat.

A few years after the publication of *Bureaucracy and Representative Government,* Migué and Bélanger (1974) proposed an amendment to the Niskanen model. They argue that bureaucrats are foremost concerned with managerial discretion and that it is the discretionary budget, which they define as the excess of revenues over minimum cost, that is being maximized. Their model departs from Niskanen's in predicting inefficiency rather than overproduction. Niskanen (1975) later conceded that the utility of a bureaucrat could be a function of both the discretionary budget and output. Migué and Bélanger point out, however, that discretionary resources depend on a large budget (ibid., 46). Consequently, the revised model also assumes that it is in the bureaucrat's interest to get a larger budget. The major propositions of the model that concern us in this book, that is, that bureaucrats attempt to and succeed in obtaining larger budgets, are therefore left intact.

The budget-maximizing bureaucrat model can be interpreted in two different ways. On the one hand, there is a formal model, with strong assumptions. Budgets are the sole component in the bureaucrats' utility function; consequently budget maximization is the only objective being pursued and all bureaucratic strategies are geared toward that specific goal. Bureaucrats are faced with a complete passive sponsor, who is left with a choice between bureaucrats' budget-output combination and zero budget and output. On the other hand, there is the informal model, with weaker assumptions. Bureaucrats are presumed to want larger budgets, not necessarily to attempt to maximize them. Bureaucratic strategies are mainly, but not exclusively, targeted at budgetary increases. Finally, in their dealings with sponsors, bureaucrats have only a relative advantage, based on asymmetric information.

The two models can be found in Niskanen's *Bureaucracy and Representative Government*. In this book, we focus primarily on the informal model, with its more nuanced assumptions. It is this informal model that inspires most of the discussion in Niskanen's book as well the debate in the literature. For instance, Niskanen acknowledges that "for some bureaucrats, for some time, budget maximization may not be a property of rational behavior (that is, consistent with the maximization of their utility)" (1971, 41). He also notes that it is not always but "under most conditions" that the bureau enjoys an "overwhelmingly dominant power" in its relationship with the sponsor (ibid., 30). Likewise, he explicitly states: "Bureaus do not, in fact, present their sponsors with an all-or-nothing choice. But the offer of a total output for a budget, *under many conditions,* gives them the same type of bargaining power." (ibid., 25, our italics). We are therefore concerned with the central ideas contained in the budget-maximizing bureaucrat model rather than with its formal aspects.

Even putting aside its most formal aspects, the budget-maximizing bureaucrat remains a theoretical construction. The model is useful only to the extent that it aptly describes and explains reality. In *Bureaucracy and Representative Government,* Niskanen acknowledges that he "does not present the set of critical tests that are ultimately necessary to confirm . . . this theory. This theory is developed primarily to interest others in taking it seriously enough to participate in the complex process of making the critical tests" (1971, 8). A number of empirical studies have tested specific predictions of the model. Twenty years after the publication of the book, it is appropriate, we believe, to review the evidence and to offer an overall assessment of the empirical validity of the model.

The model has spurred a lively debate. Much of that debate has been theoretical and polarized. The typical reactions have been either to take for granted the assumptions of the model and to derive additional propositions, or to reject it out-of-hand as a simplistic and ideologically biased caricature of bureaucratic behavior. Our approach is different. Here is an important theory that has some intuitive appeal. The theory should be taken seriously.

Let us examine the empirical evidence and determine to what

extent that evidence tends to confirm or discredit the model. It should be stressed at the outset that the model does not have to be accepted or rejected as a whole. Some of the propositions may be valid and others may be dubious or clearly wrong. This is why it is important to consider separately the two central assertions of the model; that bureaucrats *attempt to* and *succeed in* maximizing their budgets. The two assertions are of course related to each other. If the first is wrong, clearly the second cannot be right. The reverse, however, does not hold. It is quite possible that bureaucrats attempt to, but do not succeed in, maximizing their budgets. Likewise, the model may explain the behavior of certain types of bureaucrats, but not of others, and apply in certain contexts, but not in others.

The objective of the book is straightforward: to assess the empirical evidence on whether bureaucrats attempt to and succeed in maximizing their budget. The evidence to be considered is extremely varied. Because the model is couched in general terms, it applies to many diverse domains. As the book amply demonstrates, many intriguing hypotheses can be deduced from the theory, and there are many different ways to test some of its implications. Indeed the whole book is predicated on the belief that no particular test of the theory is decisive by and of itself and that it is wise to examine a wide array of findings, based on different methodologies and approaches (qualitative and quantitative), in order to offer a fair assessment of the model's merits and limits.

We look at all kinds of evidence that are directly or indirectly relevant to the argumentation of the budget-maximizing bureaucrat model. There are data and observations about bureaucrats' and sponsors' behavior, motivations, and strategies, as well as the outcomes of these strategies. We reject the position (Friedman 1957) that one should never test assumptions directly, only their implications, that is, the predictions that can be deduced from the assumptions. While we acknowledge that in many cases it is impossible to test the assumptions and that the only approach in such situations is to examine the implications, we cannot see any reason not to test the assumption directly, whenever possible; it is (trivially) true that one implication of an assumption is the assumption itself (if A, then A). And a case can be made that the more direct the test, the more powerful it is (for a similar argument, see Tsebelis 1990, 32).

We have selected ten specific topics directly related to the budget-maximizing bureaucrat model. For each topic, we asked a scholar to write a review of a given portion of the literature; some authors were also able to present new data and to conduct additional tests of the theory. In each case, the objective is to determine, from the particular perspective reviewed, whether the available evidence tends to confirm or discredit the model and, if appropriate, to suggest alternative explanations of bureaucratic behavior.

The book appropriately starts with a reflection by William Niskanen, the author of *Bureaucracy and Representative Government*. We asked him to tell us how much of his model has survived the test of his own reassessment. The answer is clear: he maintains the basic outlines of the theory but modifies the maximand, which is the discretionary rather than the total budget.

The model's most central assumption is that bureaucrats benefit from increased budgets. Consequently, the first review essay, by Robert Young, examines the link between budget size and growth and the bureaucrat's career. The question he deals with is simple but crucial: does the evidence support the proposition that bureaucrats obtain higher salary increases and faster promotions when they are in bureaus that are growing faster than normal? If there was no such link, it would not make much sense for bureaucrats to attempt to maximize their budget.

We then move from interests to strategies. The question is whether the different strategies adopted by bureaucrats are consistent with the budget-maximizing model. Laurence Lynn looks at the qualitative evidence conveyed in case studies in order to determine to what extent bureaucrats do indeed seek to maximize their budgets. Likewise, Colin Campbell and Donald Naulls ascertain the amount of budget-maximization orientation that emerged from in-depth interviews of senior officials in central agencies in the United States, Britain, and Canada.

Even if bureaucrats do press for larger budgets, there is no guarantee they actually obtain them. Three chapters evaluate the power of bureaucrats in the budgetary game. Peter Aucoin looks at the budgetary process and, more specifically, at budget restraint

procedures established by politicians seeking to control bureaucrats suspected of attempting to maximize their budget. The mere
existence of these new control procedures indicates that politicians
believe that the first basic assumption of the model is valid. If
bureaucrats are as powerful as the second assumption of the model
asserts, however, these efforts at control are bound to fail. Aucoin
reviews the literature on restraint budgeting and evaluates the relative efficacy of the various mechanisms put in place.

— The two chapters by Roderick Kiewiet and Andrew Dunsire are
concerned with the actual impact of bureaucrats on budgetary
outcomes. Kiewiet reviews the quantitative literature on the oversupply, inefficiency, and oversight hypotheses, as well as on other
implications of the model. Dunsire examines the special case of
conservative governments committed to reducing the role of the
state. He evaluates, on the basis of empirical evidence on public
expenditure, employment, and wages in the United Kingdom in
the decade 1975–1985, the applicability of the Niskanen model in
explaining policy outcomes.

— We thereafter broaden the perspective and consider whether public sector employees differ from their private sector counterparts in
their political behavior and attitudes. André Blais, Donald Blake,
and Stéphane Dion examine the voting behavior of bureaucrats in
eleven countries and ascertain its consistency with a budget-
maximizing strategy. If bureaucrats have an interest in larger budgets for their bureaus, it is also in their interest, as bureaucrats, to
deal with politicians who are positively disposed toward the
growth of public expenditure; at the polls, public sector employees
should support those candidates and parties standing for greater
state intervention. Likewise, to the extent that bureaucrats benefit
from larger budgets, they should be more favorable to state intervention in general. Donald Blake examines the hypothesis that
bureaucrats are more leftist in their political orientation.

— In the model, the bureaucrat is an individual actor pursuing his
or her own individual interest. Bureaucrats are also members of
organizations committed to defend their interests as a group. Public sector unions are the most important of these organizations.
Jean-Michel Cousineau and Anne-Marie Girard review the econometric evidence on the public sector unions' impact on wages,

fringe benefits, employment, and total public expenditures and determine to what extent the findings are consistent with the Niskanen model.

The last chapter, by Guy Peters, adopts a broad perspective and analyzes the evolution of public expenditure, employment, and wages in Western Europe and discusses the potential link between the changes that have taken place and bureaucratic interests; have these changes benefited senior civil servants, and can they be interpreted as the capacity of the bureaucracy to exert political power?

As we noted at the outset, none of these chapters, by itself, allows one to reach definitive conclusions on the merits and limits of the budget-maximizing model. Yet every chapter presents, reviews, and discusses pieces of evidence that throw some light on the validity of the model. We firmly believe that a fair assessment of the model must take into account empirical findings stemming from many diverse perspectives and approaches. We hope that the book will contribute to a more complete knowledge of the numerous but scattered empirical observations of social scientists of various disciplines, which directly or indirectly tend to confirm or discredit the Niskanen model. In the conclusion, we highlight what we take to be the major findings, both in support and in opposition to the model.

REFERENCES

Bendor, Jonathan. 1988. Review article: Formal models of bureaucracy. *British Journal of Political Science* 18:353–95.

Downs, Anthony. 1967. *Inside bureaucracy.* Boston: Little, Brown.

Friedman, Milton. 1957. *Essays in positive economics.* Chicago: Univ. of Chicago Press.

Goodin, Robert E. 1982. Rational politicians and rational bureaucrats in Washington and Whitehall. *Public Administration* 60(1):23–42.

McLean, Iain. 1987. *Public choice: An Introduction.* Oxford: Basil Blackwell.

Marx, Karl. 1970. *Critique of Hegel's philosophy of rights.* Cambridge: Cambridge Univ. Press.

Migué, Jean-Luc, and Gérard Bélanger, 1974. Towards a general theory of managerial discretion. *Public Choice* 17(1):24–43.

Miller, Gary. 1977. Bureaucratic compliance as a game on the unit square. *Public Choice* 29(1):37–51.

Mitchell, William C. 1974. Book review. *American Political Science Review* 68(4):1775–77.

Mueller, D. C. 1989. *Public choice II.* Cambridge: Cambridge Univ. Press.

Niskanen, William A. 1971. *Bureaucracy and representative government.* Chicago: Aldine Atherton.

———. 1973. *Bureaucracy: Servant or master? Lesson from America.* London: Institute of Economic Affairs.

———. 1975. Bureaucrats and politicians. *Journal of Law and Economics* 18(3):617–44.

Parkinson, C. Northcote. 1962. *Parkinson's law and other studies in administration.* Boston: Houghton Mifflin.

Tsebelis, George. 1990. *Nested games: Rational choice in comparative politics.* Berkeley: Univ. of California Press.

Tullock, Gordon. 1965. *The politics of bureaucracy.* Washington, D.C.: Public Affairs Press.

Wade, L. L. 1979. Public administration, public choice and the pathos of reform. *Review of Politics* 41(3):344–74.

1

WILLIAM A. NISKANEN

A Reflection on *Bureaucracy and Representative Government*

Twenty years ago, when I completed *Bureaucracy and Representative Government* (1971), I sensed that I had something important to say. At that time, however, I could not have imagined that this book would be the spring for a growing, if somewhat meandering, stream of political economy literature, much of which I have not read and some of which I have not been aware. I have been honored by the many bright younger scholars who have criticized, developed, and now tested my theory of the behavior of bureaus. And the conference at which the chapters in this book were first presented provided a rare opportunity for me to meet those whose names I have known and those who have made the most recent contributions to this literature. I also want to use this occasion to acknowledge how much I have learned from the many contributors to this literature, especially those who have been most critical of my own approach to this topic.

This chapter summarizes my reflections on the theory of the behavior of bureaus. How much of this theory has survived the test of my own reflections? What would I change? In other words, what would be my general approach if I were to write a new book on this topic?

These reflections, as were the perspectives in my book, are strongly influenced by the combination of my professional experience and the contributions of others. At the time I wrote the book, I had worked for a dozen years as a defense analyst, within the

13

Editor of Regulation magazine

office of the secretary of Defense and in two leading defense research organizations. I was also intrigued to learn that the only prior economic analyses of bureaucracy had also been written by "outsiders." Neither Ludwig von Mises nor Anthony Downs, for example, ever had a tenured university appointment, and Gordon Tullock, who was trained as a lawyer, based his book on his experience in the U.S. Foreign Service.[1] The academic economic community, in brief, had never addressed the behavior of bureaus.

Since completing my book, both my own professional experience and the contributions of others to this topic have been much broader. My own subsequent experience includes two White House positions, two academic appointments, my current position as chairman of a policy institute, and—most important in terms of my reflections on this topic—a position as an executive in a very large private firm. The most recent work on the behavior of bureaus has now been embedded in the academy, with both the strengths and biases that this implies. My own subsequent experience and the contributions of others have both reenforced some parts of my earlier perspective on the behavior of bureaus and led me to change my perspective in some important ways. This chapter, thus provides a twentieth-anniversary summary of my reflections on the theory of the behavior of bureaus, and I owe a debt to those who invited me to write this chapter for inducing me to organize these reflections.

The Core Elements of a Theory of the Behavior of Bureaus

The central insight of conventional economics is that the provision of private goods and services is an *incidental* effect of the incentives and constraints of consumers, entrepreneurs, and employees. In other words, the provision of private goods and services is an effect, but is not the direct purpose, of any participant in the private economy. Similarly, the central insight of the literature that is now described as public choice is that the provision of government services is an incidental effect of the incentives and constraints of voters, politicians, and bureaucrats. Although this perspective on government services is now more broadly shared, one should recognize how radical this perspective was first perceived and, among some groups, is still perceived.[2]

Any theory of the behavior of bureaus must be based on the relationship between bureaucrats and politicians. My own incentive to explore this was based on a recognition that there is a significant "agency problem" in this relationship; in other words, the incentives of bureaucrats do not lead to behavior that is fully consistent with the interests of politicians. My judgment is that there is a much more substantial agency problem between politicians and voters, but that must be another story for another day. Such agency problems, of course, are not unique to the public sector. My own experience in a very large private firm led me to conclude that there is also a significant agency problem between private managers and shareholders. In a private economy with extensive property rights and competitive firms, however, the interests of both consumers and employees are quite well served.

The first insight that led to my theory of the behavior of bureaus was the observation that some of my best friends are government officials. As are most of my other friends, these officials are characteristically intelligent, industrious, and genuinely committed to their organization. They do not, however, fit the polar stereotypes of government officials. They are neither the selfless mandarins portrayed by the public administration literature from Confucius to Woodrow Wilson, nor are they the dumb, lazy, or corrupt bureaucrats portrayed by populist fiction and editorial cartoons. Most government officials, from my experience, seem much like their counterparts in business and the professions. And I was also disturbed to recognize that some of the major policy failures of our time were due to "the best and the brightest" of these officials.

This observation was the seed that led me to question the prevailing theories that explain the behavior of bureaus in terms of the presumed distinctive attributes of bureaucrats and then to develop a theory based on their distinctive incentives and constraints. My reflections, based on my own subsequent experience and the contribution of other scholars, have led me to modify my perspective in some detail, but my basic approach to the study of bureaucracy has survived this reflection.

The seven core elements of my theory of the behavior of bureaus that have survived this reflection are summarized below.

(1.) The first element of this theory, thus, is that bureaucrats are much like officials in other organizations. Their behavior will differ, not because of different personal characteristics, but because of the incentives and constraints that are specific to bureaus.

A footnote: this assumption does not deny that bureaucrats may have different characteristics, nor would the theory be refuted by observed differences in these characteristics. People will choose to work in organizations in which the rewards are most consistent with their own preferences. In effect, people "choose their own pond," and different ponds will attract people with different preferences and characteristics (Frank 1985). The conventional theory explained the behavior of bureaus in terms of the distinctive characteristic of bureaucrats, but this confused cause and effect. My theory is consistent with the observation that those who choose to work in the distinctive environment of a bureau may have distinctive personal characteristics. An assumption that bureaucrats have different characteristics, thus, may be correct but is redundant. It is crucial, however, to recognize that bureaus are very different from private firms, most importantly in those characteristics summarized in the following paragraphs.

(2.) Most bureaus face a monopoly buyer of their service, usually some group of political officials. The effective demand for the output of a bureau is that of this political sponsor, rather than that of the ultimate consumers of this service.

(3.) Most bureaus are monopoly suppliers of their service. More specifically, most bureaus face a downward-sloping effective demand function, even if there are alternative actual or potential suppliers of the same or a similar service.

(4.) The bilateral monopoly relation between a bureau and its sponsor involves the exchange of a promised output for a budget, rather than the sale of its output at a per-unit price.

(5.) As in any bilateral monopoly, there is no unique budget-output equilibrium between that preferred by the sponsor and that preferred by the bureau. The sponsor's primary advantages in this bargaining are its authority to replace the bureau's management team, to monitor the bureau, and to approve the bureau's budget. The bureau's primary advantage is that it has much better information about the costs of supplying the service than does the sponsor.

6. The sponsor's role in this bilateral bargaining over budget-output combinations is further weakened or modified by two other conditions. The sequence of prior budget-output decisions provides relatively more information about the sponsor's effective demand for the bureau's service than about the cost of providing this service. In addition, the sponsor does not have sufficient incentive to monitor the bureau, because it shares only a small part of the benefits of more efficient performance by the bureau (Niskanen 1975); in other words, efficiency monitoring is a public good among legislators and voters. This leads the sponsor to use its authority primarily to capture part of the bureau's surplus in ways that serve the specific interests of the sponsor group, rather than the interests of the broader group of legislators and voters.

7. Finally, neither the members of the sponsor group nor the senior bureaucrats have a pecuniary share in any surplus generated by the bureau. The effect of this condition is that the surplus will be spent in ways that indirectly serve the interests of the sponsor and the bureau, but not as direct compensation.

The above characteristics, I suggest, should be the core elements of a theory of the behavior of bureaus; in other words, these are the elements of my earlier theory that have survived my own reflections on these issues. As in my book, these elements can be modified to explore special cases, such as when bureaus provide several services for a single budget, sell part of their output at a price, or compete to provide some service. But I need not expand on these special cases in this chapter.

Some Suggested Changes to the Theory

Several comments on my book, plus the developing empirical evidence, have led me to change my views on three elements of my theory. This section develops on these suggested changes.

What Do Bureaucrats Maximize?

One other question must be addressed to complete a theory of the behavior of bureaus: What assumption about the behavior of senior bureaucrats best corresponds to the assumption that business executives act to maximize the profits of their firm? Specifically, what, if anything, do bureaucrats maximize? My views on this question, which I will develop, have changed over time. The specific model of the behavior of bureaus developed in my 1971 book assumes that bureaucrats act to maximize the budget of their bureau. This seemed to be a plausible assumption and was consistent with the observation that the opportunities for promotion within each bureau increase with the level of the bureau's budget. Given the distinctive characteristics of bureaus and the political markets in which they operate, this assumption led to the conclusion that bureaus supply a larger-than-optimal output (in terms of the demand revealed by the political authorities), but that the production of this output, except in a special case, is generally efficient.

For various reasons, I now believe that this is not the best assumption on which to build a theory of the behavior of bureaus. (I recognize that this is an awkward conclusion to announce in a book on the budget-maximizing bureaucrat) As I wrote my book, I was uncomfortable with this assumption, because my personal observation was that inefficiency in production was the more general case, not a special case in the demand-constrained region of output. The subsequent empirical evidence also indicates that the salaries of bureaucrats are only weakly related to the level and growth of their bureau's budget.[3]

Fortunately, an early comment on my book by Jean-Luc Migué and Gérard Bélanger (1974) suggests an approach that both generalizes and simplifies my model in a way that resolves this inconsistency. They suggest an assumption, more consistent with that of a profit-maximizing firm, that bureaucrats act to maximize their bureau's discretionary budget, defined as the difference between the total budget and the minimum cost of producing the output expected by the political authorities. Since neither the bureaucrats nor the political authorities, however, can claim this discretionary budget as personal income, this surplus is spent in ways that serve *how exactly?*

the interests of the bureaucrats and the political authorities. Some part of this discretionary budget will be spent in ways that serve the bureau, such as additional staff, capital, and perquisites. The remainder will be spent in ways that serve the interests of the political review authorities. The distribution of this surplus between spending that serves the interests of the bureaus and that which serves the interests of the review authorities, as in any bilateral bargaining, will depend on the relevant information, alternatives, and bargaining strategies available to the two parties. This assumption leads to somewhat different conclusions: the budget of a bureau is too large, the output (again in terms of the demand revealed by the political authorities) may be too low, and the production of this output is uniformly inefficient.

An interesting part of the bargaining between a bureau and its political sponsor concerns the distribution of this surplus (the discretionary budget) between spending that serves the interests of the bureaucrats and that which serves the interests of the political review agents, but the distribution of this surplus (as in any bilateral monopoly) is not determinate. The political review agents exercise their authority to threaten more thorough monitoring as a means to capture some part of the discretionary budget in types of spending that serve their special interests (such as the relative use of factor inputs and the geographic distribution of employment and contracts). The bureaus, in turn, share some part of the discretionary budget with the review agents as the price of spending the remainder in ways that serve the bureau. The distinctive conclusion of this modified model is that bureaucratic inefficiency is the normal condition. Bureaucrats and politicians will differ on the distribution of the bureau's surplus, but neither group has sufficient incentive to reduce the excess spending.

Isn't this what they are supposed to do? I don't see it!

My prior model of bureaucratic behavior should now be recognized as a special case.[4] Bureaucrats who have a special preference for the *output* of their bureau—the "zealots," to use the term suggested by Anthony Downs (1967)—have an incentive to discipline inefficiency in order to expand the output beyond the level that maximizes the discretionary budget. The behavior of the zealots could as well be described as output maximizing, and any assumption about budget-maximizing behavior (along with its negative

There shouldn't be incentive to reduce spending because reduce spending = reduce services to the community

connotations) can be dropped entirely. The zealots, however, should expect to be opposed by those bureaucrats and political officials whose interests are served by spending the discretionary budget in other ways that they prefer. As a rule, I suggest the zealots are likely to be frustrated. My own long career as a policy analyst (a zealot for efficiency) has led me to conclude that efficiency in government cannot be much improved without changing the basic institutions and processes that affect the demand for and supply of government-financed services.

The implications of the difference between my prior model and the modified model can be efficiently summarized (see table 1.1, which is similar to one included in my book but deletes the special cases where firms or bureaus exercise factor-price discrimination). The table summarizes the output, revenue, and cost levels of both private firms and bureaus facing the same demand and cost conditions. For bureaus, these results are the opening budget-output bid in the bargaining with their sponsor; they approximate the outcome of this bargaining only in the limiting case where the sponsor is passive with respect to every dimension of this offer other than the distribution of the bureau's surplus.

The first two columns of this table present the familiar result that a monopolistic private firm will produce an output equal to one-half that produced by a group of competitive firms (facing the same linear demand and cost functions). The second two columns present a similar result: a surplus-maximizing bureau will produce an output equal to one-half that produced by an output-maximizing bureau. Both types of bureaus spend any monopoly rent specific to the bureau or the existing management team, but in different ways. The surplus-maximizing bureau will spend this rent in ways that serve the interests of the bureaucrats and the political review authorities. The output-maximizing bureau will spend this rent in expanding output beyond the optimal level.

One should also focus on the different outcomes of a competitive industry and a surplus-maximizing bureau facing the same demand and cost conditions (the second and third columns of this table). In the case presented, a bureau will produce a somewhat lower output (and factor surplus) than a competitive industry, but this case is specific to conditions of increasing unit cost. For condi-

TABLE 1.1
Equilibrium Variables for Private Firms and
Bureaus Facing the Same Demand and Cost Functions (dollars)

| Variable | Private Firm | | Bureau | |
	Monopolistic	Competitive	Surplus Maximizing	Output Maximizing
Output	50	100	83.3	166.7
Revenue	7,500	10,000	13,194	19,444
Average	150	100	158.3	↞ 116.7
Marginal	100	100	116.7	33.3
Costs	4,375	10,000	7,986	19,444
Average	87.5	100	95.8	116.7
Marginal	100	100	116.7	158.3
Factor surplus	313	1,250	868	3,472
Consumer surplus	1,250	5,000	0	0
Organization surplus	3,125	0	5,208	0

tions of constant unit cost, a surplus–maximizing bureau will produce the same output as a competitive industry, but will absorb the consumer surplus in spending that serves the interest of the bureaucrats and the review authorities.

Again, it is important to emphasize that this comparison is specific to conditions in which the demand faced by a competitive industry is equal to the effective (derived) demand faced by a specific bureau. A bureau facing a passive sponsor generates no consumer surplus within the derived demand faced by the specific bureau. Any consumer surplus generated by the total supply of a government service, in this case, depends on the difference between the total demand for the service and the derived demand faced by a specific bureau; this difference, in turn, depends on the cost of supplying this service by a private firm, another bureau, or a different management team, and the authority and incentives of the political review authorities to reallocate budgets among the actual or potential alternative sources of supply. Only in the limiting case where the review officials are completely passive and the bureau is the only potential supplier of a specific service does the bureaucratic supply of the service generate no consumer surplus. Any potential contribution of a bureau to consumer surplus, thus, is entirely dependent on conditions external to the bureau.

Considering the outcomes of a competitive industry as optimal, this analysis leads to the following general conclusions about the behavior of bureaus facing a passive sponsor.

1. The budget of the bureau is too high.

2. The output of a surplus-maximizing bureau will be too low if it faces increasing unit costs and will be about optimal if unit costs are constant. The output of an output-maximizing bureau is always too high.

3. For a surplus-maximizing bureau, the budget per unit of output is too high, but a passive sponsor would have little incentive to reduce this surplus except to capture some part of it in spending that serves their political interests. An output-maximizing bureau, in contrast, is efficient in production, but only at the expense of an output that is too high.

These conclusions differ from those in my 1975 article only in that I now regard the surplus-maximizing bureau as the usual case and the output- (or budget-) maximizing bureau as a special case. I have known numerous zealots in the bureaucracy; indeed I have been one. For several reasons, however, such zealots are unlikely to dominate a bureau for very long, because their behavior reduces spending that serves the interests of other bureaucrats and the political review authorities.

What Do Sponsors Maximize?

Most of the analysis in my 1971 book was based on an assumption that a bureau's sponsor is an unbiased sample of the legislature but is passive in its review of the bureau's proposal. In other words, the effective demand represented by the review committee was assumed to approximate that of the median voter in the legislature, but the sponsor's activities were assumed to be limited to approving or rejecting the bureau's proposal without any bargaining with the bureau to achieve an outcome that is superior for the legislature. Some of the analysis also explored the implications of a self-selection process that would lead the review committee to represent those legislators with the highest relative demand for the service provided by the bureau but, again, one that is passive in its review activities.

Of course, congressional committees and other budget review authorities are not passive. The budget review process involves substantial effort to elicit additional information, considerable bargaining between the sponsor and the bureau, and almost always leads to outcomes somewhat different from the bureau's opening proposal. These review committees have ample authority and several possible bargaining techniques to achieve a wide range of budget-output outcomes. The important contribution by Gary Miller and Terry Moe (1983), for example, explores the effects of a range of sponsor bargaining techniques for conditions that assume an unbiased sponsor and a budget-maximizing bureau. The important issue is how the review committees use their authority and bargaining techniques, to what effects, and to whose benefit.

What, if anything, do review committees maximize? These sponsors are not passive, but neither are they neutral agents of the whole legislature, voters, or the public interest. As mentioned earlier, efficiency monitoring is a public good, within the review committee, the legislature, and among voters. My current judgment is that the behavior of the review committee is best evaluated by assuming that they maximize the political interests of members of that committee, subject to the approval of the committee proposal by the whole legislature. I have not worked out the full implications of this assumption for the budget-output outcomes of the bargaining process with a surplus-maximizing bureau and, to my knowledge, neither has any other scholar. My current judgment, however, is that most of this bargaining involves the distribution of the bureau's surplus between spending that serves the interest of the sponsor and spending that serves the interest of the bureau. In that case, as in both my initial and revised models, very little of the net benefits of the bureaucratic supply of government services accrues to the general population. This issue, however, is not yet resolved and should be the highest priority for subsequent research.

What is the Range of Budget Bargaining?

The theory developed in my book assumed that bureaus bargain with the political review authorities over the full range from a zero budget to the proposed budget. As a former budget official, I knew better; this implicit assumption was an oversight but one with important implications. In fact, budget bargaining is usually restricted to a range from some base budget to the proposed budget, and the base budget is often the most recent budget. The implications of the smaller range of bargaining were first developed in an important series of articles by Thomas Romer and Howard Rosenthal (1979).[5] The most important conclusion of their model is that the level of the approved budget increases with the *difference* between the base budget (what Romer and Rosenthal term the *reversion level*) and the budget preferred by the decisive voter. The magnitude of the expected overspending in this model will be less than that in my initial model if the base budget is larger than zero.

Their cross-sectional studies of spending per student in Oregon and New York school districts indicate that spending is generally higher than that preferred by the median voter. For districts in which the base budget is higher than the preferred budget, average spending per student is about equal to the base budget. For districts in which the base budget would not be sufficient to keep the schools open, average spending per student is about 15 percent higher than in districts in which the base budget would be just sufficient. In addition, spending per student increases with the size of the school district, a reflection (in part) of the stronger monopoly power of larger districts. These extraordinarily careful empirical studies are probably the strongest evidence for my general theory of the behavior of bureaus.

The modified model developed by Romer and Rosenthal also suggests several interesting implications for the rate of change in government spending. In general, an increase in the preferred budget relative to the base budget will increase the approved budget by an even larger amount. If the base budget is defined in nominal dollars, for example, the approved budget will increase faster than the rate of inflation even if there is no increase in the real preferred budget. And even if the base budget is indexed to the price level, the real approved budget will increase at a higher rate than the increase in demand for the service. In any political system in which those that determine the proposed budget have a higher relative preference for either the discretionary budget or the output of some service, the approved budgets will be higher than that preferred by the decisive voter, whether in a legislature or among the general voters. As a consequence, both the time-series and cross-sectional data on government spending reflect a complex interaction of popular demands for government services and the personal preferences of those politicians and bureaucrats who have the authority to set the budget agenda.

Some Suggestive Evidence

Even a cursory examination of the recent performance of the public sector provides some evidence consistent with two implications of my revised theory of the behavior of bureaus: (1) the increase of real government expenditures is likely to exceed the increase in demand for government services; and (2) much of the increase in real government expenditures is likely to be waste—that is, expenditures that may serve the interests of the suppliers of the services and the political officials, but that do not increase the output of these services. A more comprehensive theory of the political system and more precise empirical methods, of course, would be necessary to estimate the specific effects of the popular demand for government services, supply conditions specific to each service, the role of politicians, and the supply of these services by bureaus. For these reasons, the following evidence is only suggestive, and further work is necessary to identify the effects of these several conditions.

A broad range of evidence is consistent with the overspending and inefficiency hypotheses of my revised model (1975). None of these tests, unfortunately, is sufficient to distinguish between a political and a bureaucratic explanation of these conditions.

The most general evidence for the overspending hypothesis is the difference between the cross-sectional and time-series patterns of government spending. The best studies of the cross-sectional data, such as those by Borcherding and Deacon (1972), conclude that the income elasticity of demand for most services provided by state and local governments is less than unity. Over time, however, expenditures for these services have increased relative to income. In a later study, Borcherding (1977) concludes that the cross-sectional evidence on the popular demand for government services explains only about half of the increase in government spending in the United States. One possible explanation of this difference is that the cross-sectional studies on government expenditures may underestimate the income elasticity of demand; this seems unlikely, because the cross-sectional studies of the demand for private goods and services generally yield higher estimated elasticities than do the time-series studies. The more plausible explanation is that the combination of political and bureaucratic conditions lead government expenditures to increase relative to the popular demand for government services.

Several other types of evidence are also consistent with the overspending hypothesis. Government grants to other governments lead to an increase in spending by the recipient governments that is far higher than the effect of an equal increase in personal income in the recipient jurisdiction (Courant, Gramlich, and Rubinfield 1979). My own study of the popular vote for the president confirms the common perception that a tax increase reduces the vote for the candidate of the incumbent party (1979). Both of these findings indicate that government spending is higher than would be the case if politicians and bureaucrats were unbiased, albeit imperfect, agents of the median voter.

One implicit hypothesis of my bureaucracy model (in either its original or revised form), as first recognized by Thomas McGuire (1981), is that the revealed (negative) price elasticity of demand for government service should be higher than unity, whatever the elasticity of the underlying popular demand; in other words, an increase in the unit cost of government services should reduce spending for these services. The evidence for this hypothesis is generally supportive but mixed. The revealed price elasticity for most state and local services, according to the Borcherding and Deacon study, appears consistent with this hypothesis. And my own (as yet unpublished) study of the demand for defense, applying the Borcherding and Deacon test equation to the U.S. time-series data, reveals a strongly negative price elasticity for defense services. These studies suggest that conditions, including waste, that increase the unit cost of government services sharply reduce the output of such services as local education and defense. These results are contrary to the common perception that the demand for government services is price inelastic, but they are not a sufficient test of my bureaucracy model because the elasticity of the underlying population demand is not (cannot be?) known.

A large and growing body of evidence has documented the inefficiency in the production of government services, at least in terms of those outputs of value to the general electorate. The aggregate evidence is more disturbing but less widely known than is the selective evidence of high prices for defense equipment and scandals in the housing program. During the past decade in the United States, for example,

• total real expenditures for defense increased 60 percent without a significant increase in the level, readiness, or sustainability of the military forces;

• real expenditures per student in the public primary and secondary schools increased 40 percent without any increase in high school graduation rates or student test scores; and

• real expenditures per person on medical care increased 60 percent without a significant effect on average health status.

For the general population, most of the increase in real spending for these services must be considered to be waste.[6]

There is an inherent difficulty in attributing the shares of the total waste in government services to the separate effects of politics and the bureaucracy. Where waste has been apparent for some years without provoking a political response, one must assume that this waste serves some other political objective; in that sense, revealed waste is there for the same reason that the programs are there—because it meets some political demand. Waste that has not yet been revealed, however, is more likely to be a consequence of the bureaucratic supply of government services. By its nature, the unrevealed waste is not (cannot be?) known. At this time, I must confess that I do not know how to pose a testable hypothesis about the shares of the total waste (the discretionary budget of a bureau) that is attributable to these two effects. I am prepared to conclude that the public sector does not serve most of us very well.

Conclusion

In retrospect, I suggest, we and other scholars have made a major start toward understanding the behavior of bureaus. Moreover, I am encouraged that bureaus and regulatory agencies have become a recognized field of study in university departments of both economics and political science, and that we seem to be learning from each other. My own reflections on this subject lead me to several general conclusions:

1. The basic structure of the theory outlined in my 1971 book will continue to be the most useful approach to understanding the behavior of bureaus. Specifically, it will continue to be more useful to focus on the distinctive characteristics of bureaus and the political institutions and processes in which they operate than to explain the behavior of bureaus in terms of the distinctive attributes of bureaucrats.

2. My prior assumption that bureaucrats act to maximize their budgets, I suggest, should now be dropped entirely in favor of an assumption that they act to maximize their discretionary budget.

3. A great deal of useful research remains to be done. Most of the subsequent research, I suggest, should focus on the characteristics of the political environment in which bureaus operate. Who reviews a bureau's proposed budget? What are their incentives and constraints? What are the effects of different rules (the "effective constitution") of the cabinet, legislative committees, legislatures, and the popular vote? What are the effects of different rules for determining the base budget and the long-term effects of a sequence of votes? What determines the distribution of the discretionary budget between spending that serves the interests of the review authorities and that which serves the interests of the bureaucrats. How much of the problems that may be attributed to bureaucratic supply are really due to the incentives and processes in the cabinet and legislature?

More work on the structure of the bureaucracy will also be valuable. What are the effects of actual or potential competition from private firms or other bureaus? What are the effects of potential future employment in other bureaus or in private organizations on the behavior of bureaucrats? What are the effects of changes in the compensation structure or the rules for promotion and termination? On examination, some of these effects will prove to be interrelated; the availability of private alternatives to a government service, for example, may lead to multiple-peaked preferences for the government service, increasing the problems of achieving a political decision and increasing the variance of outcomes.

Over the past twenty years, we have learned that private firms and markets are more complex than the prior simple models suggested. During this same period, we have only started to converge on a simple model of bureaus and political markets. That is an important start, but only a start. I will read with interest and some pride how research on this issue develops.

NOTES

1. For the primary pre-1971 contributions by economists to the theory of the behavior of bureaus, see Ludwig von Mises (1944); Gordon Tullock (1965); and Anthony Downs (1967).

2. For a strong recent critique of the public choice approach, see Steven Kelman (1987).

3. For a careful study of the relationship between public employee salaries and agency growth, see Ronald Johnson and Gary Libecap (1988).

4. For a model of bureaucratic behavior in which the utility of a bureaucrat is a function of both the discretionary budget and output, see Niskanen (1975).

5. This model was first developed and tested on Oregon school district data by Thomas Romer and Howard Rosenthal (1979). The most recent version of this model with tests based on New York school district data is reported in Thomas Romer, Howard Rosenthal, and Vincent Munley (1987).

6. For a detailed evaluation of the recent U.S. defense buildup, see Niskanen (1988). The summary of spending and output for the U.S. education and medical sectors is from a monograph in progress.

REFERENCES

Borcherding, Thomas, ed. 1977. *Budgets and bureaucrats: The sources of government growth.* Durham, N.C.: Duke Univ. Press.

Borcherding, Thomas E., and Robert T. Deacon. 1972. The demand for the services of non-federal governments. *American Economic Review* 62:891–900.

Breton, Albert, and Ronald Wintrobe. 1975. The equilibrium size of a budget-maximizing bureau: A note on Niskanen's theory of bureaucracy. *Journal of Political Economy* 83:195–207.

Courant, Paul, Edward Gramlich, and Daniel Rubinfield. 1979. The stimulative effects of intergovernmental grants: Or why government money sticks where it lands. In *Fiscal federalism and grants in aid,* ed. Peter Miezkowski and William Oakland. Washington, D.C.: Urban Institute.

Downs, Anthony. 1967. *Inside bureaucracy.* Boston: Little, Brown.

Frank, Robert. 1985. *Choosing the right pond.* New York: Oxford Univ. Press.

Gonzalez, Rodolfo, and Steven Mehay. 1985. Bureaucracy and the divisibility of local public output. *Public Choice* 45:89–101.

Johnson, Ronald, and Gary Libecap. 1988. *Agency growth, salaries, and the protected bureaucrat.* Tucson: Univ. of Arizona, Research Group for Institutional Analysis.

Kelman, Steven. 1987. *Making public policy.* New York: Basic Books.

McGuire, Thomas. 1981. Budget-maximizing governmental agencies: An empirical test. *Public Choice* 36:313–322.

Migué, Jean-Luc, and Gérard Bélanger. 1974. Towards a general theory of managerial discretion. *Public Choice* 17.

Miller, Gary J., and Terry M. Moe. 1983. Bureaucrats, legislators, and the size of government. *American Political Science Review* 77.

Mises, Ludwig von. 1944. *Bureaucracy.* New Haven, Conn.: Yale Univ. Press.

Niskanen, William A. 1971. *Bureaucracy and representative government.* Chicago: Aldine Atherton.

———. 1975. Bureaucrats and politicians. *Journal of Law and Economics* 18:617–43.

———. 1979. Economic and fiscal effects on the popular vote for the president. In *Public policy and public choice,* ed. Douglas W. Rae and Theodore J. Eismeier. Beverly Hills, Calif.: Sage.

———. 1988. *More defense spending for smaller forces: What hath DOD wrought?* Policy Analysis 110. Washington, D.C.: Cato Institute.

Romer, Thomas, and Howard Rosenthal. 1979. Bureaucrats vs. voters: On the political economy of resource allocation by direct democracy. *Quarterly Journal of Economics* 93:563–87.

Romer, Thomas, Howard Rosenthal, and Vincent Munley. 1987. Economic incentives and political institutions: Spending and voting in school district referenda. Pittsburgh, Pa.: Carnegie Mellon University.

Tullock, Gordon. 1965. *The politics of bureaucracy.* Washington, D.C.: Public Affairs Press.

2

ROBERT A. YOUNG

Budget Size and
Bureaucratic Careers

In Niskanen's influential model, a bureau with a monopoly to supply a public service confronts a sponsor with the power to fund its operations at various levels. The outcome is that the bureau may produce too much output efficiently, or the right amount inefficiently; in either case, the bureau is larger than necessary for the efficient provision of optimum output. In this model of excess government, some driving force toward growth is provided by the sponsor's interest in satisfying client groups. But because bureaucrats control information about service production costs, the real motive power lies in the efforts of bureaucrats to obtain larger budgets. This pressure flows in turn from assumptions about bureaucratic utility. As Niskanen put it originally: "Among the several variables that may enter the bureaucrat's utility function are the following: salary, perquisites of the office, public reputation, power, patronage, output of the bureau, ease of making changes, and ease of managing the bureau. All of these variables except the last two, I contend, are a positive monotonic function of the total *budget* of the bureau during the bureaucrat's tenure in office" (1971, 38).

Since Niskanen wrote, the notion that bureaucrats benefit from larger budgets has become commonplace. Bennett and Johnson (1980), for example, state flatly: "The public-sector manager who can achieve a rapid expansion in the programs under his direction can expect to benefit directly in terms of rank, salary, prestige, and perquisites of office" (109). Such sweeping contentions abound in the literature on public finance and bureaucracy.

In this chapter I am concerned with the dynamic links between bureaucratic utility and behavior. The focus is upon the interests and behavior of bureaucrats through their careers, in the course of which they may anticipate having a long tenure in one office, or changing positions and bureaus many times, or even ceasing to be bureaucrats. Do these different career expectations alter the incentives described and the behavior predicted by Niskanen? In particular, is it really worth trying to get the bureau's budget increased now in order to get ahead later?

To approach these questions, the following section briefly discusses the notion of careers and distinguishes between kinds of bureaucrat. The next section reviews the few studies that ask whether people working in government agencies actually have benefited when budgets have increased. The evidence on this point is not conclusive, but it offers little support to the Niskanen thesis. Next and more impressionistically, I examine the ways that people do get ahead in the bureaucratic worlds of advanced industrial countries. It seems that career progress is not necessarily related to achieving larger budgets; the relationship between agency growth and bureaucratic rewards, if any, is a contingent one. I conclude with some suggestions for future research and with observations about the status of Niskanen's theory. Throughout, I accept the assumption that bureaucrats want to maximize personal utility in the form of salaries, power, and so on. The core question is: What must they do now to achieve more of these in the future?

Careers and Bureaucrats

One can think of a career as a path through life, or especially through the working life (although many bureaucrats, like many academics, would find it hard to draw the distinction). People vary in the extent to which they conceive of themselves as having a career, as moving along some structured trajectory; indeed, large numbers of people think simply of work, not career, and many probably do not realize they have had a career except ex post facto.

Other individuals of course, are highly career conscious. Future oriented, they plan their route, a path that leads usually, but not always, to senior posts. Others, between these extremes, may seek generally to get ahead, with periodic reassessments of what this means. Of course, expectations and targets may sink or rise over time.

It is evident that individuals vary in the discount rate they apply to anticipated future benefits. The careerist is willing to suffer much temporary hardship for future gain; the plodding employee who dimly perceives a future rather like the present may not be so willing to make current sacrifices. Hence the salience and the perceived magnitude of the net present value of future benefits vary among bureaucrats. Second, it is worth noting that the most rational career planners may misapprehend, if only temporarily, the objective reward structure within which they are operating. Their information about it may be incomplete. They may also miscalculate, playing their cards wrong against the competition—and competition does exist when rewards are at stake. Finally, the career payoff structure may be changed, and so the behavior of those calculating within it (if motivation is constant) must also shift.

It is useful to distinguish between three types of bureaucrats now, not according to their orientations toward the future, but according to their position. First are blue- and white-collar employees filling routine jobs. Of the public servants in Western countries, these bureaucrats constitute the vast majority. For them, collective bargaining over wages and advancement through seniority are the chief sources of material rewards, while security of tenure provides the shelter from downside risks. These bureaucrats have no direct influence over budgets and, in most cases, their numbers pose a free-rider problem for whatever collective action would help to get bigger budgets for their particular agency. The second type of actor is the agency head or manager. This is a bureaucrat with some budgetary authority. He or she may negotiate directly with politicians (Niskanen's "sponsors") over budgetary allocations; much more commonly, he or she deals with superior bureaucrats about these and other matters. Across countries there are large variations in how and from whom budget allocations are obtained, and how many actors get them.[1] There are also great differences, even within national bureaucracies, in the normal length of tenure of particular managerial positions.

Finally, among bureaucrats, there is very small residual category of people who represent the new blood transfused into bureaucratic systems. All such systems, unlike the orderly, enduring structures depicted by Weber, seethe with competition. But bureaucracies seethe slowly. Heclo puts it best: "Left to their own devices, bureaucrats battle about stability and change in much the same way gardens encroach on each other, through a slow, twisting struggle where only the most rigorously enduring species will see the light of day" (1977, 144). Because bureaucratic competition is incremental and self-centered, these organizations are not left alone, but are tended. In each system there is some way of introducing new people to hurry things along. In the United States, these are the political executives—those called "politicos" by Campbell (1983). In other systems, like Canada's, young recruits into central agencies are often sent laterally into line departments at senior levels. In more closed systems like those of the United Kingdom, Japan, or France, there are the "fast-trackers," very small cadres of highly educated youths admitted largely by examination, with the expectation that they will lead bureaucracies in the future (Plowden 1984; Pempel 1984; Suleiman 1984). Political executives in the United States have quite different career patterns than normal civil servants; so do fast-trackers, who are strongly career oriented in every system.

These simple distinctions among bureaucrats will help now in confronting the core problem: Is it the case that these individuals' desires for future benefits translate effectively into bureaucratic pressure on sponsors for growth in current budgets? Before examining how and whether this outcome occurs, it is essential to review the evidence that bears on the prior question of whether agency growth actually does produce career rewards.

Bureaucratic Returns to Agency Growth

Given the attention that the Niskanen thesis and its predecessors have attracted, the paucity of careful empirical work that assesses its adequacy is remarkable. The weak form of the basic proposition (bureaucrats benefit from larger budgets) is much more testable than the strong form (bureaucrats try to maximize budgets) or the perfect form (bureaucrats always succeed), but it still defines an academic battleground where the major exchanges have been snipings of example and counterexample, rather than big salvos of carefully analyzed data. The few systematic studies of which I am aware, however, are unanimous in offering little support, even to the weak proposition that bureaucrats become relatively better-off when the budget of their bureau grows disproportionately.

Hood and Dunsire (1981) have assembled a large set of quantitative data on the U.K. bureaucracy, and Dunsire (1987) tested some Niskanen-inspired hypotheses. He found, first, that over the 1972–1983 period, British government expenditure increased 36 percent in real terms. This did not translate into bureaucratic growth (and the more rapid promotions it is thought to engender). In fact, total staff numbers fell. Did the remaining bureaucrats capture the expenditure increase in the form of higher salaries? Only in part: although salaries rose faster than inflation, total salaries grew by less than the total spending increase. And the powerful senior bureaucrats fared worse than most. While total civil service pay rose 336.5 percent and the retail price index rose 300.8 percent, the salaries of undersecretaries, deputy secretaries, and permanent secretaries increased by 224.9 percent, 191.3 percent, and 136.9 percent, respectively. In a period of budgetary expansion, the top people lost a lot of ground. "Either these people are not motivated in the way the theories assume, or they are extraordinarily inept in looking after their own interests" (119). Of course, the top civil servants could have forgone salary increases while appropriating nontaxable perks for themselves. There was indeed a detectable rise in the numbers of personal secretaries and administrative group staff, but this growth was very slight (115–16).

Dunsire also conducted a brief analysis at the departmental level for the 1971–1982 period. In six of ten departments, significant positive correlations were found between the share of total government budget and the share of total civil service staff. In four of ten departments, such correlations were found between budget share and share of top staff. If one presumes that having more staff and

senior civil servants constitutes a benefit for departmental bureaucrats, then here is some evidence it is associated with higher budgets. But the results were not consistent: "Whether or not the
predictions of the theory of bureaucratic behaviour are realized
seems to depend upon the department chosen for the analysis"
(121).

Dunsire's findings about the ability of bureaucrats to capture
immediate benefits are mixed. They are also not definitive because
of the aggregate nature of the analysis. Even departmental figures
can conceal very different relationships between staffing and budgets at the branch, agency, and group levels. More important for
our purposes, aggregate analysis can say little about the links between budgets and careers. If staffing is reduced, for example,
while budgets are constant, many salaries in the unit may increase.
Similarly, when bureau staff numbers fall, opportunities for promotion may increase—or they may not: it depends upon the level
at which the cuts were made. Career analysis requires disaggregation to the individual level, simply because without further assumptions or more precise information it is impossible to know
how individuals have actually been affected by changes in the
overall resources of the departments within which they function.
Simple correlations between budgets and staff complements reveal
nothing certain about how these changes have affected the current
fortunes and career prospects of bureaucrats within the unit.
Grandjean (1981) analyzed a 1 percent sample of white-collar
federal employees in the United States, following their careers
over the 1963–1977 period. On the supposition that career patterns
vary with individual attributes, and with organizational and historical contexts, civil service entrants were divided into five cohorts
(pre-1963, Great Society, Vietnam, Nixonomics, and Watergate).
The regression model solved for rewards (position advances and
salary increases) as a function of employee characteristics, geographic location, seniority, and agency. It explained between 80
percent and 90 percent of the variation in salary change for the
individuals within the cohorts. Most variance (40–50 percent) was
accounted for by human capital differences, which suggests that
promotions and raises do reflect to some extent a rational personnel selection process (1069).

The effects on career success of the bureau's growth (as measured in employee numbers) were more complex. In faster growing departments, entry-level salaries tended to be higher than in others. But the overall chances of "upward prestige mobility" were not highest in those departments that expanded greatly through association with the major public agenda items of the day; that is, HEW/HUD (the War on Poverty), Defense/State (Vietnam), and the Veteran's Administration (post Vietnam). More mobility was found in the other, residual departments, the "category for which growth during the period of study, though slow, was steadiest" (1079). Interagency differences in salary changes and promotions were more strongly associated with characteristics of agencies other than short-run fluctuations in size, and especially with the occupational structure dictated by the bureau's mission—medicine in Veterans' Affairs, for example—and with the internal grade structure. Finally, despite the generally negative findings about career success in fast-growing departments, Grandjean found some evidence of a "ground-floor" phenomenon: early entrants to bureaus that subsequently became the vehicles for major national policy objectives tended to advance rapidly, and they continued to do so even while later cohorts languished in the same bureaus (1081). This provides some limited support for the view that rewarding careers for a few are more likely in fast-growing agencies. However, policy shifts of the magnitude of Vietnam or the Great Society are beyond the capacity of bureaucrats, especially young entrants, to create. They can ride the wave, and they can try to prolong it, but essentially they were lucky enough to have had the right skills in the right place at the right time.

There are some problems with Grandjean's analysis, especially the grouping into cohorts, the aggregation of residual bureaus, and the absence of data on bureaus' budgets. But the results essentially highlight the elements constituting human capital as causing career success. Interbureau differences in growth rates seem to have relatively little systematic effect on promotion prospects and salary increases. The effects that do exist are mainly caused by occupational structures peculiar to bureaus and by massive changes in national priorities. In these conditions, the rational bureaucrat probably could best advance through investing in education. Nevertheless, it appears that both steady agency growth and the ground-floor phenomenon can help advance bureaucratic careers a little, other things being equal; in Grandjean's view, "the hypothesis that organizational growth creates opportunities for career achievement, while useful, is incomplete" (1088).

The most sustained investigation of this hypothesis has been conducted in the American context by Johnson and Libecap (1987, 1989). They analyzed two random samples from the central personnel data file, for 1980 and 1985, using in each instance over 15,000 cases representing GS (white-collar) employees from forty-five agencies. Solving for salary in 1980, they found large effects ($R^2 =$ .73) to be associated with education and experience: substantial differences did remain across agencies (1987, table 4), but much of this could be attributed to occupational structures and classification procedures (20). Turning to the effect of agency growth on salaries, through analyzing changes in the agency earnings differentials between 1980 and 1985, Johnson and Libecap found only one significant relationship, for the sample taken as a whole (1989, table 2). But the coefficient of only .044 implied that "an agency must more than double its size in order for salaries to increase by 4.4 percent relative to an agency that did not grow." (1989, 446) Further analysis was done on administrative and professional employees, who, if not the only ones to benefit from growth, might well be the only people capable of securing it. This produced a smaller, insignificant coefficient and, in two of the subperiods, the sign on the coefficient was negative. Excluding the large group of Department of Defense employees and controlling for occupation produced still weaker results and another negative coefficient. These nonconfirmatory results held when a budget growth measure was introduced into the equations. Moreover, the absence of a relationship was symmetrical; in cases of employment decline, "the salaries of those individuals who remain with the agency do not appear to be greatly affected by staffing change" (1987, 26). Johnson and Libecap concluded:

> The notion that the salaries of bureaucrats are closely tied to the fortunes of the agency has been an important part of the literature dealing with bureaucratic behavior and the growth of government.

Yet, the results presented in this paper do not reveal a strong significant linkage between changes in staffing and salaries within an
agency. For the typical federal white-collar employee, promoting
growth does not appear to be the way to increase salaries. (1989,
448)

An alternative hypothesis suggested by Johnson and Libecap
concerns civil service rules that emphasize seniority and time in
service. The latter is a major determinant of salary growth, as step
increases within grades are almost automatic in the U.S. federal
service. They are withheld from fewer than 1 percent of bureaucrats (1989, 436). Similarly, seniority provides protection against
cutbacks. Since there is usually more than enough salary money
available to cover the allocated slots, senior people can be protected when cuts are made. Even reduction-in-force procedures
have worked mainly through attrition rather than layoffs.

The Johnson and Libecap study provides powerful evidence
from sophisticated, careful work directed right at the heart of
the Niskanen thesis. It does not support the view that bureaucrats' remuneration is significantly related to the growth of their
agencies. There are, however, certain lacunae in the analysis, and
logical loopholes remain open. First, the time period is short.
Some salary effects of growth may take longer than five years to
show up. Second, the analysis focuses only on salaries, neglect-
ing the perks, patronage, and extra leisure that agency expansion
may bring. As well, the data cover only the GS 1–15 grades,
and so leave out the Senior Executive Service, precisely the bureaucrats who manage budgets and negotiate with sponsors: we
do not know how agency growth affects them (although their
salaries are tied to the upper GS levels, so the opportunity for
raises is limited). Most important, the analysis sweeps over the
bureau. It covers some very large departments like Transportation, Labor, and Justice, as well as some smaller agencies. Yet
in the U.S. bureaucracy many budgetary decisions and career
moves occur at lower levels, in individual bureaus (Heclo 1977,
116). Aggregate data can obscure the competition within departments that takes place between budgetary unit heads who may
be seeking to increase their own budgets and salaries. Again,

however impressive is the nonsupport delivered by Johnson and Libecap for the view that agency growth and bureaucratic rewards are related, the proposition is not entirely eliminated by their work.

It remains to report on one further test that did focus on the microlevel. For the province of Ontario, Jack (1987) identified bureaucrats at the director level and above, for whom data are available on both salaries and the budgets they administer. The analysis covered two periods of time, and was designed to test whether bureaucrats who responded to overall government policy stances were rewarded. The first era, 1970–1975, was one of expansionary fiscal and expenditure policy. Then an abrupt shift in July 1975, marked by an extraordinary budget, ushered in an era of restraint that lasted until 1979. Both the expansionary and the restraint eras were subdivided into a two-year performance period (fiscal years 1971–1972 to 1973–1974, and 1975–1976 to 1977–1978) and a single reward period (1974–1975 and 1978–1979). The study included all bureaucrats who had been in the same position and responsible for the same functions for a whole performance period. They also had to be somewhere in the public service during the relevant reward period, so that their salary subsequent to performance could be determined.[2] Simply enough, the expectation was that bureaucrats achieving relatively high budget increases in an expansionary atmosphere would be rewarded with larger salary increases; it was also thought possible that those managing to compress budgets relatively more during the restraint era might be rewarded with above average salary increases.

The comparison of changes in budgets and salaries revealed a more complex picture, though the effects were not strong in either era. During the years of government expansion, salary increases were associated with budgetary increases during the performance period ($r = 0.44$). However, salary change in the reward period was negatively associated with prior salary changes ($r = -0.36$). This result suggests that those bureaucrats not receiving large raises in the first period tended to catch up later; so it speaks to steady career progress. A regression equation solving for salary change in the reward period as a function of previous budget and salary changes produced a strong negative coefficient on salary change. The independent effect of having achieved higher budgets was positive (0.035) but insignificant. In the restraint era, the picture was different. Changes in budgets were negatively related with immediate changes in salaries ($r = -0.02$) and also with salary change in the reward period ($r = -0.08$). The regression analysis confirmed that budgetary growth had a negative (although insignificant) effect on salary in the reward period. However, the independent effect of past salary increases was both positive and significant. In this era, those bureaucrats who had benefited during the performance period continued to gain in the reward period. We do not know why they were differentially rewarded, but expanding budgets produced neither immediate nor longer-term rewards.

While this was an elegant, microlevel test, it had obvious weaknesses. Only senior managers were studied, there were no controls for occupation, the time period was short, and benefits other than salaries were not considered as rewards. Nevertheless, the notion that bureaucrats do benefit from budget increases failed once more to find empirical confirmation.

Bureaucratic Careers

The few extant quantitative tests of the proposition underlying Niskanen's model show little support for it. The objective relationship between agency growth and bureaucrats' salaries is slight at best, so even the weak form of the Niskanen thesis—that bureaucrats do benefit from larger budgets—does not stand up very well. This provides little motivational underpinning for the stronger form of the thesis—that bureaucrats actually try to maximize budgets.

Nevertheless, all the studies have weaknesses, and the empirical question about the objective nature of incentive structures must be left unresolved. In this section, I explore the question from a different angle: How do bureaucrats actually get ahead in their careers? The study of career paths and constraints may shed further light on bureaucrats' motives. In particular, it may allow us to assess whether salary, reputation, perks, power, and so on are related in the future to efforts to increase the bureau's budget now. This may help specify the structural variables that should make bureaucrats more or less inclined to press for larger budgets.

Framing generalizations about the factors conducive to bureaucratic career success is risky. There is enormous variation across countries. For example, personnel systems in which salary and status are attached to people, as in Germany, can be expected to produce very different incentives and self-perceptions than those in which position is all, such as the United States. There, "In an operational sense an official who is not appended to a particular job is not a civil servant but a 'rated eligible' " (Heclo 1977, 137). There are also differences across bureaus. As Savoie (1990) has reminded us about Canada, a powerful component of the bureaucracy consists of central agency "guardians" whose mission it is to oversee and control public expenditure; success in such bureaus depends, presumably, on other criteria than increasing budgets. Public bureaucracies also are characterized by changing environments and expectations. Positions may gradually become political or the reverse, and bureaucrats, unlike their private sector counterparts, "face scheduled disruptions in policy continuity in the form of elections" (Buchanan 1974, 343).

It is safe to say, nevertheless, that bureaucrats generally get ahead through promotion. They may report that helping achieve the goals of the agency or the pleasure of working with others most motivates them, but material incentives are also important (Peters 1978, table 4.2). With few exceptions, it seems that challenging responsibilities, a congenial work environment, high status, metropolitan locations, professional autonomy, and the chance to exercise constructive influence all accompany the higher salaries and retirement benefits found at more senior ranks (Pearce and Perry 1983, table 1; Dunleavy 1985, table 2).

Promotion and Seniority

For most civil servants the normal route to promotion is continuous service. This is true for the great majority of blue- and white-collar workers in routine jobs. It also holds for higher level professionals and managers in some countries, such as Italy and Germany. In the latter, promotion is by seniority, "with performance as a secondary criterion" (Mayntz 1984, 59). Seniority-based systems induce stable career expectations. And to the extent that the criteria of promotion stress time in service, there is less material incentive for efficiency or for doing a good job—whatever that may imply in the eyes of superiors. When promotion decisions are made in a central personnel agency rather than the bureau, this effect is strengthened, as it also is when civil service unions are strong. Under these conditions, immediate material rewards, the prospect of inevitable advancement, and the pull of pension benefits may combine to make people abide as bureaucrats, but alienation, withdrawal, and shirking are also likely (Balk and Gummer 1986; Lasson 1978, 42–80).

In such an environment, is there an incentive to increase budgets? Across the entire public service, there clearly is. Larger budgets are necessary to accommodate larger salaries for all. Pressing for such increases is precisely what civil service unions and staff associations try to do. In fact, when promotion and salary increases cannot be awarded by superiors in the bureau as a function of performance, the incentive to press for bureaucracywide benefits is strengthened. These collective agreements, however, do not differentially affect rewards and budgets at the bureau level, or within bureaus.[3] Career advancement then seems to require individual planning in order to acquire new skills and change job categories (Dresang 1984, 239–43).

Another individual strategy of bureaucrats, however, could produce government growth. One common argument making the link between budgets and promotion is that new personnel added beneath an incumbent can result in his or her promotion. Throughout a system, such desires could create constant pressure for expansion. The benefits of new subordinates, however, must be weighed against the costs of change and increased supervisory effort. It is not always evident that this calculation leads to new hires, as Niskanen recognized in his original formulation. Further, the notion that adding bureaucrats will produce more leisure for incumbents assumes that the quantity of work is fixed. An interesting study by Hannaway (1987) suggests that bureaucrats can create a lot of work for each other, so that the marginal increase in leisure produced by an extra bureaucrat may be very small. Finally, with respect to promotion, the addition of underlings is a strategy that cannot be successful very often, in the absence of an extraordinary demand for the bureau's services. Especially where seniority is important, the benefits of striving for extra subordinates seem small when compared to the accrual of annual increments, the sure accession to higher rank upon the retirement of superiors, and the returns to investing in personal skills.

Indeed, one could maintain that most bureaucrats become better off when agencies shrink rather than when they grow. Early retirement programs are an obvious case in point, as they open new opportunities for promotion. It is true that the removal of subordinates can cause downward reclassification for managers in some systems, and it is strongly resisted on those grounds (Savoie 1990, 209–10). In the United States, though, this is a slow process, and where rank is not tied to position but inheres in the bureaucrat, the problem is nonexistent. To tenured employees, personnel cuts seem to pose little direct threat of job loss, because the main technique used, apart from reducing intake and retiring staff early, is attrition or "normal wastage" (Peters 1985, 251; Fry 1988, 5). Over a short period (in career terms), attrition rates of 2 percent per year produce substantial room for upward mobility, and if salary savings are not entirely clawed out of the agency, there are surpluses for redistribution to the survivors. These are genuine benefits, although it may take time to implant the corporate culture within which this reality becomes apparent (Dolezal 1988). Of course, there are also real social and psychic costs of downsizing; yet the heaviest ones are not borne by the remaining bureaucrats. Moreover, even the short-term morale problems associated with cutting exercises may be less substantial than the enduring malaise created in stagnant bureaus by withdrawal, transparent shirking, and very aggressive competition for the few available promotion opportunities (Morgan 1981, 6).[4]

In sum, for most tenured bureaucrats it is not obvious that pressure in favor of larger budgets and more staff will be present, strong, effective, or even in their interests. But most of these people have little direct influence on budgets, and their occupational qualifications often preclude movement to the higher ranks. What about senior bureaucrats and those who have good prospects of reaching the top? Can they progress most by expanding their current budgets?

Selection Processes

The formal criteria for promotion in most systems can be read in the manuals of civil service agencies and particular bureaus. Much less is known about informal criteria, especially those operative near the top of public bureaucracies. In the case of the United Kingdom, for instance, Ridley (1983, 189) mentions quality of analysis, constructive ideas, judgment, written and oral expression, numerical ability, relationships with others, management of staff, reliability, professional knowledge, and potential. These are very subjective criteria of quality—and an appropriate appreciation of them might itself qualify one for higher office in the United Kingdom; hence Seers's caustic remark that the "chief requirement for a successful career is still conformity" (1968, 96).

Across countries there is much variation in the degree to which such criteria are applied centrally. In France, a great deal depends on one's image within the Corps; in Canada, the United Kingdom, and Japan, suitability for advancement is assessed by the whole senior public service; in the United States, the situation is fragmented, with judgments being made both within departments and by officials and politicians in Congress and in the White House. Whatever the structure, however, promotions inevitably are decided by the bureaucrat's superiors. These can be either other bureaucrats or politicians.

Breton and Wintrobe (1982) have emphasized that bureaucrats are both superiors and subordinates. Managers have an interest in making exchanges with subordinates in order to secure their compliance; that is, to induce them to use their discretion in various informal ways so as to advance the managers' projects. But if a manager seeks promotion, he or she is aware that good performance is defined by his or her own superiors. So careerist managers are caught in a delicate balance, having to buy the loyalty of their own subordinates so as to invest in meeting their superiors' requirements. Breton and Wintrobe (133–38) suggest that larger budgets can be useful in securing subordinates' compliance, be-

questionable!

cause more perks and promotions can be traded for supportive behavior. When growth is not penalized from above, then the manager who attains larger budgets is in the happily congruent position of being able to buy more loyalty to deliver whatever results are conducive to promotion.

And yet the average civil servant actually can be better off in a smaller department. Cutting the absolute size of budgets can similarly still leave managers with more discretionary resources to exchange with their (remaining) subordinates for supportive behavior. Under these conditions, managers can better invest in meeting their superiors' requirements. Further, if superiors' criteria of good performance stress efficiency and agency downsizing, then managers have a positive incentive to cut budgets if they want promotion.

Ignoring politicians for the moment, this suggests that advancement toward the bureaucratic summit depends on demonstrated acceptance of the norms prevailing there. (By *norms*, I simply mean collective understandings about appropriate behavior.) Norms are themselves the object of competition, and they do shift along with the structures of incentives within which behavior occurs. But groups of senior public servants must have enough consensus about them to make promotion decisions. In centralized parliamentary systems, the relevant cabal often consists of permanent department heads. In other systems, the group with power over promotions may be located in particular departments or agencies. Whatever the case, there appears to be no necessary reason for such groups to reward managers who have managed to maximize their budgets.

Of course innovation and expansion will sometimes tend to meet with approval. In Canada, Morgan (1981, xix) describes the "ideology of creativity" that led to rapid promotions for young, growth-oriented program planners during the 1970s. But norms can be such as to lead to rewards for restraint. Sorenson (1987) describes the common interest of Norwegian bureau heads in constraining the more aggressive ones among them, because government deficits and inflation pose the threat of lower economic growth and less tax revenue. Similarly, Hood and Dunsire (1981, 79) recount how bureaucrats responsible for nationalized industries in the United Kingdom tried to cut subsidies and force the firms to be more self-sufficient by charging higher prices; instead, the Heath government allocated large budget increases to the sponsor departments against their wishes. Perhaps the most common outcome of senior bureaucratic collusion is an orientation neither to growth nor to downsizing. Peters argues that departments may settle for a fair share of the resource pie along with policy autonomy: "The agencies are in competition, but this competition is limited by the costs of that competition to the preservation of the relative position of the agency and its control over central policy concerns. Thus, to the extent that the bureaucracy as a whole has any unified policy concerns, they will frequently be over the preservation of the status quo" (1978, 175).

In such environments, the costs to bureaucrats of pressing for larger budgets rise. These costs are not only the direct ones of negotiating, preparing background papers, and so on (Dunleavy 1985, 305), but also the costs to reputation that accrue when managers break ranks and buck the prevailing consensus. What counts for promotion in public bureaucracies, where the criteria of a job well done are vague, is a willingness to adopt the behavior that finds acceptance at the top.

Sooner or later in a career, bureaucrats' prospects depend in part on politicians. In some systems, this influence is pervasive; Pempel (1984) describes, for example, how the senior Japanese bureaucracy is "sewn into the web" of conservative politics. In other systems, especially ones closed to lateral entry, politicians' influence on promotions is marginal or indirect, as in the United Kingdom (Plowden 1984; Ridley 1983, 195). In Italy, seniority may rule supreme, but ministers choose the *direttore generale,* and very flat salary schedules render highly significant the perks and appointments awarded at the minister's discretion (Cassese 1984, 56). In France, not only is service in a minister's office a vital tour for young graduates of the ENA and the Polytechnique (Gournay 1984, 76), but the unique system of Corps service makes movement into electoral politics costless for bureaucrats; indeed, a summit of the public service career is becoming a minister oneself (Suleiman 1984, 119–28). Especially for the young high-flyers, sensitivity to the prevailing political views about policy and government expansion can improve promotion probabilities, particularly when careers are not structured mainly within single bureaus.

The U.S. case is unique in this regard. Senior career bureaucrats are dependent on Congress and associated client groups for appropriations, and they have a strong incentive to form links with these actors, not just in order to advance but also to protect their own positions in the fierce Washington world (Heclo 1977, 141; Aberbach, Putnam, and Rockman 1981, 96). Forging closer links with the Executive Office of the President, on the other hand, is dangerous, as it may lead to political tainting and termination after a regime change (Heclo 1977, 180, 185–86). Hence flows the horizontal resistance within bureaus to the White House and to its appointed political executives, despite their power to advance the careers of like-minded bureaucrats (ibid. 213–20). It is precisely this resistance—rather than inefficiency or bloated budgets—that executive branch reorganizations have been designed to overcome (Crenson and Rourke 1987).

As for the political executives, their tenure is short and their lines of communication to the cabinet and the White House often turn out to be uncertain. They can also be hurt by the career civil servants, and so they may either "go native" in the bureau (Heclo 1977, 172, 109–11) or act so as to maximize their own later returns (which may or may not require larger budgets). It is worth noting, too, that 85 percent of these appointees have had previous government experience (Brauer 1987, 177). Their political affiliations have enabled them to leapfrog tiers of career bureaucrats.

So, normal promotions at the peak of bureaucracies, as well as the career prospects of fast-trackers and political appointees, depend significantly on the approval of politicians. This pushes the essential problem of government growth back to the relationship between bureaus and sponsors, a full treatment of which is impossible here. It is noteworthy, though, that politicians are not mere pawns in this bilateral game. Some simple negotiating tactics are available to political overseers, should they prefer to use them (Miller and Moe 1983; Sorensen 1987). It may also be rational for politicians to invest in control devices (Breton and Wintrobe 1975), and there is some evidence both that such devices can be effective (Connolly 1986) and that politicians believe them to be so (Pearson and Wiggington 1986). The imposition of controls may be easier in a parliamentary than in a presidential system, but cuts and controls are available to politicians anywhere, should they want to enforce them.

Exit

It remains to consider briefly the effects of mobility on bureaucrats' incentives to expand budgets and staff. Presumably, to the extent that the probability of changing positions increases, commitment to any bureau falls, as does the incentive to press for staffing growth and larger budgets. It is clear that systems vary greatly in the extent to which careers are confined to single bureaus.

In the United States, bureaucratic mobility is low. More than one interagency change is rare in a typical career, and such moves usually happen early (McGregor 1974; Scism 1974). Especially in professionalized, technical occupations, careers tend to be confined to a single bureau; in fact, within many agencies, promotion corridors are so precisely defined that they are sometimes called *tubes*. In Japan, on the other hand, as many as one-third of senior bureaucrats have served in three or more agencies (Pempel 1984, 96), and in Germany, mobility is greater still, with transfers occurring even between levels of government. France is the extreme case: membership in the Corps endures while positions in line departments (except Defense), central agencies, ministers' offices, universities, state enterprises, politics, and the private sector can all be temporary roosts for the lifetime servant of the state.

Civil servants also leave public bureaucracies entirely. To the extent that this is probable, bureaucrats have an incentive to concentrate on matters other than the size of next year's budget. In particular, they will try to increase their human capital while in office. Bureaucrats may also behave in office, in part, in response to extragovernmental incentive structures, so building a reputation that can translate into future benefits. Obviously this behavior need not be growth promoting. In most systems, it is through exit prospects as well as high-level lateral entry that the private sector penetrates the state bureaucracy. Long-lived Japanese bureaucrats retiring ("descending from heaven") at fifty to fifty-five years of age are a clear case in point. France, once more, is the exception, as statist technocrats colonize the private sector between official engagements.

Again, the United States seems unique. The large number of political executives have extremely short tenures; Brauer (1987, 174–175) reports an average of two and a half years. These civil servants incur large costs in their jobs. Over 55 percent indicated they made financial sacrifices to take their position, and 62 percent reported greater stress in their government jobs than before. Yet these appointees tend to increase their earning power by holding office, and political service often leads to career changes into business and law (ibid., 181–83, 187–89). It is hard to see how these individuals have any necessary interest in budget maximization. But neither can they control the career service–Congress axis, in this curious system where executive attempts to control the bureaucracy are so evident, yet so impotent.

Conclusion

The main finding of this survey is that current research indicates that there exists little relationship between the growth of bureaus and the career prospects of bureaucrats. There is no strong empirical support for the view that civil servants obtain higher salary increases and faster promotions when they are in bureaucracies that are growing faster than normal. Several studies have found positive correlations between agency growth and career progress, but these are generally very small and are not uniform across departments.

This finding appears to undercut one of the major motivational pillars of the Niskanen thesis. Objectively, any benefits likely to accrue to bureaucrats who succeed in obtaining larger staffs and budgets for their agencies seem so small that in career terms budget-maximizing behavior simply does not pay. Nevertheless, the evidence is not broadly comparative, research designs have not been ideal, and the possibility remains that bureaucrats could create pressure for larger budgets if they act as though they believe that the proposition is true.

Next, I asked whether it is in the interests of bureaucrats to press for budget increases if they want material rewards and especially promotion, which is the most effective way to increase utility. The answer is not simple. It depends on the kind of bureaucrat in question and on the career structure within which he or she is operating. The great majority of civil servants have little direct control over budgets, and they achieve greater benefits through seniority, collective bargaining, and training. Managers may have an incentive to secure larger budgets in order to exchange discretionary benefits for compliant behavior by subordinates. Yet it is possible to design bureau-shrinking exercises that, while temporarily disruptive, leave managers with increased discretionary resources. Moreover, promotion-oriented managers take cues from their bureaucratic superiors and ultimately from their political masters. To the extent that bureaucrats operate in an environment where budget reductions are rewarded, rational bureaucrats interested in promotion will tend to cut their budgets.

Several structural factors may also help determine the probability that bureaucrats will manage to compress budgets. One is the extent to which promotions are made according to merit rather than on the basis of seniority. Another is whether promotion decisions are made centrally rather than within the bureau. A third is the probability of exit to a different agency or to the private sector. When merit can be rewarded, when it is defined outside of the bureau, and when commitment to any particular agency is reduced by likely exit, then norms of budgetary restraint have a better chance of taking hold. Downsizing is also easier, probably, when budgetary allocations flow from a unified executive rather than a spending-oriented legislature with which senior bureaucrats have to forge alliances.

In sum, we find little empirical or logical support for the core Niskanen thesis about bureaucrats' interests. Still, one cannot say that the model does not work at all. There is not much evidence for it insofar as bureaucratic careers are concerned, but even here more research is desirable before one can side with Jenkins and Gray in stating: "A Gresham's law of model development in which the simple but invalid drives out the complex but realistic serves little but dogma" (1983, 184–85).

As several analysts have suggested, more work is needed in specifying types of bureaucrats and in distinguishing between components of the budget. Much more quantitative study of career paths is worthwhile. Special attention should be focused upon interagency mobility and the process of personnel osmosis between bureaucracies and the private sector. Qualitative research on the informal criteria of promotion also seems desirable, although difficult in practice; it would be easier to examine bureaucrats' perceptions of the structure of opportunity that lies before them. Particular attention should be devoted to bureaus where cuts in staff and budgets have been substantial: What happened to those who initiated the change and to those who survived the cuts?

Finally, it would be illuminating to study the typical educations received by high-caliber bureaucratic entrants, on a cross-national basis. One theme of this chapter has been the importance at the summit of bureaucracies of particular kinds of ethos and expectations, and it would be worth knowing what intellectual baggage the current generations of fast-trackers are carrying to the top. Directly or indirectly, an important influence on all of them was *Bureaucracy and Representative Government*. Niskanen's thesis undoubtedly has shaped our general views of government, and it has also helped to change the incentive structures within which public servants work and strive for betterment.

NOTES

1. It is a measure of the infancy of bureaumetrics and of the complexity of modern governments that no systematic, let alone comparative, data are available on the depth of disaggregation of budgetary authority throughout whole bureaucracies or even on the degree of disaggregation of budgetary allocations made by politicians (the latter being an important indicator of political control or responsiveness to narrow client groups).

2. The extent of bureaucratic change in this stable province is shown by the fact that this search yielded only twenty-one observations in the expansionary era and thirty-eight in the restraint era.

3. A partial exception may exist in the case of highly specialized bu-

reaus where particular job categories are concentrated (such as "forester" in departments of the interior). Professional associations may press the case for reclassification and salary increases. In the U.S. system, at least, there seems to be considerable scope for agency-specific job reclassifications. But for nontechnical subordinates in countries with more centralized personnel administration, the prospects for widespread "classification creep" seem small enough to discourage collective efforts at the bureau level toward this end.

4. Agency restructuring can open new opportunities for careerists. It can produce major changes in occupational classifications, for example. More generally, Dunleavy (1985) argues persuasively that the character of bureaucratic life in small, central, elite, control-function agencies corresponds with the real desire of many senior bureaucrats and fast-trackers. Such restructuring represents an area of possible congruence between smaller budgets and bureaucrats' utility.

REFERENCES

Aberbach, Joel D., Robert D. Putnam, and Bert A. Rockman. 1981. *Bureaucrats and politicians in western democracies.* Cambridge, Mass.: Harvard Univ. Press.

Balk, Walter L., and Burton Gummer. 1986. Career disaffection among public service professionals: Analysis and recommendations. In *Bureaucratic and governmental reform,* ed. Donald J. Calista, 321–36. Greenwich, Conn.: JAI Press.

Bennett, James T., and Manuel H. Johnson. 1980. *The political economy of federal government growth: 1959–1978.* College Station: Center for Education and Research in Free Enterprise, Texas A & M University.

Berry, William D., and David Lowery. 1984. The growing cost of government: A test of two explanations. *Social Science Quarterly* 65(3): 735–49.

Brauer, Carl. 1987. Tenure, turnover, and postgovernment employment trends of presidential appointees. In *The in-and-outers: Presidential appointees and transient government in Washington,* ed. G. Calvin Mackenzie, 174–94. Baltimore, Md.: Johns Hopkins Univ. Press.

Breton, Albert, and Ronald Wintrobe. 1975. The equilibrium size of a budget-maximizing bureau: A note on Niskanen's theory of bureaucracy. *Journal of Political Economy* 83(1): 195–207.

———. 1982. *The logic of bureaucratic conduct.* New York: Cambridge Univ. Press.

Buchanan, Bruce, II. 1974. Government managers, business executives, and organizational commitments. *Public Administration Review* 34(4): 339–47.

Campbell, Colin. 1983. *Governments under stress: Political executives and key bureaucrats in Washington, London, and Ottawa*. Toronto: Univ. of Toronto Press.

Cassese, Sabino. 1984. The higher civil service in Italy. In Suleiman 1984a, 35–71.

Connolly, E. F. H. 1986. Controlling local government expenditures: The case of Northern Ireland. *Public Administration* 64(1): 83–96.

Corson, John J., and Paul R. Shale. 1966. *Men near the top: Filling key posts in the federal service*. Baltimore, Md.: Johns Hopkins Univ. Press.

Crenson, Matthew A., and Francis E. Rourke. 1987. By way of conclusion: American bureaucracy since World War II. In *The New American state: Bureaucracies and policies since World War II*, ed. Lewis Galambos, 137–77. Baltimore, Md.: Johns Hopkins Univ. Press.

Dogan, Mattei, ed. 1975. *The mandarins of Western Europe: The political role of top civil servants*. New York: Sage.

Dolezal, Peter. 1988. Strategies for successful downsizing. *Bulletin* of the Institute of Public Administration of Canada 11(2).

Dresang, Dennis L. 1984. *Public personnel management and public policy*. Boston: Little, Brown.

Dunleavy, Patrick. 1985. Bureaucrats, budgets and the growth of the state: Reconstructing an instrumental model. *British Journal of Political Science* 15(3): 299–328.

Dunsire, Andrew. 1987. Testing theories: The contribution of bureaumetrics. In Lane 1987, 94–144.

Fry, Geoffrey K. 1988. The Thatcher government, the financial management initiative, and the "new civil service". *Public Administration* 66(1): 1–20.

Goodin, Robert. 1975. The logic of bureaucratic back scratching. *Public Choice* 21 (Spring): 53–67.

———. 1982. Rational politicians and rational bureaucrats in Washington and Whitehall. *Public Administration* 60(1): 23–41.

Gournay, Bernard. 1984. The higher civil service of France. In Smith 1984, 69–86.

Grandjean, Burke D. 1981. History and career in a bureaucratic labour market. *American Journal of Sociology* 86(5): 1057–92.

Hannaway, Jane. 1987. Supply creates demands: An organizational process view of administrative expansion. *Journal of Policy Analysis and Management* 7(1): 118–34.

Heclo, Hugh. 1977. *A Government of strangers: Executive politics in Washington.* Washington, D.C.: Brookings.

———. 1984. In search of a role: America's higher civil service. In Suleiman 1984a, 8–34.

Hood, Christopher, and Andrew Dunsire. 1981. *Bureaumetrics: The quantitative comparison of British central government agencies.* Westmead, England: Gower.

Jack, Stephen. 1987. The success of slashers: A test of Niskanen's budget maximization theory. B.A. thesis, University of Western Ontario.

Jenkins, Bill, and Andrew Gray. 1983. Bureaucratic politics and power: Developments in the study of bureaucracy. *Political Studies* 31(June): 177–93.

Johnson, Ronald N., and Gary D. Libecap. 1987. Agency growth and bureaucratic salary structure. Unpub. paper. Montana State Univ. and Univ. of Arizona.

———. 1989. Agency growth, salaries and the protected bureaucrat. *Economic Inquiry* 27 (July): 431–51.

Lane, Jan-Erik, ed. 1987. *Bureaucracy and public choice.* London: Sage.

Lasson, Kenneth. 1978. *Private lives of public servants.* Bloomington: Indiana Univ. Press.

Lewis, Gregory B., and Meesung Ha. 1988. Impact of the baby boom on career success in federal civil service. *Public Administration Review* 48(6): 951 56.

McGregor, Eugene B., Jr. 1974. Politics and the career mobility of bureaucrats. *American Political Science Review* 68(1): 18–26.

Maynard-Moody, Steven, Donald D. Stull, and Jerry Mitchell. 1986. Reorganization as status drama: Building, maintaining, and displacing dominant subcultures. *Public Administration Review* 46(4): 301–10.

Mayntz, Renate. 1984. The higher civil service of the Federal Republic of Germany. In Smith 1984, 55–68.

Miller, Gary J., and Terry M. Moe. 1983. Bureaucrats, legislators, and the size of government. *American Political Science Review* 77(2): 297–322.

Morgan, Nicole. 1981. *Nowhere to go? Possible consequences of the demographic imbalance in decision-making groups of the federal public service.* Montreal: Institute for Research on Public Policy.

Niskanen, William A. 1971. *Bureaucracy and representative government.* Chicago: Aldine Atherton.

Pearce, Jone L., and James L. Perry. 1983. Federal merit pay: A longitudinal analysis. *Public Administration Review* 43(4): 315–25.

Pearson, William M., and Van A. Wiggington. 1986. The effectiveness of administrative controls: Some perceptions of state legislators. *Public Administration Review* 46(4): 328–31.

Pempel, T. J. 1984. Organizing for efficiency: The higher civil service in Japan. In Suleiman 1984a, 72–106.

Peters, B. Guy. 1978. *The politics of bureaucracy: A comparative perspective.* New York: Longman.

———. 1985. The United States. Absolute change and relative stability. In *Public employment in western nations,* ed. Richard Rose, 228–61. New York: Cambridge Univ. Press.

Plowden, William. 1984. The higher civil service of Britain. In Smith 1984, 20–39.

Rainey, Hal G. 1979. Perceptions of incentives in business and government: Implications for civil service reform. *Public Adminstration Review* 39(5): 440–48.

Ridley, F. F. 1983. Career service: A comparative perspective on civil service promotion. *Public Administration* 61(2): 179–96.

Rose, Richard. 1984. The political status of higher civil servants in Britain. In Suleiman 1984a, 136–73.

———. 1985. The programme approach to the growth of government. *British Journal of Political Science* 15(1): 1–28.

Savoie, Donald J. 1990. *The politics of public spending in Canada.* Toronto: Univ. of Toronto Press.

Scism, Thomas E. 1974. Employee mobility in the federal service: A description of some recent data. *Public Administration Review* 34(3): 247–54.

Seers, Dudley. 1968. The structure of power. In *Crisis in the civil service,* ed. Thomas Balogh et al., 83–109. London: Anthony Bland.

Shafritz, Jay M., Albert C. Hyde, and David H. Rosenbloom. 1986. *Personnel management in government: Politics and process.* 3d ed., rev. New York: Marcel Dekker.

Smith, Bruce L. R., ed. 1984. *The higher civil service in Europe and Canada: Lessons for the United States.* Washington, D.C.: Brookings.

Sorensen, Rune J. 1987. Bureaucratic decision-making and the growth of public expenditure. In Lane 1987, 63–75.

Suleiman, Ezra N., ed. 1984a. *Bureaucrats and policy making: A comparative overview.* New York: Holmes & Meier.

———. 1984b. From right to left: Bureaucracy and politics in France. In Suleiman 1984a, 107–35.

Warren, Ronald S., Jr. 1975. Bureaucratic performance and budgetary reward. *Public Choice* 24 (Winter): 51–57.

3

LAURENCE E. LYNN, JR.

The Budget-Maximizing Bureaucrat: Is There a Case?

Like the Peter Principle and Murphy's Law, the budget-maximizing bureaucrat has achieved an honored status in the folklore of public management. The notions, as formulated by Niskanen—that bureaucrats are self-interestedly rational, not simply obedient implementors of public law, and that political institutions reward budget and output expansion—seem to hold great promise for illuminating the dynamics of policy making and for explaining how the level and efficiency of bureaucratic provision of goods and services are determined.

The primary objective of this chapter is to evaluate the Niskanen model, drawing on evidence from case studies. Relying on evidence from cases risks reintroducing into the discussion of bureau behavior the kind of intellectually effete institutionalism that Niskanen was attempting to counter with his rigorous public choice model. Cases are subject to a wide variety of selection and interpretation biases. Drawing on specific cases, a clever rhetorician can not only confirm the infinite complexity of the world but also can find support for almost any plausible conjecture about that world.

As I share Niskanen's preference for parsimonious models with predictive power, I shall discipline my evaluation of evidence from cases by resolving to challenge the model only when the evidence seems to me compelling and when a less parsimonious formulation seems both feasible and necessary to an understanding of

59

bureaucratic behavior. In other words, the model will be given the benefit of the doubt. I conclude that a number of theoretical problems with Niskanen's approach must be resolved if the model is to have value in predicting bureaucratic behavior in typical cases.

Although the number of potentially usable case studies is large, a relatively small proportion treat the interplay between institutional contexts and bureaucratic behavior with sufficient subtlety to shed light on the appropriateness of the Niskanen model. To enlarge the body of relevant evidence, in addition to the case studies, I shall include systematic inquiries by social scientists based primarily on interviews and field observations, cases prepared for use in classroom teaching, biographical and autobiographical works by former public officials, and journalistic and anecdotal material. For practical reasons, the evidence is drawn exclusively from recent U.S. experience, albeit from a wide variety of policy domains and from all levels of government.

Before proceeding to examine the evidence from cases, however, I want to state my understanding of the model that I am attempting to evaluate and indicate the kinds of case-grounded evidence I consider relevant to the evaluation.

The Model Explicated

This chapter is based on the version of Niskanen's model set forth in his 1975 *Journal of Law and Economics* article. Budget-maximizing behavior is a prediction derived from a model in which bureaucrats are assumed to maximize their utility within a specific institutional context.

For bureaucrats, utility is a function of income—salary and fringe benefits—and perquisites, a variable representing a wide variety of desirable end states: access to emoluments, a favorable reputation, power, patronage, and the like. Both income and perquisites are postulated as being positive functions of the bureau's output and of its discretionary budget, which is the difference between the maximum budget that can be obtained from a bureau's sponsor for a given output and the lowest cost for which that output can actually be produced, thus creating a kind of profit. This profit is appropriated indirectly by the bureaucrat in the form of income (say, through higher salaries permitted by a higher position grade structure financed by budget growth) or of perquisites created by the uses to which discretionary resources are put. The shapes of bureaucrats' utility functions may in theory differ from bureau to bureau and from bureaucrat to bureaucrat, but, in Niskanen's view, they tend to be quite similar.

The utility-maximizing bureaucrat is transformed into a budget-maximizing bureaucrat by a set of specific institutional factors. The bureau is postulated as a monopoly supplier of a particular output and is assumed to exchange a total output for a total budget from its sponsor, a legislative body assumed to be a monopsonist. The availability of information is assumed to be asymmetrical: only the bureaucrat has accurate information on the minimum cost at which a given output can be produced, and that information can be obtained by the sponsor only at a cost. The sponsor's demand function for the bureau's output, that is, its marginal budget offer function, is given and declines as a function of the size of the budget.

How, then, do we obtain evidence from cases bearing on the hypothesis that bureaucrats maximize their budgets? As Niskanen himself notes, available aggregate data on bureau budgets and outputs are jointly determined by bureaucracy and by representative government, that is, by both supply and demand conditions; estimates of the partial effects of specific structural characteristics are exceedingly difficult to obtain from such data. Are observed changes in budgets explained by shifts in demand or by changes in the conditions of supply? Declining or stable budgets, and attenuated budget requests, for example, are not inconsistent with the assumption that bureaucrats seek to maximize their budgets, all else being equal. Thus it is exceedingly difficult to determine if the particular assumptions of the model hold.

In the light of these difficulties, an examination of cases has some potential advantages. Ideally, we should be able to identify the specific behavior of bureaucrats and the specific institutional factors with which the behavior is associated, perhaps even forming conjectures concerning partial effects on behavior of variations in these factors. Further, we can gain some insight into the motives of bureaucrats: what they want and why. Using their testimony and that of observers and associates, we can attempt to identify behavior overtly or covertly designed to secure or protect budgetary resources; behavior that reveals participants' goals, preferences for bureaucratic outputs or outcomes, or preferences for institutional arrangements, such as maintenance of a bureau's monopoly position, which are preconditions to budget maximization; and behavior consistent with alternative specifications of such a model that would lead to revised formulations and predictions.

In reality, however, bureaucrats may be reluctant to reveal their motives or preferences, or even their behavior, to other actors or to observers either out of self-interest or fear of reprisals. Budget-maximizing behavior—indeed, as we shall argue later, budget-minimizing behavior—may be covert or clandestine. Explanations may be deliberately deceptive and self-serving. Unfortunately, because cases are written to serve various purposes, it is often difficult to distinguish actual behavior and its consequences, as corroborated by dispassionate observers, from self-described behavior, and its alleged consequences, of questionable veracity. For this reason, evidence from cases asserting the actual shape of bureaucrats' preference functions or their evaluations of strategic payoffs associated with specific institutional circumstances must be interpreted with caution.

I will first present evidence that seems to bear directly, albeit imperfectly, on the behavior and on the implied utility functions of bureaucrats. Then, evidence bearing on the institutional contexts within which bureaucrats function will be discussed. The implications of these findings for the theory of the supply of goods and services by bureaus will be discussed in the final section.

Bureaus and Budgets: Evidence from Cases

What Do Bureaucrats Want?

The most robust conclusion concerning what bureaucrats want, based on evidence from cases, is that they want control over discretionary resources.

"During the March revisions round of cutting from their budgets, the cabinet members started to dig in their heels. They were facing OMB [U.S. Office of Management and Budget] proposals that hit them where it hurt: in their administrative expenses budgets" (Stockman 1986, 138). This kind of bureaucratic behavior is typical of that reported by David Stockman in his richly textured account of his efforts to reduce the size of the federal budget during the early years of the administration of President Ronald Reagan. "Dollars are dollars," said one Reagan appointee in response to Stockman's proposals to cut overhead accounts and small discretionary programs. "I've got to have some discretion in my priorities" (ibid.).

Although Stockman's evidence concerning the behavior of cabinet officers is the most explicit and, in view of the administration's espoused commitment to reducing expenditures, the most telling indicator of bureaucratic commitment to control discretionary resources, other evidence from cases is fully consistent with the proposition that bureaucrats place a high value on access to and control over discretionary resources. A variety of ploys and tactics is used to enlarge the discretionary budget.

• Cases concerned with public management in state and local government, for example, often reveal how grants from higher levels of government, or even from private sources, are used to initiate innovations or to free public officials from the encumbrances of state and local personnel and budget systems (Lynn 1980).

• Executive administrations at all levels of government may put forward optimistic projections of revenues to forestall stringent review of appropriations requests, which might lead to the elimination of fat.

• Bureaucrats seldom reduce their base budget when activities justifying particular expenditures are terminated, preferring to divert the excess appropriations to discretionary uses, perhaps in the guise of the original activity.

• In a similar spirit, bureaucrats may argue for a fair share of an enlarged budget even though a specific cost- or output-based justification is absent, or else they might contrive such a justification.

Indeed, it is intellectually fashionable to celebrate public entrepreneurs who are able employ a wide variety of tactics to achieve and exploit significant autonomy in directing the uses of public resources. Budgetary resources, argues Steven Cohen, a researcher with experience in government, "are the capital needed for entrepreneurial risk taking. The odds of successfully implementing a risky strategy are enhanced by possessing extra resources (1988, 103; see also Doig and Hargrove 1987, 8). Eugene Lewis concludes in his study of three well-known U.S. public entrepreneurs that "the public entrepreneur distinguishes himself from others in that he uses organizations and their resources to achieve great aims with minimal direction from the other elements in the political system" (1980, 18). As director of the Federal Bureau of Investigation, for example, J. Edgar Hoover "never had a budget request denied" (ibid.). In directing the U.S. Navy's nuclear programs, Admiral Hyman Rickover "commanded financial and human resources far beyond those of his putative superiors" (ibid., 20).

Stockman's evidence suggests, however, that cabinet officers, even in the fiscally conservative Reagan administration, went beyond protecting discretionary resources and argued strongly for maintaining or expanding their agencies' outputs and overall budgets. Official after official is described as having advocated higher expenditures and larger programs than OMB thought consistent with the president's priorities. One was described as "a sucker for every spending proposal that came along" (Stockman 1986, 141). Another "submitted a forty-five-page appeal for restoration of 'devastating' OMB budget cuts" (ibid., 361). Still another took his complaint against a 2.6 percent reduction in departmental staffing levels directly to the president (ibid., 138–39).

Indeed, consideration of the evidence in cases leads to the strong impression that few bureaucrats—whether career officials or appointed executives—believe that appropriations are adequate to produce the levels of output that are mandated by authorizing statutes or that are required if the bureau is to fulfill its mission. Most bureaucrats regularly seek to demonstrate to sponsors the existence of unmet needs, deficiencies in the quality of output, inadequate enforcement, insufficient outreach, and the like.

In terms of Niskanen's model, however, this evidence has somewhat ambiguous implications. It most probably suggests that bureaucrats seek to induce a positive shift in the sponsor's demand function for the bureau's output. This is not quite the same thing as, though not inconsistent with, budget maximization, a point to which I shall return.

Not all bureaucrats, and especially not all political appointees, are overt advocates for higher total output and spending, however. Reagan appointed many zealous budget cutters to key executive positions. Some Reagan administration officials, for example, openly courted legislative reprisals, but praise from the White House, by taking to budget reduction with alacrity (Kennedy School of Government 1984, 1983). Said one, simply: "My job . . . was to cut the budget for this agency" (ibid., 5). A former associate said of Anne Gorsuch, Reagan's appointee to be administrator of the Environmental Protection Agency: "Early on, she had a tendency to think in terms of broad brush strokes. And the broad brush strokes were that the EPA bureaucracy was bloated and that the enforcement arm was an unfair burden on business" (Kennedy School of Government 1984).

In state and local agencies, it is not unusual for officials to seek reputations for maintaining control over spending, eliminating waste, fraud, and abuse from budgets and for achieving gains in efficiency that save money. A deputy commissioner of mental retardation, under court order to seek higher expenditures for state schools for the retarded, complained that such court decrees undermined managerial and fiscal discipline, precluding managers from having to make choices (Kennedy School of Government 1987b, 12). Services for clients who fell outside the decree received little new funding.

The impression is strong, moreover, that few career bureaucrats welcome explosive or even extraordinarily large increases in their budgets, even when thrust upon them by willing sponsors. Career bureaucrats typically try to maintain an even keel approach that will eventually lead to a greater total through gentle increases, even though the prospects of a sharp rise at first might seem tempting (Wildavsky 1979, 19–20). In a similar interpretation, Douglas Yates argues that "Bureaucracies . . . doubtless seek to increase their budgets, but they do this in a limited and guarded fashion" (1982, 90).

Even these demurrers do not point to the complete story of the attenuated nature of bureaucrats' goals, however. Case studies further reveal that bureaucrats engage in goal-oriented activities that appear to have little or nothing directly to do with expanding the bureau's output, and thus with budget maximization.

• The professed goals of one state commissioner of mental health, for example, were to safeguard the rights of mentally ill persons, to involve family members and consumers in policy making, and to care for patients in the least restrictive environment. These goals might well have permitted reduction in budgets for expensive state institutions (Kennedy School of Government 1987c).

• The goals of the director of the U.S. National Highway Traffic Safety Administration were to see that rule-making standards resulted in cars being designed to the capabilities of safety research vehicles, to issue standards in a timely manner in order to enhance the agency's reputation for competence, and to attend to the needs and concerns of purchasers and operators of motor vehicles in formulating agency policy. These were goals with only modest implications, if any, for the agency's budget (Lynn 1987, 131–34).

• The primary goal of a state human services administrator was to improve methods of insuring that contracts with nonprofit service providers led to achievement of agency program objectives; again, a goal with no obvious budget implications (Kennedy School of Government 1979a).

• A state environmental commissioner during the expansionary period of the early 1970s concentrated on replacing the traditional litigation-based approach to enforcing air pollution control orders with a system of administrative penalties that would alter the incentives of potential polluters by increasing the costs of noncompliance with administrative orders (Lynn 1980). This change was accomplished with a modest expenditure of discretionary funds.

The number of such examples of bureaucratic commitment to quality, due process, access, and similar types of goals that appear to be unrelated in any direct way to output and budget expansion could easily be proliferated.

The interpretation of such evidence most consistent with the Niskanen hypothesis is that the concept of a bureau's output is exceedingly ambiguous and seldom reducible to an easily measured dimension. Each of the above officials, it might be argued, is seeking to maximize something that can be interpreted as a bureau output: safeguarded rights, conforming vehicles, individuals served in a least restrictive environment, services meeting agency standards, instances of voluntary compliance with administrative orders, episodes of identifiable consumer influence on agency policy, and the like.[2] (It is similarly difficult to define unambiguously an agency's minimum cost to produce a given output—a subject to which we will return later.) Thus their behavior is consistent with Niskanen's model. These rather abstract definitions of output, however, are unlikely to be the definitions used by actual sponsors and bureaucrats. Expanding output in this kind of abstract sense is probably not what they think they are doing—indeed, they may think they are contributing to budgetary restraint—a possibility with complex implications for analysis of bureaucratic behavior.

Partly because output is an ambiguous concept, participants in policy making and budgeting are more likely to frame issues in less abstract, often more input- or activity-oriented terms. It is conventional wisdom among students of public budgeting that budgeting serves diverse, often conflicting purposes: expenditure control and fiduciary accountability, the management and allocation of agency resources among agency structures, and the planning and determination of the desired mix, quality, and level of agency outputs (Lynn 1987, 195). Public budgeting formats, systems, and staffs are likely to reflect all three purposes. Indeed, it is plausible to argue that the administrators of the budget function are largely input oriented, that bureaucrats are primarily activity or program oriented, and that appointed and elected executives are the government actors most likely to be, but are by no means always, goal or output oriented. Budgeting is thus a complex game in which each type of participant is contending for diverse types of advantage.

This view of budgeting is not inconsistent with Niskanen's model. It suggests, however, that the concept of minimum cost, the relationship between cost and output, and the incentives governing the dissemination of information on costs are likely to be rather ambiguous in practice.

Another fundamental question raised by these examples is the relationship between an agency's output and its budget. In the case of what we may call regulatory outputs (Wolf 1988, 38), the quantity may depend, perhaps for demand-induced reasons, more on the effective organization of internal administrative processes than on the purchase of additional inputs. In the language of the Niskanen model, managerial activity is directed at absorbing discretionary resources into the production of monitored output, or, alternatively, at reallocating discretionary resources discovered within the organization toward monitored inputs and activities. One example of this type of bureaucratic strategy is reducing discretionary resources in the hands of subordinate officials and shifting control over discretionary resources upward, behavior that is consistent with the spirit of Niskanen's model and poses an issue to which we shall return.

Of great interest in this regard is the increasing resort by public officials to "unappropriated public spending" (Leonard 1986, 13)—including direct disbursing of financial claims, assuming liability for future payments, and consuming assets—and to forms of government action, such as regulation, the costs of which are borne by the private sector or by other levels of government. In terms of Niskanen's analytic framework, the public officials' perquisites may indeed by functions of the bureau's output and discretionary budget, but the expansion of output can often be accomplished with little or no expansion of the bureau's budget.

That this occurs with increasing frequency does not necessarily undermine the budget-maximization hypothesis; it suggests, rather, that budget maximization may be only one means to achieve utility maximization. Bureaucrats, in other words, do indeed appear to maximize some function of income and perquisites, but the constraints within which they operate include parameters in addition to their own bureau's budget: corporate profits (in some sectors), state and municipal budgets (or the discretionary resources incorporated therein), and other external sources of discretionary resources.

Indeed, the net effect of sponsors and bureaucrats seeking indirect forms of output expansion may be little or no actual output or input expansion but, instead, reallocations of costs among levels of government and between the public and private sectors and increases in the minimum cost for which outputs can be produced by bureaus. It is generally held that increases in federal expenditures for social services in the 1970s represented a shifting of costs for traditional services from nonprofit and state agencies to the federal budget. Allowing states to match federal grants with private donated funds, for example, led to expansions in state contracting with private organizations that, though it might have led to an increase in competition, allowed these organizations "to restructure their debt, raise salaries, and/or improve their physical plants through the internal reallocation of costs (Smith 1988, 6).

This suggests a formulation of bureaucratic behavior similar to Niskanen's formulation of sponsor behavior. Just as sponsor oversight of a bureau is costly, so too is securing additional budgetary resources costly to a bureaucrat. Bureaucrats might be supposed to engage in it up to the point at which marginal gains no longer outweigh marginal costs. When the relative cost of securing additional budgetary resources falls, for example, as when some kind of shift in political mood induces sponsors to spend more on a problem, program, or an agency, or when amendments to statutes create new funding opportunities, bureaucrats can be expected to devote more attention to budget-expanding strategies. But when budgets are tight, bureaucrats shift to other strategies.

Yet another complication in defining a bureau's output bearing on budget maximization is the familiar one of collective goods. Most publicly provided social welfare goods and services, for example, have the character of collective goods. That is, their intended social benefits—an equitable distribution of income, equal access to social opportunities, full utilization of a society's human resources, safe and healthful neighborhoods, and social insurance or the guaranteed availability of help to those experiencing a dramatic reduction in well-being—are enjoyed by all citizens, whether or not they have paid for them. Thus social welfare bureaucrats face the general problem that the public at large may express support for the collective goals of equity and assisting the needy but may be reluctant voluntarily either to tax themselves to pay for social programs or to reveal the value they place on the outputs.

Under such circumstances, bureaucrats may become entrepreneurs actively seeking ways to induce voluntary support for social programs through making political arrangements that attract political support. They can attempt, for example, to design programs in accord with the wishes of organized groups of service providers:

physicians, vocational rehabilitation counselors, mental retardation or child development specialists, psychologists, or police. Alternatively, they can seek to employ court rulings, regulations, or other coercive measures to compel support for public provision. They can promise rewards such as the elected executive's support for other, unrelated programs. Entrepreneurial bureaucrats seeking to overcome free-rider problems look in practice a lot like Niskanen's budget-maximizing bureaucrat in that they are often overtly committed to output and budget expansion. But their goals, in general, require more complex characterization. Douglas Yates states the following general proposition: "Bureaucracies tend gradually to enlarge their roles over a wide spectrum of policy making functions—spending money, designing new programs and bureaucratic units, developing new regulations, expanding their evaluation of lower-level governments, and increasing their control of the flow of information" (1982, 90).

How Are Bureaucrats Rewarded?

Most evidence concerning bureaucrats' utility functions, including that just cited, is inconclusive because it almost inevitably confounds supply and demand considerations. Budgeting, argues Wildavsky, is a matter of scanning the environment for cues and clues as to "what will go" (1979, 24). Based on the evidence in cases, what can be said about what will go, that is, about reward structures?

Stockman describes the dense network of interrelationships between the U.S. Congress and the federal bureaus, the lifeblood of which is budgetary resources. On the one hand, and particularly at the federal level, political appointees who seek to be influential in the issue networks in which their agencies participate often feel compelled to be advocates for spending. Many of Reagan's appointees, for example, professed to be engaged in political survival strategies when advocating higher expenditures. "Justice's budget would grow and grow," said Stockman, "as the Attorney General came up with more and more schemes to show that the administration was 'committed' to aggressive 'internal defense' [crime prevention and deterrence] in order to avoid being embarrassed by Congressional democrats" (1986, 141).

On the other hand, having a reputation for economizing is not necessarily inconsistent with maximizing the bureau's budget, especially at state and local levels of government. Agencies led by officials who are committed to economy in administrative functions or to managing programs that happen to have weak constituencies often experience steady growth in staff, budget, and responsibility. The rewards of apparently frugal and efficient management often come in the form of expanded responsibilities and being entrusted with additional appropriated funds (Kennedy School of Government 1987a). Further, officials who publicly bow to legislative or executive demands for budgetary discipline may do so knowing that political reprisals against the administrator and lawsuits by interest groups will "take them off the hook" with agency constituencies. It is a game that is well understood by all participants, and they play it to their advantage.

The evidence suggests, then, that political reward structures can be changeable, inconsistent, and subtle. Consider the following two examples.

In the early 1970s, the secretary of health, education, and welfare proposed to publish regulations that would "limit drug reimbursements under programs administered by his Department to the lower cost at which the drug was generally available unless there is a demonstrated difference in therapeutic effect" (Kennedy School of Government 1980). Implementation of such a proposal, which would have had the effect of rewarding the prescribing of generic instead of brand name drugs, would have reduced, not increased, the department's budget, further enhancing the reputation of an official known to be fiscally conservative. Such a straightforward outcome was not to be, however.

Several groups were involved in the bargaining that preceded the adoption of a final solution: a legislative committee on antitrust and monopoly whose long-standing goal had been to reduce drug prices charged consumers; top government health officials, some concerned with program administration, who favored it, and others concerned with the dangers of overregulating medical practice, who opposed it; a pharmaceutical manufacturers' association representing large, research-based pharmaceutical companies marketing brand name drugs and vigorously opposed to the regulation; the American Medical Association, whose journal depended on revenues from the large pharmaceutical companies; an association of professional pharmacists, which saw an opportunity to augment their professional standing by supporting generic prescribing; and an association of retail druggists, which saw an opportunity to increase the profitability of dispensing drugs but was opposed to the approach of the pharmacists.

After three years of conflict and negotiation among these groups, the published regulations created an excruciatingly complex process for determining, for individual drugs, what the maximum allowable cost would be. The likely impact on either the department's budget or on consumer budgets could not be determined. In summary, conflict among those with a stake in the outcome created a highly ambiguous reward structure for the bureaucrats involved.

Later in the decade, the director of the National Highway Traffic Safety Administration found herself caught in a tangle of interests involving the president of the United States, facing difficult economic policy choices because of a recession in the automobile industry; the federal office of management and budget, generally skeptical of spending by the department and directed by a close associate of the president; the secretary of transportation, a presidential appointee and a former and probable future elected official; two authorizing committees and two appropriations committees of the U.S. Congress, each with a distinctive viewpoint on automobile safety issues; a militant and politically influential consumer advocacy group, the former and, it turned out, future employer of the agency director; a well-financed research institute sponsored by the automobile insurance industry that produced cost and output information competitive with that of the bureau; and the automobile industry, comprising a few large automobile manufacturers, which were not always in agreement, and the contentious and powerful union of automobile workers, usually in conflict with the manufacturers.

As in the previous example, the outputs and budgets of this

bureau were a product of conflict and negotiations among actors with sharply divided interests. Under a fiscally conservative president, these actors were less concerned with the size of the budget or the level of output per se than with specific policy issues and with their particular budgetary and other impacts.

Depending on how the bureaucrat perceives the political reward structure and the time period over which rewards are sought— elected office? a high-paying industry job? a reputation justifying promotion within the administration? future opportunities with other administrations? a future job with one's past employer?— utility maximizing may lead to overt efforts to control or reduce expenditures, to reallocate expenditures among outputs, to shift costs through regulations, or to other strategies. It is generally likely to lead to efforts to differentiate outputs, to selective advocacy of various bureau activities, and to strategic behavior of various kinds designed to reduce the odds of damaging political reprisals and to strengthen one's constituencies.

Although the evidence from cases suggests the complexity of reward structures, it is not, based on my perusal of it, inconsistent with the conjecture that, all other things—and there are a great many of them—being equal, expansion in agency and program budgets and outputs is generally held to be a symbol of managerial prowess, and bureaucrats' income and perquisites, in an expected value sense, can plausibly be postulated as being positively related to a bureau's output and to control over discretionary resources that can be converted into symbols of growth and innovation. Aaron Wildavsky expresses a related notion: "Perhaps the most useful axiom would be that agency people seek to secure their other goals so long as this effort does not result in an over-all decrease in income" (1979, 19–20).

But, even within the public choice framework, there is more to it than that. Concerning the importance of the institutional environment, three conclusions can be drawn from the evidence in cases.

• Institutional contexts and the reward structures to which they give rise are generally more complicated than the simple bilateral monopoly model postulated by Niskanen.

• Public budgeting is characterized by a pattern of competition and conflict among various actors in the budgetary process who have different stakes in the outcome. These patterns of interaction within the institutional environment seem to have a strong bearing on the extent to which utility maximization leads to budget maximization.

• Budgeting is concerned with measurable outputs to only a limited and inconsistent extent. Often sponsors are seeking to exchange an appropriation not for a total output but for a distribution of appropriated funds among particular classes of inputs or activities, perhaps located in designated legislative districts.

The kinds of behavior characteristic of a world of many actors linked to each other through strategic interactions are especially clearly illustrated in a case concerning the Massachusetts Bay Transit Authority (Kennedy School of Government 1979b, 1979c). The actors include the transit authority, its chief executive officer, its advisory board, representing local governments whose residents were taxed to pay for transit services, its five-member board of directors, and its unions. The bureau comprised several operating divisions, each with its own interests and budget office. In addition, the advisory board had a budget committee with its own staff.

The chief executive officer viewed the MBTA budget as his primary instrument for achieving and maintaining central direction and control of the bureau. He knew that the advisory board—equivalent to Niskanen's sponsor—always cut MBTA's budget request and, in addition, that any savings in operating costs would be pocketed rather than reinvested. He knew, further, that his subordinate departments both padded their budget requests and expected that any cost overruns would be covered by late-year supplementary budget allotments. He was aware, finally, that he knew far less than his department managers about the actual costs of providing transit service. He was thrust into the center of a complex budgetary game: "We made a decision, right or wrong, that the budget would be as tight as we could make it. We would leave nothing deliberately for the Advisory Board to cut out." This left his sponsor pleased but nonetheless wary (Kennedy School of Government 1979c, 8). The director was later rewarded with the directorship of the largest municipal transportation authority in the country.

This particular case illustrates many of the features of Niskanen's model: a bilateral monopoly, information asymmetries, cost-conscious sponsor oversight, and, we may infer, utility-maximizing behavior by the chief executive officer. It is clearly questionable, however, whether utility maximization in this particular context leads to budget maximization in Niskanen's sense. The rewards lay, rather, *in maintaining fiscal discipline while seeking internal reallocations of control over discretionary resources*. My impression is that, in times of fiscal restraint, the structure of rewards often induces such behavior.

The Utility-Maximizing Bureaucrat: Additional Considerations

A number of Niskanen's conjectures stand up rather well to the disparate body of empirical evidence one gathers from cases. Undoubtedly the most important is that bureaucratic behavior is governed by the structures of rewards embedded in the institutions of representative democracy. In my judgment, the evidence I have reviewed is consistent with the notions that bureaucrats exhibit stable preferences, that their preferences are for both material and nonmaterial rewards, and that these rewards are, interestingly often, positively related to the bureau's output and to the amount of discretionary budgetary resources controlled by the bureaucrat. Niskanen's general public choice framework, in other words, seems a plausible basis for further research.

It seems unlikely, however, that the model as formulated by Niskanen would explain much of the observed variance in agency budgets and level and mix of output even if good tests could be devised. The reason for this conjecture is that the model is too parsimonious to account for significant aspects of actual institutions and bureaucratic behavior that affect output and budget determination. In the next section, I identify several respects in which Niskanen's public choice framework needs to be extended to explain actual behavior.

The Prevalence of Interactive Behavior

Few systematic accounts of bureaucratic behavior fail to notice the extent to which the actions of bureaucrats anticipate the reactions of other actors in the political process. In their study of bureaucrats and politicians in Western democracies, for example, Aberbach, Putnam, and Rockman conclude that "Policymaking is . . . a kind of dialectic, in which the 'law of anticipated reactions' normally governs the behavior of bureaucrats" (1981, 248). Wildavsky (1979) observes that "budgeting proceeds in an environment of reciprocal expectations that lead to self-fulfilling prophecies as the actions of each participant generate the reactions that fulfill the original expectations." The literature on budgeting is replete with resorts to the metaphor of games to account for the interactive character of the budgetary process.

Indeed, although Niskanen does not explore this aspect of his model, unless one of the parties is strong enough to force a solution (Niskanen assumes that sponsors passively submit to bureau domination), a bilateral monopoly is likely to lead to bargaining and cooperation concerning outputs and budgets and thus to the kind of strategic, interactive behavior one observes in practice. Budgeting is a gamelike process in which actors choose their strategies in the light of the other actors' possible responses.

The question is whether a bilateral monopoly model is sufficiently general to account for the great range of budgetary outcomes one observes in practice. More general, non-zero-sum games, either single period or multiperiod, and principal-agent models, are, at least intuitively, superior to static bilateral monopoly models with a dominant actor as frameworks for analyzing bureaucratic behavior.

In a more comprehensive formulation than Niskanen's, Jonathan Bendor and Terry Moe have created an analytic framework in which "the central outcomes of interest—government outputs, budgets, and bureaucratic efficiency—are in every sense jointly determined by the interdependent decisions of bureaucratic, legislative, and interest group participants" (Bendor and Moe 1985, 756). By modeling the interactive character of budgeting, Bendor and Moe show, for example, contrary to Niskanen's predictions, that budget maximization leads neither to gross inefficiency nor to gross over-supply of output and that maximizing discretionary resources can lead to explosive budget expansion and gross inefficiency.

The Diversity of Bureaucrats and Sponsors

Without abandoning the notion that a bureaucrat's utility is related, at least to some extent, to the bureau's budget and output, and thus to sponsor demands, through the bureaucrat's preferences for income and perquisites, it seems appropriate in light of the evidence to introduce some additional considerations.

Utility functions for appointed executives, who serve at the pleasure of elected officials, and for career civil servants are likely to differ. Argue Aberbach, Putnam, and Rockman:

> The norms of representative democracy . . . endow elected politicians with a monopoly on one essential ingredient in policymaking—legitimacy as the final decision-making authority. However expert and imaginative a civil servant in substantive terms, however skilled in winning consent from organized interests, however adept in coordinating his initiatives with others, however successful in implementation, he needs endorsement from political leaders for his actions. Constitutionally, politicians are everywhere empowered to reject the counsel of bureaucrats, although such rejection is infrequent in practice. (1981, 248)

Executive agencies, in other words, have two kinds of bureaucrats: the appointed executive, whose rewards are established in a wider political context and in the light of more diverse career aspirations, and career civil servants, whose rewards are likely to be more closely related to agency outputs and budgets. (It is possible to compound the complexity by adding central finance and budget officials and elected executives to the model.)

The usefulness to prediction of introducing this kind of distinction is, of course, an empirical question. The ubiquity of bargaining games among executive branch actors and between executive branch actors and legislators—who, themselves, can be subclassified in various ways—cannot be doubted, and such factors as information asymmetries and the payoff structure vary from context to context.

A bureaucrat's political reputation may be enhanced through successful internal reallocations of existing discretionary budgets, or through shifting costs to other levels of government or to the private sector, or through cutting fat. Those of Reagan's appointees who sought to reduce their agency's budget were not acting irrationally; they were facing different reward structures. For a political appointee, perquisites and even income may depend on being associated with an administration's substantive policy achievements, with reshaping agendas of issues and alternatives, with supplying satisfactions of various kinds, perhaps in symbolic form, to administration and agency constituencies, or with successfully managing a crisis, conducting an investigation, or inducing cooperation from recalcitrant parties.

In this context, the rewards from seeking additional budgetary allocations must be compared with the rewards from other types of political activity in the light of their relative costs. Elsewhere, I argue that the relevant cost is the opportunity cost of forgoing alternative uses of a bureaucrat's time, attention, and personal political influence (Lynn 1987). Fighting an appropriations battle may not be worth it if greater perquisites in the form of an enhanced reputation can be earned in other ways, for example, by imposing regulatory restraints on other levels of government or on the private sector. Beginning with the administration of President Jimmy Carter, the evidence suggests that the rewards went disproportionately to those bureaucrats who successfully avoided or minimized contact with the regular appropriations process.

The fact that budgeting is not typically output oriented introduces another complication. Although a monopsonist, the sponsor may show little preference for securing a given output at the lowest price. Indeed, bureaucrats can be observed seeking lower appropriations for a given output than sponsors wish to allocate. If the sponsor is a legislator whose rewards are reelection and increased seniority, which depend in turn on bringing the benefits of budgetary allocations to his or her district, and the bureaucrat earns rewards in the form of discretionary resources for avoiding inefficiencies in particular programs, incentives for budget maximization are effectively reversed, the bureaucrat seeking lower appropriations, the sponsor seeking higher ones.

Most government bureaus produce a variety of outputs, and production is accomplished through reliance on specialized administrative units. Each of these outputs, and many of the specialized administrative units, is likely to have its own sponsorship. Because of the existence of positive transaction costs for conducting exchanges among these units, organizations tend to be loosely coupled, that is, they engage in cooperative exchanges only up to the point that it is worth it.

Sponsorship, too, is likely to comprise various partially overlapping and frequently shifting constituencies. Indeed, as John Kingdon has suggested, sponsorship may be organized around particular problems or around classes of "solutions" or outputs (1984). Investigators variously refer to issue networks, segmented pluralism, policy domains, partisan mutual adjustment, and other characterizations of the specialized, loosely compartmentalized, opportunistic nature of these sponsorship networks.

Neither sponsors nor bureaus, therefore, are monolithic. A bureau's budget is a result of complicated networks of strategic interaction among actors with differing purposes and influence. Budget maximization is only one of the behaviors one would expect under such circumstances. It is reasonable to expect problems of arranging for collective action on both the demand and the supply sides and to anticipate both cooperative and noncooperative outcomes.

The Ambiguity of Outputs and Costs

The outputs of most bureaus contain important elements of ambiguity. The availability and price of a good or service provided by a bureau alter the incentives of those entitled, eligible, or otherwise able to consume it. Is the bureau's output a particular good or service, is it the altered behavior implied by its consumption, or is it the consequence of the consumption? The availability of a low-cost medical treatment under the auspices of government, for example, may stimulate total consumption of that treatment and thereby improve health status. Sponsors may be purchasing the treatment, the additional consumption, or the improvement in health status. Enforcement of a regulation proscribing certain behavior may lead to punishment of violators, deterrence of viola-

tions, and the alleviation of problems associated with the pro-
scribed behavior. Again, actual and potential sponsors may value
these outputs differently.

Similar ambiguities exist in the concept of cost in large part
because of ambiguities in defining output. Day care for young
children, for example, can range from custodial protection in a
private home to highly enriched developmental programming in a
professionally staffed center. In principle, issues of what a service‾
costs are inseparable from issues of what the service is. In practice,
the two issues are often blurred, and service definition issues mas-
querade as cost issues.

These kinds of ambiguity may be what Niskanen had in mind
when he embraced the notion of a discretionary budget. A sponsor
interested in supporting specific numbers of children in publicly
financed day care, but with only general, impressionistic concerns
about the quality of that care, may be offered enrichment programs rather than custodial programs. The differences in the costs
of the two types of day care can be construed as discretionary
resources that the bureaucrat uses to obtain a perquisite: a highly
favorable reputation among child care specialists who advocate
and staff enrichment programs. Others, however, may regard this
analysis as incorporating a dubious interpretation of the term *discretionary,* thus begging the question of what that term can mean in
practice.

Concluding Note

Niskanen's primary goal in formulating his model was to explain how the level and efficiency of bureaucratic provision compare to the social optimum. The prevalence of collective action
problems in assessing both the demand for and supply of government outputs makes this question empirically intractable, although, if one wishes to know whether governments grow too
large, Bendor and Moe (1985) present a good case for a model
more complex than Niskanen's. The test of the Niskanen model's
value in public policy research lies, rather, in its value as a basis for

predicting the behavior of bureaucrats in particular institutional contexts.

The evidence from cases suggests that, in particular, frequently encountered circumstances, bureaucrats do indeed seek to maximize the amount of discretionary resources over which they exercise control; occasionally they seek to maximize their budgets as well. The problem is that it is difficult to specify a priori the circumstances under which budget-maximizing behavior will occur. Bureaucrats, at least those managing complex organizations, choose to maximize their utility from among a variety of strategies with different costs and benefits. Whether or not they choose budget-maximizing strategies is an empirical question. To say that budget-maximizing strategies are occasionally chosen, therefore, takes us only a limited way toward understanding the nature of bureaucratic supply. To go further, the evidence suggests that Niskanen's framework needs to be expanded in a variety of ways.

The value of introducing additional specifications of various kinds into the Niskanen–inspired public choice framework for predicting the behavior of bureaucrats depends on the specific questions one wants to answer. If one wishes to explain a particular agency's mix of outputs, choice of production functions, efficiency, and budget, and to predict the future course of these variables, a more complicated model of the sponsor, the bureaucracy, and the interactions between them is undoubtedly necessary.

There can be little doubt, however, that attempts to model reward structures, utility functions, and optimal strategies on the assumption of dynamic relationships between sponsors and bureaucrats can lead to important insights into the nature of bureaucratic supply. This was Niskanen's fundamental insight, and therefore his model deserves its status as seminal in the theory of bureaucratic supply.

REFERENCES

Aberbach, Joel D., Robert D. Putnam, and Bert A. Rockman. 1981. *Bureaucrats and politicians in western democracies.* Cambridge, Mass.: Harvard Univ. Press.

Bendor, Jonathan, and Terry M. Moe. 1985. An adaptive model of bureaucratic politics. *American Political Science Review* 79:755–74.

Cohen, Steven. 1988. *The effective public manager: Achieving success in government.* San Francisco: Jossey-Bass.

Doig, Jameson W., and Erwin C. Hargrove, eds. 1987. *Leadership and innovation: A biographical perspective on entrepreneurs in government.* Baltimore, Md.: Johns Hopkins Univ. Press.

Kennedy School of Government Case Program. 1979a. Contracting for human services (A). Case C14-79-268. Cambridge, Mass.: Harvard Univ.

———. 1979b. The MBTA: Budget Process (A). Case C16-79-249. Cambridge, Mass.: Harvard Univ.

———. 1979c. The MBTA: Budget Process (B). Case C15-79-250. Cambridge, Mass.: Harvard Univ.

———. 1980. Maximum allowable cost (MAC). Case C14-80-282. Cambridge, Mass.: Harvard Univ.

———. 1983. Dr. Savitz and the Department of Energy. Case C16-83-513. Cambridge, Mass.: Harvard Univ.

———. 1984. Note on the EPA under Administrator Anne Gorsuch. Case N16-84-587. Cambridge, Mass.: Harvard Univ.

———. 1987a. Denise Fleury and the Minnesota Office of State Claims. Case C15-87-744.0. Cambridge, Mass.: Harvard Univ.

———. 1987b. Judge Tauro and care of the retarded in Massachusetts. Case C15-87-739.0. Cambridge, Mass.: Harvard Univ.

———. 1987c. Pam Hyde and Ohio mental health: Shifting control of inpatient care. Case C15-97-741.0. Cambridge, Mass.: Harvard Univ.

Kingdon, John W. 1984. *Agendas, alternatives, and public policies.* Boston: Little, Brown.

Leonard, Herman B. 1986. *Checks unbalanced: The quiet side of public spending.* New York: Basic Books.

Lewis, Eugene. 1980. *Public entrepreneurship: Toward a theory of bureaucratic political power.* Bloomington: Indiana Univ. Press.

Lynn, Laurence E., Jr. 1980. The Connecticut enforcement project (A); The Connecticut enforcement project (B); The Connecticut enforcement project (C). In *Designing public policy: A casebook on the role of policy analysis,* 405–61. Santa Monica, Calif.: Goodyear.

———. 1987. *Managing public policy.* Boston: Little, Brown.

———. 1990. Managing the social safety net: The job of the social welfare executive. In *Impossible jobs in public management,* ed. Erwin C. Hargrove and John C. Gudewell, 133–51. Lawrence: Univ. Press of Kansas.

Niskanen, William a. 1975. Bureaucrats and politicians. *Journal of Law and Economics* 18:617–43.

Smith, Steven Rathgeb. 1988. Policy entrepreneurship and nonprofit agencies: The experience of the states. Paper presented at the annual meeting of the Association for Public Policy Analysis and Management, Seattle, Wash., 27–29 October.

Stockman, David A. 1986. *The triumph of politics: How the Reagan revolution failed.* New York: Harper & Row.

Wildavsky, Aaron. 1979. *The politics of the budgetary process.* 3d ed. Boston: Little, Brown.

Wolf, Charles, Jr. 1988. *Markets or governments: Choosing between imperfect alternatives.* Cambridge, Mass.: MIT Press.

Yates, Douglas. 1982. *Bureaucratic democracy: The search for democracy and efficiency in American government.* Cambridge, Mass.: Harvard Univ. Press.

4

COLIN CAMPBELL, S.J., AND
DONALD NAULLS

The Limits of the
Budget-Maximizing Theory:
Some Evidence from Officials'
Views of Their Roles and Careers

CAMPBELL: *Is there any driving motive in particular in your coming*
[into government] at this time?

RESPONDENT: *It's a combination of two things. One is that Mr.*
Reagan's . . . what Mr. Reagan wants to do here is closer to what I
would like to see done. . . . Second, my personal circumstances, eco-
nomic and otherwise, just made it possible to do so. The government's
in a strange situation right now in that the real salaries—or the
inflation-corrected salaries—at the top have declined a good bit over
the years. My present salary . . . corrected for inflation—is lower
than my first job in . . . [1962], although my position is a great deal
more responsible. . . . So, basically, the only people you can get in
these senior positions these days are . . . young people on the make
who use this as a stepping stone to something else, or people with an
independent income, or mediocre people.

—Confidential interview with Reagan administration official,
11 November 1982

The above is just one of several hundred accounts of career motivations rendered by respondents in a data set that we have been
collecting for thirteen years. One thing becomes clear in any effort
to probe the reasons why individuals enter and remain in public
service: career motives are exceedingly complicated. Respondents
(such as this one) who answer our questions honestly reveal that
several factors caused them to enter public service.

85

In most instances, these considerations include personal issues. For instance, people might say that they saw public service as a secure form of employment or an opportunity to obtain work that calls upon their academic training or substantive expertise. Public service appealed to the respondent quoted above because he had reached that stage in life where he could afford the loss of income he would incur.

In addition, the factors affecting individuals' decisions to enter government might relate to what they hope to accomplish substantively. In the case of our respondent, he obviously sought to involve himself in the process of developing and implementing policies that stood an especially good chance because of the ideological commitments of the president. However, entrants to public service need not bring with them aspirations about a specific agenda. They might simply want to serve the public as best they can.

This chapter assesses Niskanen's budget-maximization theory from the standpoint of what we know about the motives of senior civil servants, in order to illustrate some of the theory's limitations. The first part offers an empirical analysis of the budget-maximization theory from data collected through in-depth interviews with senior officials in central agencies in the United States, the United Kingdom, and Canada. This analysis attempts to examine how budget-maximizing orientations relate to officials' perceptions of their roles and career motivations.

The second part offers some reflections on the applicability of Niskanen's work to Anglo-American systems other than that of the United States—especially in light of developments in bureaucracy since 1971. In effect, we propose some caveats about the portability and durability of the budget-maximization theory. Our final analysis asserts that bureaucratic cultures vary immensely both among and within political systems. This makes it exceedingly difficult to validate a monotonic theory of bureaucratic behavior such as the one advocated by Niskanen. More recent investigations of public officials' reports of their motives and aspirations for their departments and agencies indicate a more diverse bureaucratic culture.

We turn first to an examination of how these motives and aspirations relate to budget maximization. At this stage, our data permit us to probe only the U.S., U.K., and Canadian cases.

The Case of Central Agents

In several studies we—along with George J. Szablowski of York University and John Halligan of the University of Canberra—conducted a series of in-depth interviews designed to ascertain the role perceptions, behavioral orientations, and social-demographic backgrounds of officials in central agencies. Our research centered on the U.S. (1979 and 1982–1983), the U.K. (1978 and 1986–1987), Canadian (1976), Australian (1988), and Swiss (1978) systems. For our purposes, we focus our current analysis on U.S. political appointees under the Carter and Reagan administrations, career officials under Carter, U.K. permanent officials in 1978, and Canadian civil servants in 1976.

Central agencies are departments or offices that take or share the lead in five functions with overarching importance in any executive-bureaucratic complex. These concern developing strategic plans for a government/administration and making substantive policy decisions that reflect these, devising and integrating economic and fiscal policies, allocating budgets and setting policies for the management of government resources, managing senior personnel, and—in federal systems—conducting federal-provincial relations. Those working in central agencies normally base their leverage with the government apparatus through close proximity to the chief executive or head of government (for example, the White House Office), a special role regarding the support of the cabinet or one of its committees (the Cabinet Office in the United Kingdom), or association with a minister who enjoys a privileged relationship with the president or prime minister in connection with an overarching function (HM Treasury in the United Kingdom).

In 1976, Canadian central agencies included the Prime Minister's Office (supporting the prime minister), the Privy Council Office (the prime minister and cabinet), the Federal-Provincial Relations

Office (the prime minister and cabinet), the Treasury Board Secretariat (serving a cabinet committee), and the Finance Department (working for the finance minister). In 1979, U.K. central agencies took in Number 10 Downing Street (supporting the prime minister), the Cabinet Office and the Central Policy Review Staff (the prime minister and cabinet), the Civil Service Department, and HM Treasury (the chancellor of the exchequer). In both 1979 and 1982–1983, U.S. central agencies consisted of the White House Office and the Executive Office of the President—the latter, including the Office of Management and Budget—and the Office of Personnel Management (the president), and the Department of the Treasury (the Treasury secretary). The number of respondents in the four groups are Canada—ninety-two; the United Kingdom—forty-one; the United States (1979)—sixty-three appointees and sixty-nine career officials; the United States (1982–1983)—sixty appointees.

Measure of Budget Maximization

The purpose here is to describe the construction of a scale of budget maximization from this study of central agency officials. From this we were able to secure a measure of the degree to which these senior bureaucrats focused on budget maximization and, later, to explore how this orientation relates to their perceptions of official roles and career motivations.

The interview agenda did not include direct questions as to the utility of increased resources, but a series of questions focusing on an evaluation of their agency's role and performance provides indirect information on budget-maximization orientations among the respondents (see appendix to this chapter). The general goal in the construction of this simple additive scale, as required by the budget-maximization model, was to be sure that weighting was given to respondents who were focusing on their own agency or bureau and were asserting their own personal utility for the benefits that greater resource allocation can claim.

The first question was, Is (the agency) role being adequately performed? How so? A weight of one was given to those with a neutral, negative, and strongly negative response to capture those focusing on problems within their own agency. Next, if the response was neutral to strongly negative, they were asked to diagnose the problem with the following prompt: What is wrong? Up to three responses were possible, with weighting on those dealing with inadequate resources, budgets, or personnel.

In reaction to this probe on what was wrong, the open-ended responses were coded into twenty-two different categories. What is interesting to note is the limited degree to which the respondents focused on inadequate resources, budgets, and personnel, which formed only three of the categories. The emphasis was on, among other things, mandate deficiencies, organizational and access obstacles, and planning and information problems.

We then prompted respondents to focus on whom or what they blamed for their problems. We assessed up to an additional two points if they placed some of the fault at the feet of politicians—cabinet members or legislators—and if they associated their problems with the magnitude and complexity of the difficulties they faced outside their agency, as opposed to those who saw the fault lying within their own agency. This weighting attempted to reflect within the budget-maximizing model that bureaucrats, in failing to maximize budgets, tend to blame those areas of government that have control over their resource allocations.

We then asked officials, How might performance of your department/agency be improved? We assigned up to three additional points if they prescribed increases in resources, budgets, or personnel. Also, in order to include an aspect of their own personal utility, an additional point was added if they indicated that they believed change in their department's situation should be sought and another additional point if they in fact believed that it would actually come about. This attempted to capture those who indicated that their activities could result in increased resources.

The scale resulted in a range from zero, for those who failed to obtain a single point for budget maximization, to eleven for the three respondents who received weighting on each item. Table 4.1 summarizes the results for country, administration, and position. Among the five groups, career civil servants under Carter attained the highest mean, followed by Carter appointees, Canadian respondents, U.K. officials, and Reagan appointees. The scale's reliability

TABLE 4.1
Budget-Maximizing Scores by Country

Country or Administration	Mean	Standard Deviation	N
All countries	2.77	2.61	325
United Kingdom	2.46	2.29	41
Canada	2.92	2.42	92
United States	2.76	2.77	192
Reagan politicos	1.70	2.46	60
Carter administration	3.25	2.77	132
Career	3.42	2.89	69
Politicos	3.06	2.65	63

of alpha .66 is relatively strong (standardized alpha is .65). The omission of any single item but one would reduce alpha rather than raise it.

On an institutional or positional breakdown (table 4.2) those bureaus traditionally concerned with budgetary restraint throughout the bureaucracy, the so-called guardians—"Finance and Treasury" departments—scored higher than the other central agencies. For the other central agencies that are on the support- and policy-driven side—or more regularly referred to as the spenders—the scores are lower for Canada and the United States and higher for the United Kingdom, compared to their respective counterparts. What may be appearing here is a positional effect. The bureaucratic culture for the guardians in the United States and Canada that focuses on the budget process has resulted in their favoring the budget as a solution to their own problems, while those on the policy-driven side do not favor it as strongly. The expectation of the budget-maximizing model suggests that those on the policy side should perceive the importance of the budget as a primary instrument but that is not entirely supported by these results.

Also, the budget-maximization scores reveal important differences between the Carter and Reagan administrations. Under the "Finance and Treasury" category, the Carter career officials and politicos scored much higher than the Reagan group. Within the other central agencies, the Carter career officials and politicos

TABLE 4.2
Budget-Maximizing Scores by Agency

Agency	Mean	Standard Deviation	N
Finance and Treasury			
All countries	3.02	2.51	194
United Kingdom	2.43	2.12	23
Canada	3.25	2.30	60
United States	3.02	2.68	111
Reagan politicos	1.34	1.55	23
Carter administration	3.46	2.74	88
Career	3.64	2.85	57
Politicos	3.12	2.55	31
Other central agencies			
All countries	2.39	2.72	131
United Kingdom	2.50	2.54	18
Canada	2.31	2.55	32
United States	2.40	2.85	81
Reagan politicos	1.91	2.88	37
Carter administration	2.81	2.79	44
Career	2.33	2.90	12
Politicos	3.00	2.78	32

scored respectively lower than their counterparts in the "Finance and Treasury" category, while the Reagan group scored higher than their "Finance and Treasury" counterparts.

The maximizer scores for the five groups fit pretty well with what we might expect. We might anticipate the Carter career officials to score higher than any other group for two reasons. The fragmentation of the U.S. bureaucracy engenders budget maximizing, and the permanent bureaucracy in 1979 operated under a Democratic administration, which still held a relatively expansive view of the role of government. The Canadian central agents exceeded the maximizing tendency of their British counterparts, probably because of the degree to which the representational imperative in Ottawa impinges on executive-bureaucratic politics. Given the philosophic underpinnings of their administration, it makes sense that Reagan appointees show only a very weak interest in maximization.

Influences on Adoption of Maximizing Orientations

We selected a number of variables that might help us to ascertain what contributes to the adoption of budget-maximizing roles in the five groups. The first of these takes in respondents's views of their responsibilities and their stylistic approach to their work; the second probes officials' orientations toward government service. Table 4.3 summarizes—for each group—the mean scores of respondents with the orientations of characteristics depicted by the variables on the maximization scale.

Examining the relationship among responsibilities, styles, and maximization, we come first to the officials' views of their roles. We collapsed the emphasis of officials' responses into three categories— strategic and policy planning, allocation of resources, and economic and fiscal policy (individuals were allowed more than one response). In all five groups, those who related their work to allocation of resources registered the strongest orientations toward maximization—although the gap in the Carter appointee group between those involved with the role and those engaged in economic and fiscal policy is minute (3.26 versus 3.25). This suggests that budgetary gamekeepers believed that they required increased resources to adequately curtail the incursions of poachers!

With regard to work style, there were three categories—policy and priority planning, management and implementation, and communication (both within and outside of one's agency). A similar result to the one that emerged in the preceding cluster suggests itself here. Those who styled themselves as managers and implementors rate the highest as maximizers—except in the Canadian group, in which they are slightly edged out by those who saw themselves as involved in setting policies and priorities (2.95 versus 2.29). In all cases but the Carter appointee group, those whose approach involved communication within their agency attained the lowest maximizer scores.

The next cluster of variables—mandate focus—concerns officials' perceptions of the span of their agencies' responsibilities for which they bear some obligations. Again allowing for multiple responses, individuals could mention one part, several related parts, or the entire mandate as coming in some way under their

TABLE 4.3
The Budget-Maximizing Bureaucrat: Description of Groups

| | Carter | | | | | | Reagan Politicos | | | United Kingdom | | | Canada | | |
| | Politicos | | | Career | | | | | | | | | | | |
Description	Mean	SD	N	Mean	SD	N	Mean	SD	N	Mean	SD	N	Mean	SD	N
ALL GROUPS	3.06	2.65	63	3.42	2.89	69	1.70	2.46	60	2.46	2.29	41	2.92	2.42	92
AGENCY RESPONSIBILITIES															
Strategic and policy planning	3.05	2.72	39	3.54	2.73	22	1.89	2.65	39	2.40	2.37	20	2.29	2.47	45
Allocation of resources	3.26	2.54	23	3.66	2.85	39	2.00	2.57	26	2.64	2.31	17	3.14	2.19	58
Economic and fiscal policy	3.25	2.42	20	3.40	3.08	32	1.71	2.53	28	1.87	1.58	16	2.58	2.42	34
WORK STYLE															
Policy and priority planning	3.00	2.59	60	3.47	2.89	67	1.81	2.54	54	2.46	2.29	41	2.95	2.47	84
Management and Implementation	3.68	2.71	22	3.60	3.12	25	2.00	3.40	24	2.80	2.25	10	2.93	2.93	33
Communications	3.32	2.73	25	2.93	3.10	16	0.85	1.29	28	1.80	2.94	5	2.42	2.47	35
MANDATE FOCUS															
Entire mandate	1.85	2.41	7	0.00	0.00	1	2.14	3.00	14	3.00	2.58	13	3.30	3.19	13
One part of mandate	3.34	2.91	29	3.55	2.90	55	1.42	2.47	33	2.64	2.17	14	3.13	2.22	61
Several parts of mandate	3.17	2.63	29	2.65	2.84	15	1.80	2.15	21	2.00	2.17	17	2.39	2.47	38

(continued)

TABLE 4.3 continued

| | Carter | | | | | | Reagan Politicos | | | United Kingdom | | | Canada | | |
| | Politicos | | | Career | | | | | | | | | | | |
Description	Mean	SD	N	Mean	SD	N	Mean	SD	N	Mean	SD	N	Mean	SD	N
MOTIVE FOR GOVERNMENT SERVICE															
Idealism, public service	3.00	3.22	16	4.50	3.17	22	1.77	2.04	9	2.33	2.25	15	3.12	2.83	24
Special scholastic training	2.78	3.11	14	3.86	2.88	23	1.71	2.83	32	2.54	2.25	11	2.72	1.84	11
Desire to be "Where the action is"	2.16	1.72	6	4.54	3.67	11	1.85	2.79	20	3.37	2.26	8	3.60	2.61	25
Previous career experience	2.75	2.34	24	2.75	2.49	8	1.55	2.12	9	2.62	1.68	8	3.28	3.19	14
Specific policy interest	4.42	2.29	7	3.25	2.50	4	3.00	0.00	1	0.00	0.00	1	3.21	2.51	14
Career opportunity	3.19	2.63	21	2.88	2.67	42	1.18	1.88	27	1.93	1.94	15	2.91	2.38	58
Partisan political commitment	3.00	2.82	29	6.66	1.52	3	1.52	1.54	17	2.85	3.07	7	2.14	2.47	7
GOALS															
Making government responsive	3.10	2.71	20	3.05	3.13	18	1.63	1.80	11	3.57	3.25	7	2.86	3.02	15
Improving planning and decision making	2.80	2.31	21	4.15	3.28	20	2.16	3.39	18	2.92	2.23	14	2.89	1.93	29
Improving a specific policy	2.95	2.28	20	3.33	3.16	27	1.79	2.46	29	2.17	2.06	17	3.48	2.76	31
Improving personnel	4.00	3.60	9	4.40	2.83	10	3.60	3.04	5	2.40	2.07	5	4.15	3.07	13

Giving best possible advice	2.16	2.20	12	3.47	3.01	23	1.18	1.90	32	2.30	2.35	13	3.09	1.64	11
General overarching goals	4.57	3.90	7	1.00	1.00	3	2.18	3.31	11	2.50	2.12	2	1.83	2.08	12
Having an impact	3.00	2.92	8	4.33	3.50	6	2.11	3.51	9	0.50	0.70	2	3.45	1.96	11
Personal satisfaction	2.88	2.71	9	3.00	2.78	9	1.71	1.88	7	6.00	1.41	2	3.04	2.02	21
Facilitating policy and decision making	1.40	2.06	10	4.50	3.53	2	0.81	1.16	11	3.00	3.16	4	3.40	3.40	10

PART OF JOB WOULD MISS IF LEFT
GOVERNMENT

Impact in specific policy sector	3.11	2.36	17	3.14	2.96	7	2.25	2.81	24	0.00	0.00	0	2.16	2.78	6
General policy impact	2.90	2.60	21	4.03	3.08	32	1.58	2.20	17	2.66	2.64	12	3.68	2.44	35
Atmosphere and challenge	2.88	2.60	43	3.00	2.67	37	1.59	2.28	32	1.91	1.99	23	2.83	2.47	55
Variety of problems	3.00	3.21	7	3.85	4.14	7	1.50	2.12	2	3.60	2.70	5	3.53	2.77	15
High caliber, stimulating colleagues	2.33	3.82	6	3.33	3.07	6	1.80	1.75	10	3.11	2.61	9	2.42	2.41	19
Sense of public service; team work	3.35	3.77	14	3.92	3.47	15	2.62	3.15	16	3.15	2.60	13	2.87	1.99	16
Intellectual challenges	2.85	1.77	7	3.33	4.16	3	2.50	4.27	6	2.50	1.30	8	5.00	2.44	6
Instrumental opportunities of job	2.60	3.28	5	2.66	2.93	12	1.40	2.26	32	3.25	2.98	4	2.68	1.66	16

Note: SD = standard deviation.

purview. The results in this cluster come out less straightforwardly than in the previous two. We had anticipated that the narrower the officials' focus, the more they would lean toward maximization. The results for both Carter groups bear this expectation out. In the other three groups, however, those citing some responsibility toward the entire sweep of their agencies' mandates scored the highest as maximizers.

The next set of clusters—orientation toward government service—includes variables based on respondents' renderings of why they entered government, what they have derived a sense of accomplishment from during their careers, and what they would miss if they left public service. In the cluster tapping respondents' motives for coming into government, their responses fell into seven categories: idealism and a desire to serve the public, scholastic training, desire to be "where the action is," cognate experience in a previous career, a specific policy interest, an opportunity for advancement, and partisan/political commitments. Multiple responses were allowed in this and the other career orientation clusters.

Similar patterns emerge from the maximization scores of those registering various reasons for entering public service as appeared under the responsibility and style clusters. Career officials in the United States, the United Kingdom, and Canada who came into government because they wanted to be close to the action—that is, they wanted to obtain a sense of having an influence in government—produced relatively high average maximization scores (respectively, 4.54, 3.37, and 3.60). As groups, Carter and Reagan appointees and Canadian officials who cited a specific policy interest as motivating their entrance to government all rated high as maximizers (respectively, 4.42, 3.00, and 3.21). Carter career officials yielded two especially interesting findings. Those claiming a general interest in public services ranked high as maximizers (4.50). And the three Carter career people who brought a partisan political commitment with them when they first started attained by far the highest level of maximization of any groups in table 4.3—fully 6.66! The data associated with motives for seeking government careers thus point to deep commitment to public service, a desire to be in the thick of things, or an interest in a specialized policy field as the orientations most related to maximization

A look at maximization scores among those giving various responses to our question on what officials have tried to accomplish during their careers uncovers some very strong results. In all respondent groups—with the exception of the British—officials who have placed a high priority on the development and management of personnel strongly favor maximization. In two groups—Reagan appointees and the Canadians—officials who made some mention of a personnel orientation yielded the highest scores; in the two Carter groups, such officials ranked second in maximization.

Since publication of *Bureaucracy and Representative Government* (Niskanen 1971), concerns have arisen over whether excessively stringent cuts in government—that is, those that lead to excessively low pay or overload among remaining officials—have induced an erosion of the human resources necessary even for minimalist governance (Levine 1988). We see in our officials' emphasis on personnel management the degree to which practitioners believe that a relationship exists between staff efficiency and effectiveness and their compensations and resources.

Moving to what officials would miss if they left public service, the data present one strongly counterintuitive finding. As we have noted, Niskanen's budget-maximizer theory rests heavily upon the assertion that officials view the expansion of the resources in their policy field as serving their personal utility. In their responses to our questions about what they would miss if they left, government officials gave thirteen different types of responses, which we have collapsed into eight categories. Here we devised a variable— instrumental opportunities of the job—which includes five values. These relate more to anticipated changes in the respondents' personal utility than to missing the substantive dimensions to the job. The values included the opportunity to manage a large number of people, the facilities and material to conduct research or carry out one's responsibilities, lifestyle issues (such as a decent living or security), an opportunity denied in other sectors (such as professional advancement for women or minorities), and an outlet for a profession not well represented in the private sector.

With respect to the instrumental opportunities variable, the

U.S. data suggest the exact opposite of what we might expect with those whose personal utility becomes entwined with the resource situation of their organization. Those who would miss their jobs due to loss of instrumental opportunity score lower than any other motivation group in maximization. That is, those seeking optimal personal utility place little emphasis on resource increases and more emphasis (as budget minimizers) on mandate deficiencies, organizational and access obstacles, and planning and information problems.

In the epigraph at the beginning of this chapter, a 1982 respondent argues that Reagan officials entered government for one of three reasons—they were young and upwardly mobile, they had independent means, or they were mediocre. We should note in this regard that 53 percent of Reagan appointees would have missed the instrumental opportunities connected with being in government, whereas only 8 and 17 percent of Carter appointees and career officials, respectively, gave responses that fit into this category. An equal proportion of Reagan appointees took a leaf from the movie *Being There* and dwelt on how they would miss the atmosphere—challenge and excitement—of working in government. These officials scored a bit higher on maximization than those stressing personal utility (1.59 versus 1.40). However, they still fell short of their group mean.

A proactive, passive split between the two administrations begins to take shape when we look at which officials scored high as maximizers. With both political groups, those who would miss the feeling that they were serving the public lean the strongest toward maximization—although the Reagan respondents' scores fall considerably short of the Carter appointees (2.62 versus 3.35). Carter career officials registering the highest (4.03) on maximization were the 46 percent of respondents who would have missed the sense that they were having an impact on policy. Of the U.S. groups, those who presented themselves as actively engaged with the project of governance come out as maximizers. On the other hand, those simply sopping up the atmosphere and seeking instrumental opportunities prove to be minimizers.

This analysis reveals that among and within the political systems there is some degree of variability of bureaucratic cultures in regard to budget maximization. As stated above, there are differences in the degree of budget maximization between the various countries— from 2.92 for Canada, to 2.76 for the United States, to 2.46 for the United Kingdom. There are also positional differences in degrees of budget maximization between the Finance and Treasury side versus the other central agencies, with the latter being consistently lower. More to the point, there are differences in the degree of budget maximization expressed between the Carter and Reagan administrations, 3.25 and 1.70, respectively. The analysis of the relationships between budget maximization and roles and career motives reveals that a personal utility perspective of career is associated with somewhat limited concern with budget maximization.

The comparative salience of the Niskanen budget-maximization theory in relation to the differences between Anglo-American systems is assessed below.

The Niskanen Theory and Bureaucratic Culture

Niskanen's *Bureaucracy and Representative Government* obviously has had a tremendous impact on thinking about bureaucracy both in the United States and elsewhere. For instance, his monograph *Bureaucracy: Servant or Master? Lesson from America* (1973) and the fact that Margaret Thatcher made it required reading at the outset of her government, point up the influence of his thought in the United Kingdom. Indeed, the Niskanen approach—along with other theories that are public-choice oriented—have contributed to the development of programs designed to inculcate in senior officials a greater ability to clarify their objectives and minimize their claims on resources. This was revealed, for example, by the differences in the budget-maximization scores of the Carter and Reagan respondents. With the emergence of managerialism in the United Kingdom, Canada, Australia, and New Zealand, we find that increasingly Whitehall-style bureaucratic systems evaluate the performance of senior officials on the basis of how effectively and efficiently they utilize their resources (Aucoin 1989; Boston 1987; Considine 1988; Fry 1988; Fry et al. 1988; Keating 1988).

Any scholar who has attempted a cross-national comparison of bureaucratic cultures has to question how readily a theory developed to describe the behavior of bureaus in the United States might adapt itself to a similar task in a Whitehall/Westminster system of government. The upper levels of the U.S. public service differ substantially from those in Whitehall/Westminster systems. In the United States, political appointees penetrate down four levels in administrative hierarchies below the cabinet-level head of a department or agency. This means that they will fill all posts of deputy, under, and assistant secretaries, as well as roughly half of the deputy assistant secretary positions. This contrasts sharply with the practice in Whitehall/Westminster systems, where permanent heads serve as the deputy to the cabinet-rank minister, and career civil servants fill all the remaining slots in the administrative hierarchy.

Permanent officials in the United States tend to spend the bulk of their career within highly specialized offices and bureaus without moving between units—let alone departments (Heclo 1977, 116–20). In Whitehall/Westminster systems, officials move frequently both within and between departments. Indeed, some studies of career routes in the Canadian public service suggest that the more frequently officials change departments the more rapidly they rise to the most senior posts (Chartrand and Pond 1970, 48–49; Doer 1981, 46, 63; Borins 1986, 194).

The tendency for U.S. career officials to focus their career in one relatively narrow field of government contributes greatly to the ossification of relationships between civil servants, congressional staff, and interest groups in U.S. policy sectors. Scholars have characterized the institutional sclerosis (Olson 1982, 50–52) originating from rigid client-patron relationships in the United States variously as "subgovernment," rule by "iron triangles," and "atomization" (Aberbach, Putnam, and Rockman 1981, 94–100; Ripley and Franklin 1980; Rose 1976, 161; Heclo 1978, 102–05; Aberbach and Rockman 1977).

We might expect that the infusion of political appointees to U.S. departments and agencies would offset the tendency of career officials to follow overly specialized career routes. However, if we differentiate between politicos and amphibians among appointees, it becomes clear that the latter often become intensely specialized.

Politicos obtain appointments mostly on the basis of their adeptness at political operations, whereas amphibians usually draw both upon detailed knowledge of some substantive policy field and upon some previous experience working in that area within government (Campbell 1986, 200–01).

Hugh Heclo has maintained that amphibians—whom he terms "public careerists"—comprise a de facto higher civil service (1984, 18–20). As such, they consciously prepare themselves to be policy professionals in specialized issue areas. They usually have advanced degrees; they routinely parlay experience in previous administrations into higher posts in the same field the next time they serve in government; in the private sector they keep their public profiles high either by employment in Washington think tanks or associational headquarters or by taking on projects or assuming posts that keep them in touch with the capital.

Niskanen posits a symbiosis between the interests of top-level officials and legislative committees that cannot be assumed in Whitehall/Westminster systems. Even if it did exist, it would not have the same effect on budget maximization. Niskanen asserts that the members of legislative committees seek to maximize the net benefits of specialized areas of government activity to their constituents (1971, 159). They, therefore, share a mutual interest with bureaucrats in the expansion of programs.

Two conditions must prevail in order for this symbiosis to operate as a major factor in executive-legislative relations. To begin, legislators must have the power to form specialized committees with mandates going beyond the term of a parliamentary session. They also must be able to determine the membership of these committees without interference from the political leadership of the executive branch. In the cases of the U.K., Canadian, Australian, and New Zealand systems, none of the legislatures satisfied these criteria in 1971. While all of these systems have made some progress toward security of mandate and tenure in the past twenty years, they currently have achieved—at best—fledgling status when compared to congressional committees in the United States.

The second condition for symbiosis between bureaucrats and legislators builds upon the first (Polsby 1968, 166). It requires that what the legislative committee does in the policy process makes a difference. That is, the committee's hearings and deliberations actually exert consistent and substantive sway over the formulation and implementation of policies and the allocation of resources to competing programs.

Nelson Polsby terms legislatures whose committees possess a capacity—independent of the political executive—to mold and reshape laws and budgets as "transformative" (1975, 277). No Whitehall/Westminster legislature has attained this position. No matter how they have advanced toward security of mandate and tenure in committees, they still operate with strict party discipline. This makes it highly unlikely that a committee dominated by the government party will actually take stances that conflict substantively with the political executive. Thus, we cannot posit a meaningful symbiosis between Whitehall/Westminster bureaucrats and legislators, because any linkages that have developed would still fall far short of producing transformative consequences.

To be sure, symbiosis can arise elsewhere in the policy process as well as in the relationship between legislators and bureaucrats. And these strong mutual interests can place upward pressures on budgets. For instance, many Northern European political systems have developed complex networks of consultative bodies designed to mediate the views of political executives, bureaucrats, legislators, and various client groups within policy sectors. As Johan Olsen points up in his study of political institutions and the welfare state, such mechanisms place expert bureaucrats in a position where they provide the critical nexus between ministers and organized groups (1983, 90–96). Eventually, they view themselves as "key players in public policymaking—as defenders of different institutions, agencies values, and clients" (Olsen 1988, 243–44).

Mancur Olson has pointed up the extent to which the U.K. bureaucracy maintains strong links with interest groups (1982, 77–79). Indeed, he attributes a considerable degree of institutional sclerosis in the United Kingdom to the multiplicity of groups that enjoy special relationships with patron departments. These fight in the corner of clients, so that comprehensive policy coordination becomes very difficult. The resulting fragmentation of Whitehall decision making has greatly hampered Britain's ability to respond in a timely way to the economic pressures of the past two decades.

The links between Whitehall and U.K. interest groups, however strong, constitute much less even matches than those found in other Northern European countries. Most interactions occur in private meetings between officials and group representatives. Most consultations occur without the benefit of routinized bodies that provide a forum in which parties with contesting views can reach mutually acceptable agreements. Officials can readily conceal their activities and the information upon which they base their decisions by cloaking themselves in a veil of secrecy. Even the consumers of officials' advice—ministers—lack alternative guidance. That is, they rely almost entirely upon career civil servants to staff policy initiatives and to oversee the implementation of programs.

It becomes questionable at times whether ministers—let alone legislators—wield transformative sway over policies and their implementation. Officials must take interest groups into account. However, they rarely enter into a symbiosis with these groups that would approximate the reciprocity of official/group links achieved in the United States. As James B. Christoph puts it, Whitehall departments enjoy monopolies over administrative resources in most policy sectors, which makes it very difficult for ministers and groups alike to contest their received wisdom (1975, 32–36; see also Campbell 1983, 57, 128–30).

The leverage of career public servant does not necessarily translate into budget-maximizing behavior. This largely owes to the immense power of HM Treasury in reviewing the expenditure plans of individual departments. Some important institutional features buttress the Treasury's role. Since 1974, an increasing proportion of government programs have come under a "cash limit" regime. Now, over two-thirds of expenditure runs not according to parliamentary mandates to perform certain functions but rather must stay within specified cash expenditure ceilings. This discipline has greatly reduced cost overruns based on special pleading about unexpected events or higher-than-anticipated inflation.

Also, Treasury officials work closely with the financial officers of departments to reach agreement on the guidelines for making bids for new money or identifying savings. This process—called the public expenditure survey (PES)—ends with a consensus document that ministers agree to before the summer recess of Parliament. Further negotiations take place around the fringes during the fall. However, ministers have already taken on board the central elements of the PES. An informal body—termed the Star Chamber and chaired by a senior cabinet minister—settles the handful of disputes that remain after the fall round of bilaterals between the Treasury and departments.

The process accomplishes two things that tend to limit disagreements and special pleading. The entire cabinet rarely discusses specific expenditure issues. And the prime minister lets cabinet colleagues—the chancellor of the Exchequer, the chief secretary of the Treasury, and the chairman of the Star Chamber—take most of the blame for tough decisions. He or she generally avoids direct involvement with spending ministers' appeals.

Together, these features of the British system take us some way toward an explanation of why the United Kingdom has stayed out of deficit trouble such as that experienced by the United States and Canada. The public sector borrowing requirement in the United Kingdom has declined from over 9 percent of the gross domestic product in fiscal year 1975–1976 to a surplus approaching 3 percent in 1988–1989. Since the proceeds from privatizations go into the general treasury, we should deduct 1 percent from the auspicious 1988–1989 performance.

Political executive/bureaucrat/interest group relationships in Canada contrast sharply with those in the United Kingdom. The high degree of regional, economic, and cultural segmentation of Canadian society has, since the beginning of confederation, imposed an array of representational imperatives upon the cabinet that do not exist in Britain (Campbell 1985a, 61–62). In many respects, the degree of fragmentation in Canadian society exceeds that in the United States.

The fact that Parliament functions as a nontransformative legislature exacerbates societal pressures that would make legitimation of the federal government's role difficult even if the country had a legislature like the U.S. Congress. We find embedded here a lesson for those quick to blame budget-maximizing behavior on the fragmentation of the public will by assertive legislatures. Serious dysfunctions arise when institutional arrangements try to paper over societal divisions.

Fear of the consequences of divisive public discourse tends to make party discipline in Canada even stricter than that in the United Kingdom. In many cases, working out agreements between contesting groups within secret cabinet sessions becomes the only way in which to resolve key issues without divisive controversy (Lijphart 1977, 118–29; Matheson 1976, 22–25; Punnett 1977, 65–70). In the transaction, Canadians expect that they will have spokespersons in the cabinet—especially individuals who will express the views of their region, province, locality, or ethnic/cultural group.

The representational imperatives have tended, at least since the turn of the century, to inflate the size of cabinet and increase the complexity of public service. The latter tendency takes root in the fact that Canadians will not settle for a minister without portfolio or those who simply assist senior cabinet members in various departments. To be convincing as representatives, ministers must actually shoulder responsibility for a department—preferably one whose work bears significantly on the region or group that seeks accommodation. Unwieldy government emerges as the obvious consequence of the inflation of cabinets' size and the proliferation of departments. As far back as 1912, a visiting British adviser pointed up the dysfunctions of the Canadian approach to cabinet building (Mallory 1971, 103; Wilson 1981, 329).

The growth of government in the 1950s and 1960s forced Canadian prime ministers to attempt to offset the dysfunctions of the representational imperative. From the time the Liberals resumed power under the leadership of Lester B. Pearson in 1963, through the early years of Pierre Elliott Trudeau's tenure, a system of committees emerged that—it was hoped—would improve the efficiency of the cabinet decision making. In this period, a wide array of specialized committees emerged, as well as a de facto inner cabinet. Trudeau attempted to operate the latter—the Priorities and Planning Committee—as essentially the executive council for the government.

Efforts to cope with the dysfunctions of the representational imperative with committees fell short of expectations. The cabinet, in fact, continued to expand, and the same pressures for inclusiveness in the cabinet worked their way through the committee system to the point where it became unwieldy as well. Representational requirements even kept the Priorities and Planning Committee too large for effective deliberation. Also, they often forced Trudeau to appoint ministers to the committee who attained their standing in the cabinet through representational considerations rather than their ability or even the importance of their department. It became clear that a highly routinized and specialized committee system would not do all the work required to overcome the cabinet's inefficiency.

Throughout the 1970s, Trudeau—and top career civil servants who had attached themselves to his star—developed the view that only an enhancement of the bureaucratic apparatus in the center of government could compensate for the dysfunctions of the representational imperative (Van Loon 1981, 256). As the theory went, restructuring in the machinery of government could kill two birds with one stone. It would improve the support system for the prime minister and for cabinet coordination. It would also reduce the power of the deputy heads of line departments. These officials, it was thought, had used the weakness of cabinet coordination and the uneven quality of ministers to arrogate to themselves fiefdoms that often proved impenetrable to political direction.

Trudeau and his most trusted civil service advisers grew to believe that the best way to fight departmental willfulness was through a counterbureaucracy operating out of central agencies. Interestingly, this tack corresponded to one Niskanen prescription for countering budget-maximizing behavior in the U.S. bureaucracy—strengthening the Office of Management and Budget and creating some other executive review group (1971, 221–22).

The experimental phase that emanated from this impulse in Canada brought on perhaps the greatest proliferation of units and resources ever to occur in a central agency system. However, it also proved to be an abysmal failure. Huge turf fights developed between central agencies, all of which brimmed with brand-new—the number of central agencies doubled from four to eight between 1975 and 1979—or revamped staffs, each of which tended to promote separate views of policy and programmatic rationality (French 1980; Campbell 1983).

In the face of increased fiscal stress, Trudeau and his institutional engineers devised the policy and expenditure management system (PEMS), which the latter managed to sell to the Progressive Conservatives during their short-lived 1979–1980 government (Campbell 1985a, 362–67). This fascinating budgeting approach later became known as the "pretty expensive management system."

PEMS gave each policy committee of cabinet jurisdiction over envelopes of expenditure that cut across departmental lines. Working collegially, and one step removed from their departments, ministers—presumably—would look in a more detached way at expenditure priorities within these umbrella policy fields. To facilitate the process, ministers who identified savings within their cluster of departments would keep the money rather than have it go to the general treasury. Individual ministers, thus, would find it easier to identify cuts in their departments knowing that they could bid to get the funds back for another program or, at least, see that it would be put to work in a sister department.

Two things escaped the designers of PEMS. First, just because ministers resolved resource matters in issue sectors, this did not prevent them from engaging in logrolling (Hartle 1980, 48–49). That is, mutual interests would just as likely support trade-offs of support for vulnerable programs as identification of these as dispensable. Second, ministers collectively could play the same games with the central agencies that they do as departments heads. That is, they could offer for sacrifice only those programs that were politically uncutable.

Under PEMS, the government of Canada chalked up an astronomically high public debt. In fiscal year 1982–1983, its expenditures exceeded its revenues by 50 percent. The anticipated deficit for 1988–1989 was some $29 billion. And the national debt has almost reached $350 billion. Among the eighteen nations of the Organization for Economic Cooperation and Development, only Greece, Italy, Belgium, and the Netherlands have done a worse job than Canada in controlling the size of deficits in relation to the GNP. Those who blame the budget-maximizing bureaucracy on the symbiosis between legislatures and the absence of central guidance systems in the executive branch might well reflect upon the Canadian experience.

Australia provides another instance of a Whitehall/Westminster system with a nontransformative legislature. Unlike Canada, however, it reaps the dual benefit of having an elected senate and a considerably less segmented population and federal system. The former feature greatly assists the legitimation of commonwealth government initiatives and programs. The latter assures that fewer deeply held regional, cultural, and sectoral issues require resolution in the federal arena. Both features work to minimize the effects of the representational imperative on prime ministers' efforts at cabinet building.

Notwithstanding the relatively low salience of the representational imperative in Australia, departments proliferated in Canberra to the point that the number of cabinet ministers with sole responsibility for their own bureaucratic organizations reached the upper twenties. This owed substantially to a constitutional convention whereby each minister would have to have a department of his own (Wettenhall 1989, 97). However, there would only be one department per customer.

After receiving his third mandate in July 1987, Bob Hawke successfully defied the one minister/one department convention by increasing the number of ministers to thirty, reducing the cabinet to seventeen members, and reorganizing the government into sixteen departments (Halligan 1987). In one stroke he accomplished precisely what no Canadian prime minister has had the courage to do. He squeezed the cabinet down toward a more manageable size. And he made it clear that ministers need not take on full embodiment—complete with their own departments—in order to represent.

Importantly, Hawke has pursued deficit reduction with similar resolve. He has worked through an exclusive group of economic rationalist ministers known as the Expenditure Review Committee (ERC). Through marathon bargaining sessions chaired by the prime minister, the ERC has managed between fiscal years 1985–1986 and 1988–1989 to squeeze enough savings out of departments to reduce the budget by 5.1 percent in real terms and the proportion of the GDP absorbed by the commonwealth from 29.8 to 25.6 percent. Also, it has reversed the 1985–1986 $A 5.5 billion deficit into a $A 5.5 billion surplus (Keating and Dixon 1988).

The budgetary process driven by the Australian cabinet's ERC stands in stark contrast to that under Brian Mulroney. In Canada, fully four committees—namely, Priorities and Planning, Operations, Expenditure Review, and the Treasury Board—oversee different dimensions of budget review. Only one central agency—the Finance Department—serves as the secretariat for the ERC. In Ottawa, three central agencies—the Privy Council Office, the Treasury Board Secretariat, and the Finance Department—play a strong role in the budgetary process because they provide the secretariat for one or more of the committees and/or possess the capacity to effectively weigh in with strong views about expenditure within specific policy fields.

We have attempted to focus readers' attention on the differences in civil service cultures and institutional arrangements between four Anglo-American systems. It becomes clear that the exact conditions that give rise to budget-maximizing behavior among bureaucrats in the United States do not pertain to the United Kingdom, Canada, and Australia. In the case of Canada, however, the representational imperative works on the cabinet—its size, structure, and dynamics—to mimic the circumstances of the U.S. budgetary process—without, of course, the presence of a transformative legislature. Australia has proven more adept at avoiding the tendency—found in more segmented societies that lack transformative legislatures—to make the cabinet into a surrogate representative body. We will now turn to a reconsideration of our scholarly understanding of bureaucratic cultures that is being driven by both theoretical refinements and empirical studies.

Budgets, Maximization, and Different Bureaucratic Cultures

Colin Campbell—in an article with B. Guy Peters and a subsequent review essay (Campbell and Peters 1988; Campbell 1988)—has attempted to point up the degree to which bureaucratic cultures differ. Without giving due regard to various systemic patterns, we cannot make any type of valid comparisons of officials' motives and behavior. This assertion rests largely on what scholars have found

over the past two decades about the applicability of the policy/
administration dichotomy across executive-bureaucratic systems—
even between types of units within these.

The salience of the policy/administration dichotomy strikes at
the heart of any treatment of budget-maximizing bureaucracy.
Niskanen's theory simply highlights one way in which officials
put themselves in the driver's seat so that they—not elected
authorities—determine agendas, rank priorities, and establish the
contours and extent of implementation.

Such a condition—where officials as much as politicians influence policy—would fly in the face of the received wisdom on the
role of bureaucrats that dominated thinking about public administration through the first half of this century. Since the 1950s, however, political scientists have beat a gradual retreat from this purist
notion (Aberbach, Putnam, and Rockman 1981, 2–20). In the
1950s, the view emerged that officials involve themselves in policy
but confine their interventions to relevant facts and knowledge
(Simon 1957, 57–58). By the 1960s, scholars increasingly accepted
that bureaucrats engage themselves in political calculation and
manipulation—although they respond to a narrower band of concerns and with less passion or ideology than do politicians (Landau
1962, 10; Holden 1966; Kaufman 1969, 4–5).

Aberbach, Putnam, and Rockman have identified a fourth view
of bureaucracy along the path away from the policy/administration
dichotomy. They adduce some recent literature that suggests that
some civil servants—usually at the highest levels or in the most
strategically located units—do develop and employ a full range of
behind-the-scenes political skills and passionately commit themselves to assuring specific policy outcomes (1981, 16–23).

The authors also note how these "pure hybrids" have made their
presence felt in the interlocking career ladders of politicians and
career civil servants in France and Japan (Suleiman 1974; Suleiman
1984b; Pempel 1984); in the assumption of positions specially created for outsiders in Britain and Germany (Pollitt 1975; Campbell
1983, 63–67; Mayntz and Scharpf 1975, 85–86; Mayntz 1984;
Derlien 1988); and in interventionist central agencies that foster a
superbureaucratic mentality (Campbell and Szablowski 1979).

The articles by Campbell and Peters and by Campbell attempt

to delineate precisely which types of officials fit within the pure hybrid category. Whether a civil service cadre involves itself as readily in politics as in administration turns on two issues. First, the members must hold relatively intense views about policy options—even if the norms of the system prescribe that they maintain an external image of detachment and operate privately.

Second, the officials' interests and work must call upon a high order of skill in the integration of diverse perspectives on various issues. In this regard, we should note that this criterion does not eliminate specialists as prospective hybrids. In large and complex executive-bureaucratic systems such as that in the United States, individuals working in very specialized fields still must learn how to advance the integration of policy views in highly charged environments. The sheer size of policy sectors and their high stakes force participants—no matter how much they style themselves as experts—to develop their political skills.

With regard to the type of engagement on the part of the officials in the executive-bureaucratic complex, we can identify three types of politically oriented officials. In each case, we have to consider whether the cadre operates within a context that calls upon members' ability to engage in systemwide crosscutting gamesmanship. Or does it allow them to confine their activities within a relatively narrow area of government activity—even if this constitutes a complex field in which a great deal is at stake.

First, reactive career bureaucrats fit the stereotypical mold of the incremental or intransigent bureaucrat. These officials will base their appeals and maneuvers on their superior institutional memories and subject matter expertise. They can exert immense power while cloaking their deep commitments to the status quo or their units' world views and priorities behind a veil of anonymity. High-flying career officials in British central agencies serve as an example of reactive officials involved in crosscutting gamesmanship; career office directors in the United States suggest themselves as archetypical reactive officials with a departmental focus.

Second, proactive permanent civil servants differ from their reactive colleagues in that they have carved out comprehensive or positive policy agendas. That is, they place a premium on programmatic rationality over incrementalism and collaboration with politicians over resistance. Proactive officials exert an exceptionally broad and flexible authority, which is often strengthened by an aura of association with the political executive. That is, they usually enjoy special relationships with the president or prime minister, the cabinet, or individual secretaries and ministers. Members of Canada's Privy Council Office and Australia's Department of Prime Minister and Cabinet serve as good examples of crosscutting proactive permanent civil servants (Campbell and Szablowski 1979, 13; Weller 1985, 136–39).

We would also find proactive career officials—but with departmental focuses—in the policy coordination staffs that emerged in both the U.S. and U.K. departments during the 1960s and 1970s (Heclo 1977, 151; Cornish and Clarke 1987). In both countries, these units—at least those that included significant numbers of career officials—have either disbanded or diminished in importance during the 1980s (Aberbach and Rockman 1986; Cornish and Clarke 1987).

Finally, party-political officials work within departments and agencies as policy professionals. That is, they differ from other political appointees in that their involvement in the policy process goes beyond the "switchboard" work in which pure political operatives usually engage themselves. Party-political officials usually occupy hierarchical positions within the bureaucratic organization and style themselves as policy professionals. Besides drawing upon partisan networks and credentials to obtain and do their jobs, these officials bring to their work substantial experience and expertise within specific policy sectors. Public careerists in U.S. central agencies (Heclo 1984, 18) and "promoter" state secretaries in West Germany (Mayntz 1984, 196) supply instances of party-political officials who have assumed positions that involve crosscutting gamesmanship. High-level political appointees in line U.S. departments and agencies assume similar roles—with, however, a departmental focus.

Our understanding of bureaucratic culture has been pushed from an earlier "ideal type" asserted by the policy/administration dichotomy image to a more differentiated and refined understanding. Niskanen, it should be remembered, was writing in a period of government expansion. Thus, the tendency in that epoch for bureaucracies to seek and, usually, to gain enhanced budgets absorbs Niskanen's attention. The Niskanen theory asserts a singular way in which bureaucrats demonstrate a deep-seated inclination toward budget maximization (1971, 38). This phenomenon owes to the strength of the link between an individual official's personal utility and the benefits that a robust budget can advance. These include an adequate salary, perquisites, public reputation, power, patronage, and the output of the bureaucrats' organization. Given both more recent theoretical developments asserting a pure hybrid and further empirical investigations of the motives of public servants, a less stereotypical and more varied understanding of bureaucratic culture has developed.

Conclusion

This chapter has examined Niskanen's budget-maximization theory from two standpoints. It has examined how budget-maximizing orientations relate to officials' perceptions of their roles and their career motivations. It also has assessed the comparative salience of the budget-maximization theory given the differences among Anglo-American systems.

Regarding officials' role perceptions and career motivations, we found that maximizers tend to be committed to public service as a value and dedicated to relatively specialized fields. In view of the fact that our officials work in central agencies, we were surprised to find the degree to which those focusing their work on allocations of resources throughout the bureaucratic system proved strongly inclined toward maximization. Most strikingly—in view of the central assertion of Niskanen's theory—those who viewed their career from the standpoint of personal utility came out as minimizers, not maximizers, looking for solutions for problems within their agency through mandate clarification as well as organizational, planning, and information changes.

Also, an examination of administrative and positional perceptions of budget maximization disclosed intriguing variations. Within the United States, the United Kingdom, and Canada, there were differences in consideration of budget maximization, for example, between the Carter and the Reagan administrations, and between "Finance and Treasury" versus the other central agency groups. As indicated in the later part of the chapter, different government conditions drive budget-maximization behavior. It is not only a result of the budget-maximizing (or minimizing) bureaucrats but, as in the case of Canada, the representational imperative of the cabinet that enhances budget growth; or, as in the case of Great Britain, the important role of HM Treasury and a system that contains budget-maximization behavior.

With respect to its applicability to systems other than that of the United States, we have cautioned that differences in both the structure of bureaucratic careers and the nature of power relationships—between the political executive, the bureaucracy, the legislature, and interest groups—make it highly unlikely that the conditions that lead to a high degree of budget maximization in the United States will prevail elsewhere. The Canadian system attains the closest approximation to the conditions in the United States, largely through the auspices of cabinets laboring under the burden of the representational imperative.

We have raised several questions about Niskanen's theory. These go beyond simply urging that it be fine-tuned to account for the exigencies of different bureaucratic systems. They also touch on very fundamental questions about Niskanen's core assertion connecting maximization to personal utility, In fact, maximizers tend to be expansive about what government can do and to be devoted to specific policy fields. This is quite different from being motivated by personal utility—as our surprising finding about the career motives of budget minimizers points out.

APPENDIX
Questions and Prompts for the Budget Maximization Scale: Agency and Role Evaluation Section

Is [agency] role being adequately performed? How so?

 Tone of respondent response: strongly negative, negative, neutral, positive, strongly positive.

Respondent diagnosis: What is wrong? (Twenty-two different categories, weighting of only *inadequate budget* and *personnel,* with three possible responses.)

Focus of blame: (Thirteen different categories with two possible responses).

How might the performance of [department/agency] be improved?

What remedies does respondent prescribe? (Nineteen different categories, weighting of only *increased budget* and *personnel,* with three possible responses.)

Intensity of perceived need for change.

Prognosis for change.

REFERENCES

Aberbach, Joel D., Robert D. Putnam, and Bert A. Rockman. 1981. *Bureaucrats and politicians in western democracies* Cambridge, Mass.: Harvard Univ. Press.

Aberbach, Joel D., and Bert A. Rockman. 1977. The overlapping worlds of American federal executives and congressmen. *British Journal of Political Science* 7:23–47.

———. 1986. On the rise, the transformation, and the decline of analysis in government. Paper presented at the conference on American-Canadian political economy: The 1980s and beyond, Virginia Polytechnic Institute and State University, Blacksburg.

Aucoin, Peter. 1989. Contraction, managerialism and decentralization in Canadian government. *Governance* 1:144–61.

Borins, Sanford F. 1986. Management of the public service in Japan: Are there lessons to be learned? *Canadian Public Administration* 29:175–96.

Boston, Jonathan. 1987. Transforming New Zealand's public sector: Labour's quest for improved efficiency and accountability. *Public Administration* 65:423–42.

Campbell, Colin. 1983. *Governments under stress: Political executives and key bureaucrats in Washington, London and Ottawa.* Toronto: Univ. of Toronto Press.

———. 1985a. Cabinet committees in Canada: Pressures and dysfunctions stemming from the representational imperative. In *Unlocking the cabinet: Cabinet structures in comparative perspective,* ed. Thomas T. Mackie and Brian W. Hogwood. London: Sage.

―――. 1985b. The pitfalls of a revisionism too eager by half: An open letter to Richard Van Loon. *Canadian Public Administration* 28:319–28.

―――. 1986. *Managing the presidency: Carter, Reagan and the search for executive harmony.* Pittsburgh, Pa.: Univ. of Pittsburgh Press.

―――. 1988. The political roles of senior government officials in advanced democracies. *British Journal of Political Science* 18:243–72.

Campbell, Colin, and B. Guy Peters. 1988. The politics/administration dichotomy: Death or merely change? *Governance* 1:79–99.

Campbell, Colin, and George J. Szablowski. 1979. *The superbureaucrats: Structure and behaviour in central agencies.* Toronto: Macmillan.

Chartrand, P. J., and K. L. Pond. 1970. *A study of executive career paths in the public service of Canada.* Chicago: Public Personnel Assoc.

Christoph, James B. 1975. Higher civil servants and the politics of consensualism in Great Britain. In *The mandarins of Western Europe: The political roles of top civil servants,* ed. Mattei Dogan. New York: Halsted.

Considine, Mark. 1988. The corporate management framework as administrative science: A critique. *Australian Journal of Public Administration* 47:4–17.

Cornish, Derek B., and Ronald V. Clarke. 1987. Social science in government: The case of the Home Office research and planning unit. In *Social science research and government: Comparative essays on Britain and the United States,* ed. Martin Bulmer. Cambridge: Cambridge Univ. Press.

Derlien, Hans-Ulrich. 1988. Image IV revisited: Executive and political roles. *Governance* 1:50–78.

Doer, Audrey D. 1981. *The machinery of government.* Toronto: Methuen.

French, Richard D. 1980. *How Ottawa decides: Planning and industrial policy-making, 1968–1980.* Toronto: Lorimer.

Fry, Geoffrey K. 1988. The Thatcher government, the financial management initiative and the "new civil service." *Public Administration* 66: 1–20.

Fry, Geoffrey K., Andrew Flyn, Andrew Gray, William Jenkins, and Brian Rutherford. 1988. Symposium on improving management in government. *Public Administration* 66:429–45.

Halligan, John. 1987. Reorganizing Australian government departments, 1987. *Canberra Bulletin of Public Administration* 52:40–47.

Hartle, Douglas C. 1980. Some notes on recent changes in the federal expenditures budgetary strategy and process. Unpub. paper. Univ. of Toronto, Dept. of Economics.

Heclo, Hugh. 1977. *A government of strangers: Executive politics in Washington*. Washington, D.C.: Brookings.

————. 1978. Issue networks and the executive establishment. In *The new American political system,* ed. Anthony King. Washington, D.C.: American Enterprise Institute.

————. 1984. In search of a role: America's higher civil service. In Suleimam 1984a.

Holden, Matthew. 1966. Imperialism in bureaucracy. *American Political Science Review* 60:943–51.

Kaufman, Herbert. 1969. Administrative decentralization and political power. *Public Administration* 29:3–15.

Keating, Michael. 1988. Managing for results: The challenge for finance and agencies. *Canberra Bulletin of Public Administration* 54:73–80.

Keating, Michael, and Geoffrey Dixon. 1988. Australian economic policy: Problems and processes. Paper presented at the Canadian Institute for Research on Public Policy 1988, workshop on Economic Policy-Making in Asia-Pacific Region, Bangkok, Thailand.

Landau, Martin. 1962. The concept of decision-making in the field of public administration. In *Concepts and issues in administrative behavior,* ed. Sidney Mailick and Edward H. Van Ness. Englewood Cliffs, N.J.: Prentice-Hall.

Levine, Charles H. 1988. Human resource erosion and the uncertain future of the US civil service: From policy gridlock to structural fragmentation. *Governance* 1:115–43.

Lijphart, Arend. 1977. *Democracy in plural societies: A comparative exploration*. New Haven, Conn.: Yale Univ. Press.

Mallory, James R. 1971. *The structure of Canadian government*. Toronto: Macmillan.

Matheson, W. A. 1976. *The prime minister and cabinet*. Toronto: Methuen

Mayntz, Renate. 1984. German federal bureaucrats: A functional elite between politics and administration. In Suleiman 1984a.

Mayntz, Renate, and Fritz Scharpf. 1975. *Policy-making in the German federal bureaucracy*. New York: Elsevier.

Niskanen, William A. 1971. *Bureaucracy and representative government*. Chicago: Aldine Atherton.

————. 1973. *Bureaucracy: Servant or master? Lessons from America*. London: Institute of Economic Affairs.

Olsen, Johan. 1983. *Organized democracy: Political institutions in a welfare state, the case of Norway*. Oslo: Universitetsforlaget.

————. 1988. Administrative reform and theories of organization. In

Organizing governance: Governing organizations, ed. Colin Campbell, S.J., and B. Guy Peters. Pittsburgh, Pa.: Univ. of Pittsburgh Press.

Olson, Mancur. 1982. *The rise and decline of nations: Economic growth, stagflation, and social rigidities.* New Haven, Conn.: Yale Univ. Press.

Pempel, T. J. 1984. Organizing for efficiency: The higher civil service in Japan. In Suleiman 1984a.

Pollitt, Christopher J. 1975. The central policy review staff, 1970–74. *Public Administration* 52:375–92.

Polsby, Nelson W. 1968. The institutionalization of the US House of Representatives. *American Political Science Review* 62:144–68.

————. 1975. Legislatures. In *Governmental institutions and processes,* vol. 5 of *Handbook of political science,* ed. Fred I. Greenstein and Nelson W. Polsby, Reading, Mass.: Addison-Wesley.

Punnett, R. M. 1977. *The prime minister in Canadian government and politics.* Toronto: Macmillan.

Ripley, Randall B., and Grace A. Franklin. 1980. *Congress, the bureaucracy, and public policy.* Homewood, Ill.: Dorsey.

Rose, Richard. 1976. *Managing presidential objectives.* New York: Free Press.

Simon, Herbert A. 1957. *Administrative behavior.* New York: Macmillan.

Suleiman, Ezra. 1974. *Politics, power, and bureaucracy in France: The administrative elite.* Princeton, N.J.: Princeton Univ. Press.

————. ed. 1984a. *Bureaucrats and policy making: A comparative overview.* New York: Holmes and Meier.

————. 1984b. From right to left: Bureaucracy and politics in France. In Suleiman 1984a.

Van Loon, Richard. 1981. Kaleidoscope in grey: The policy process in Ottawa. In *Canadian politics in the 1980's: Introductory readings,* ed. Michael Whittington and Glenn Williams. Toronto: Methuen.

Weller, Patrick. 1985. *First among equals: Prime ministers in Westminster systems.* London: Allen and Unwin.

Wettenhall, Roger. 1989. Recent restructuring in Canberra: A report on machinery-of-government changes in Australia. *Governance* 2:95–106.

Wilson, V. Seymour. 1981. *Canadian public policy and administration: Theory and environment.* Toronto: McGraw-Hill Ryerson.

5

PETER AUCOIN

The Politics and Management of
Restraint Budgeting

Restraint budgeting has been the order of the day for all governments in industrialized democracies for over a decade. In light of this it might be assumed that politicians have sought to exercise particularly tight control over any behavior on the part of bureaucrats to maximize their budgets in ways that afford them resources beyond what is required to engage in prescribed activities. These efforts at control, it might further be assumed, stem not only from the need to be efficient in public spending but from the view that bureaucrats do indeed seek to maximize their budgets in ways that are not efficient from the perspective of value-for-money budgeting. In this latter respect, the budget-maximizing bureaucrat thesis of William Niskanen (1971), among other propositions of public choice theory, has been particularly influential in political circles, especially in English-speaking democracies (Aucoin 1989). Although bureaucracy bashing has been a popular sport among conservative politicians over the past two decades, even politicians and governments of other ideologies have been persuaded that greater control needs to be asserted over the administrative apparatus of the state in the pursuit of restraint.

In this chapter, I outline a number of developments that have occurred in industrialized democracies that bear upon the budgetary process from the perspective of restraining expenditures. In so doing, I seek to highlight those relevant to attempts on the part of politicians, primarily in the executive branch of government, to

119

cope with, or to overcome, the presumed pathology of budget-maximizing bureaucrats. First are the efforts to strenthen the central executive capacities of governments to scrutinize, control, and reorder public spending. Second are the actual measures used in attempts to effect restraint through the budgetary process. Third are the efforts to reform management within the public sector in order that efficiencies be pursued as a norm for public managers. Each of these is treated in turn with an attempt to assess their effects on the behavior of bureaucrats.

Political Control

Central to the Niskanen thesis is the proposition that politicians have neither the incentive nor the capacity to meaningfully exercise their formal authority over bureaucrats in ways that would promote efficiency in the budgetary process. This lack of incentive arises from, among other factors, the limited utility to the individual politician of pursuing efficiency in public spending decisions across the broad spectrum of expenditures, most of which will have little, if any, direct effect on the prospects of reelection. The fragmentation of political structures, moreover, reduces the collective interests of politicians in overall efficiency. This is most applicable to the U.S. system, perhaps, but also obtains to coalition cabinet governments and even to single-party governments, where the regional or departmental interests of ministers (and legislators) diminish the collective will to pursue efficiency across the entire budget.

The advent of the perceived need for restraint has affected this variable: some politicians now see a political advantage in pursuing efficiency in public spending. This is particularly the case, of course, for political parties or leaders who have made restraint part of their explicit agenda and who see themselves as deriving public support for it. "Running against government," and succeeding, has altered the political incentive system (Maslove, Prince, and Doern 1986, 207). Even incumbents have adopted this tack, although in these instances the government is taken to be the bureaucracy (Levine 1986).

Although public support for restraint may not be as widespread as conservative politicians might like to think (see Johnston 1986), the conventional wisdom in many quarters has given legitimacy to the demands for restraint, and the now-popular opinion that bureaucracies are not efficient (and do not attempt to be) has fueled this demand. The number of restraint-minded governments that have been reelected has provided further evidence for those who are inclined to pursue restraint. It is not surprising from this perspective that among the chief instruments of restraint in many, if not most, governments have been measures to trim the personnel resources of the administrative apparatus (Sutherland and Doern 1986; Hood, Dunsire, and Thomson 1988).

The incentive to pursue efficiency via restraint should not be exaggerated. The record of governments in industrialized democracies is a modest one, at best. Decrementalism has been characterized by the same features of disjointed and minor adjustments that characterized incrementalism during the prior period of expansion. As Schick notes: "The fact that spending, in total and for most programs, has continued to rise under cutback budgeting suggests that there has been a substantial difference between appearances and action" (1988, 524).

If restraint, despite the rhetoric, has not led to a revolution in the political will of politicians to secure efficiency, then perhaps the reason lies in the capacities of politicians to do so. Here we can single out those developments that have been undertaken to strengthen the capacities of governments to effect restraint. In addition to those measures that have been taken by legislatures to play a greater role in the budgetary process (Peters, Chapter 11, this volume), three developments within the executive-bureaucratic arenas of several political systems are noteworthy.

First, in a number of political systems, there has been an increased centralization or concentration of power under the chief executive officer of government (president or prime minister) and those officers with executive authority for fiscal and expenditure policy (Kemp 1986; Hansen and Levine 1988). In these instances, more aggressive leadership behavior, rather than changes to formal structures of authority, has been the norm. These efforts have been undertaken in order to impose a greater corporate presence in government decision making, particularly under conditions of collective leadership such as in cabinet government, in order to offset the fragmentation of power inherent in the modern administrative state (Campbell 1988a). The Thatcher government in the United Kingdom and the Hawke government in Australia stand out in these regards, but they are not unique.

The point of such centralization or concentration of power is to highlight the corporate interests of a government in having the guardians of the public purse pull in the reins on spenders. In some large part, the objective is to control the spending inclinations of ministers or cabinet members responsible for line operations and who constitute the majority of the executive. At the same time, however, it is recognized that these members of the executive branch are often less able to resist the spending demands of their departmental officials than are the guardians who are one step removed from direct pressures from departmental officials, as well as from their departmental constituencies. Centralization thus not only gives greater leverage to the guardinas, it may also enable spending ministers to hide behind corporate/collective decisions in the face of criticisms, implicit or explicit, from their departmental officials and their clientele. Under these conditions, only wide-spread public criticism, and the potential loss of electoral support for the government, is likely to keep central executive authorities from pursuing their restraint policies.

Centralization has also tended to strengthen the hands of finance ministers, not only to better control total projected expenditures and actual spending, but also to use fiscal policy initiatives, including tax expenditures, for reordering the ways in which benefits are designed. More generally, centralization of this sort does make even expenditure reorderings relatively easier, in that the dynamics of collective decision making are somewhat removed from center stage. The collapse of the policy and expenditure management system (PEMS) in Canada over the past several years—notwithstanding Schick's claim (1988, 522) that it was "the only major innovation to have taken root in industrialized democracies"—illustrates the perceived need for centralization (Aucoin 1988; Campbell 1988b).

The failure of PEMS to achieve what was expected of it resulted primarily from the relative absence of restraint discipline among ministers. The expenditure envelopes assigned to policy committees of cabinet simply had too much leakage, in the sense that ministers were not able or willing *collectively* to restrain their demands within the limits of the expenditures in their sectoral envelopes. These committees became, in effect, minicabinets, without sufficient command or corporate leadership; functioning in a supposedly collegial manner did not restrain the pressures on these collectivities to act as a conglomerate of separate interests. The result has been a centralization of control over spending: first in 1986, with an operations committee headed by the deputy prime minister (the number-two minister in the cabinet) and composed of a majority of ministers with corporate responsibilities; and then in 1989, with an expenditure review committee chaired by the prime minister, modeled largely on the Australian initiative of the Hawke government.

A second development characteristic of efforts to assert political control has involved the much heralded politicization of the administrative apparatus that serves the political executive. Even in the United States, where there has been a long tradition of political appointees within the executive branch, an increased number of political appointments has been the norm of recent administrations. This has extended increasingly to line as well as to staff positions (Ingraham 1987). In political systems without this tradition, the number of political appointees in staff positions has been increased, and even line positions have been subject to some politicization as well (Kemp 1986). Further, promotions and redeployment of career bureaucrats have been made increasingly in many jurisdictions on the basis of their perceived enthusiasm for the incumbent government's policy or management orientation, if not its partisan political stripe (see Bulmer 1988).

One consequence of this development is that there has been an increasing blurring of political and bureaucratic roles. Although there are various ways in which this development may be conceptualized (Aberbach and Rockman 1988), it is clear that the simple dichotomy between politician and bureaucrat, even at the level of line organizations, increasingly does not obtain (Campbell and Peters 1988b). These various forms and shades of politicization may not be a panacea for political control of bureaucracy, but they have served to challenge the concept and reality of bureaucracy as independent of the political branch of govenrment. At the same time, these developments point to the perceived need by politicians for their own staff to provide advice countervailing that of the permanent bureaucracy or to direct the implementation of government policy from line management positions (Peters 1989, 207–09).

To the degree that certain positions once the prerogative of career bureaucrats are filled, or are perceived to be filled, by those who are considered trustworthy by those in power, there is an obvious incentive for career bureaucrats to act in ways that endear them to their political masters. Under restraint-minded regimes, the implications for those who may have been budget-maximizing bureaucrats are obvious (Dunsire, Chapter 7, this volume).

Although such measures for enhancing the political control of the bureaucracy may serve to increase political responsiveness (Campbell 1983), it is not at all obvious that the basic dynamic between spenders and guardians is substantially altered. Political appointees and bureaucrats who come under the authority of ministers who are more inclined to spend rather than restrain, whatever the policy of their government, may well take their cues from them (Bakvis 1988). The different routes to their appointments then make little difference. To the degree that there is conflict between political appointees and career bureaucrats, or political appointees/trusted career bureaucrats and other career bureaucrats, it will more likely revolve around the distribution of expenditures to programs and not whether restraint should be promoted for efficiency purposes.

A third development, and one that at first blush appears to go directly to the heart of the issue of the budget-maximizing bureaucrat, has been the use in some political systems of external, or partly external, mechanisms to promote efficiency in public expenditures. These mechanisms have relied on the use of private sector managers to assess government programs and management systems. President's Reagan's private sector survey on cost control, Japan's temporary commission on administrative reform, and Canada's task force on program review are examples of such external mechanisms (Wilson 1988). Britain and Australia, two other examples, have used private sector assistance with internal reviews (Metcalfe and Richards 1987; Halligan 1989). These kinds of initiatives are akin to special external commissions or task forces that traditionally have been used to assist governments in public policy and program innovation. The difference here is that they are now used to help trim back the state. In each case, however, the logic has been to use outsiders to counter the advice received from the career bureaucracy and to generate support and legitimacy for actions subsequently taken by government.

In the case of these recent reviews, the explicit assumption has been that private sector management is superior to public sector management, both in its willingness to pursue efficiency and in its capacity to manage financial resources in pursuit of value for money. This is hardly a new bias toward a more businesslike approach to public management, but it has been undertaken with a vengeance that heretofore has not been the norm. Not surprisingly, the principal focus has been to identify instances where the inefficient use of resources can be directly attributable to budget maximizing by bureaucrats.

The results of these reviews are difficult to assess. The massive savings that were expected in almost all instances have not materialized. This can be explained by several phenomena. (1) Governments have retreated from prescribed cuts in inefficient government spending because of the backlash from affected constituencies. (2) Public sector administrative policies restrict the authority of managers to pursue efficiencies, as defined by these external reviews—and these governments have been unwilling to alter these policies. (3) Identified inefficiencies are often the direct result of the government's public policies and not of bureaucratic pathologies; in most cases, governments have not been willing to reverse these policies. (4) Many identified inefficiencies have been already recognized by bureaucrats, themselves, but they derive from the complexity of governance, and every solution proposed by external reviews or by bureaucrats has clearly unacceptable consequences, including other kinds of inefficiencies.

At the same time, however, it is clear that these external reviews have had some effect on restraint and the pursuit of efficiencies (Schick 1988). In some instances, changes have been effected; some have even been welcomed by bureaucrats (Wilson 1988). Equally important, these reviews have acted as catalysts for those bureaucrats who have sought to effect change, not so much to emulate the supposedly superior model of private sector management, but rather to bring about desired improvements in public sector management in its own right (Plumptre 1988; Kooiman and Eliassen 1987). It is in this respect that many bureaucrats have long recognized the deficiencies in public management; they have felt constrained, however, by the political and administrative regimes within which they operate (e.g., Canada 1983). In these respects, many of the reforms that have surfaced as a result of these external reviews have had their origin in the critical analyses of bureaucrats, themselves.

Centralization, politicization, and external reviews have all been used to promote restraint and, in certain respects, to enhance the capacities of political leaders to diminish the abilities of bureaucrats to maximize their budgets. Insofar as the latter objective is concerned, politicians have acted on the assumption that bureaucrats generally do attempt to maximize their budgets. The experience of the past decade does not provide evidence to the contrary. However, to the degree that the limited success at restraint provides us with clues to the dynamics of budgeting, the experience suggests that inefficiencies in public spending also derive from those political leaders and their support staff, be they political appointees or bureaucrats, who are interested in program expansion. This includes programs with discretionary spending components (e.g., Savoie 1989) and administrative rules and regulations that reduce either the capacities or the incentives of bureaucrats to pursue efficiencies (Plumptre 1988). In this latter respect, even senior bureaucrats are middle managers, who lack the authority of their presumed counterparts in the private sectors, namely the chief executive officers of corporations.

The conclusions that this suggests are, first, that the basic dynamic is between spenders and guardians, between roles and positions in the budgetary process, and not between politicians and bureaucrats per se; and second, that bureaucrats, as subordinate officials, by themselves may not have the incentive or the capacity to pursue efficiency in budgeting (or spending). Bureaucrats, as department heads or bureau chiefs of spending agencies, should have a better grasp of the data and information pertaining to their agencies than that possessed by their political masters and their policy and budgetary support staff, but it does not necessarily follow that they have the autonomy to manipulate the structures of their budget requests (or their spending of approved budgets) to serve their own purposes. This does not rule out the pursuit of inefficiencies in order to maximize budgets; rather, it draws attention to the fact that many variables in a budget are determined by authorities external to the agency. Inefficiencies may well be the result of, but they do not always emanate from, the requests or practices of agency officials. Indeed, requests for budgetary slack and discretionary spending powers, whether explicit or hidden, are necessary for efficiency purposes, given the very real constraints on bureaucrats.

Budgetary Techniques

On the basis of his comparative study of budgetary adaptations to fiscal stress in industrialized democracies, Schick concludes that "someone returning to budgeting after an absence of a decade or more would have no difficulty recognizing current practices." The reason for this is that there is "little interest these days in big reforms of the sort that animated performance budgeting, planning-programming-budgeting (PPB), and zero-based budgeting (ZBB) in earlier decades." Adaptations, accordingly, "have tended to be piecemeal, ad hoc, and improvisational" (1988, 532).

It might be argued that the current efforts at restraint provide evidence to the effect that politicians and their policy and budgetary support staff, as guardians of the public purse, have given up on the search for budgeting techniques with which to alter their relationships to spenders, be they political executives or career bureaucrats, in the pursuit of efficiency. The fact that many of the current practices are focused on controlling the rate of growth in public spending in total gives credence to this. Prominent among restraint measures, accordingly, have been the traditional devices of across-the-board cuts, budget increases set below the rate of

inflation, freezes on hiring and replacements, limits on public service compensation, controls and entitlement adjustments set below the rate of inflation, tightening eligibility requirements for
benefits, and the like (Schick 1988; Peters 1989).

The attractiveness of these measures to restraint-minded governments lies in the relative ease with which they can be adopted.
Although they are not without their political risks, these top-down
measures require much less in the way of political and bureaucratic
transactions or budgetary analysis than do cutback exercises that
entail a wide range of individual programs, each of which must be
considered individually—and therefore, usually in considerable detail. In this respect, the above measures have a considerable advantage over the exercises required by PPB and ZBB. As top-down
exercises, they also restrict the participation of spenders, whether
political or bureaucratic, in the decision-making process.

Because such measures normally entail decisions on spending,
and in most cases do not provide detailed directives for the spending of what is approved, there is still scope for spending agencies
to influence the shape of agency budgets and expenditures. In
order to control inclinations on the part of spending agencies to
ignore restraint, however, some governments (Britain and the
Netherlands) have instituted mechanisms whereby there are actual
cash limits to budgetary allocations, at least for certain agencies or
programs. The logic here is that budgetary overruns are not to be
tolerated; overspending on certain items is thus to be compensated
for by reductions in approved expenditures in other areas of an
agency's budget.

Although the British government has reported some success
with this approach, in the Netherlands the emphasis has shifted to
greater control over decisions to commit expenditures in the first
place (Schick 1988). As was the case in Canada, with its budgetary
envelopes (which were also meant to be ceilings), the experience in
the Netherlands suggests that the most effective control over either
overruns or end runs around the prescribed process requires firm
discipline by those at the center and a capacity to anticipate likely
problems in these regards.

Firm discipline, of course, requires something other than techniques. A capacity to anticipate problems, on the other hand, can

be dealt with in part by strenthening financial control systems. The latter has occurred in many countries (Schick 1988, 529). This development has led to both increased reporting requirements on the part of spenders and more aggressive scrutiny by central departments and agencies. Advanced information technologies obviously have assisted in this. Although these monitoring exercises throughout the annual budgetary cycle have not led to additional cutbacks during the year in question (Schick 530), their watchdog function does serve to enhance the informational capacities and knowledge of central agents with respect to the existing budget bases of program expenditures. One effect is to assist central agents to identify future prospects for special restraint measures in light of a government's strategic priorities (Veilleux and Savoie 1988).

There has also been an increased tendency to refocus the program evaluation function from program effectiveness to program efficiency in order to assist in restraining budgets (Derlien 1989). This has meant that the function of program evaluation is now more closely associated with the budgetary cycle and expenditure reviews. The reaction of the Canadian task force on program review to the extensive system of program evaluation in Canadian government is illustrative here. The task force's study teams found "routine government program evaluations" to be "generally useless and inadequate for the purpose of program review" (Canada 1986, 23), notwithstanding the considerable resources that the Canadian government has invested in this function. These evaluations tend to be self-serving on the part of the sponsoring program agencies, and rarely, if ever, do they question the rationale of the programs so evaluated (23–24). This is not a surprising conclusion. The Canadian experience has been one in which the shift from a focus on outcomes to a focus on outputs, especially for evaluations conducted internally by spending agencies, has been explicitly undertaken to improve program efficiency as measured by agency managers, themselves. This avoids raising the politically difficult, and inherently value laden, judgments about the rationale of programs.

Each of the above developments—the measures used to effect restraint, the strengthening of central financial control systems, and the refocusing of program evaluation—provides evidence, if only indirectly, of the limited capacities of guardians and their agents to effect restraint and especially to reorder the spending patterns of governments in the short term. This does not imply that politicians are completely unable to control budget-maximizing behavior by bureaucrats, for some restraint, some cuts, and some efficiencies have been effected. What it does suggest is that those at the corporate center, whether they be politicians or bureaucrats, are limited in their capacities to make substantial changes in the volume or patterns of government spending in the short term. Both the complexities of the system and the interests involved restrict corporate authorities to major strategic initiatives on a limited number of fronts.

For the most part, significant improvements in efficiency must be made in a more disaggregated manner—that is, further down the line of authority and within the numerous centers of what is a highly differentiated organizational structure. This means that efficiency is first and foremost a matter of discretion within government departments and agencies. Niskanen's budget-maximizing thesis recognizes this, and indeed, it is on this very point that he constructs his argument: the need for decentralization *and* differentiation severely restricts the use of direct control by corporate authorities, accommodation among executive authorities, and centrally imposed measures of standardization to achieve policy objectives efficiently.

Although the U.S. system of congressional government, which constitutes the empirical reference of Niskanen's analysis, may be at one extreme with respect to these features of decentralization and differentiation, all national governments in industrialized democracies exhibit these features; none are near enough to the other end of the spectrum that they can easily operate without extensive de facto decentralization and differentiation. Where cabinet systems of government (especially under the Westminster model, and particularly where one party controls the executive branch of government and dominates the legislative branch) differ from the U.S. model, with its significant degree of legislative power, is that elected political officials (ministers) are individually at the apex of authority of government departments. Ministers, not bureaucrats, are the bureau chiefs of these organizations.

Many ministers have neither the time nor the inclination to engage in departmental or agency management, which devolves a good deal of power to their senior bureaucratic officials. However, the pressures on these officials to be politically responsive in support of their ministers, especially in policy advice and the management of their political environment, have resulted in a situation where even senior officials are not engaged completely in administrative affairs. Rather, much in the way of program management—and thus budgeting and spending—falls to officials down the line of departmental and agency hierarchies. It has been in recognition of these facts of public sector management that almost all governments in industrialized democracies have now shifted the primary focus of restraint to departmental and agency management.

Management Reform

The shift of focus in restraint budgeting from central executive authorities and their corporate support agencies to departments and agencies has generally followed increased political control and the deployment of the budgetary measures outlined above, although in some cases the initiation of management reform has run almost parallel to them. The shift of focus has been relative, in that major strategic decisions on policy or administrative matters, which invariably have expenditure implications, have remained a central concern of the center. This includes macrobudgetary decisions such as the total size of annual expenditure commitments and the broad patterns of their distribution across the principal sectors of government spending.

At the same time, however, budgeting has become characterized by two new features. First, many governments have moved to departmental or agency budgets that give increased discretion to their political or administrative heads to reallocate funds among programs and activities, particularly with a view to managing the implications of restraint with respect to departmental or agency priorities. Second, departments and agencies have greater flexibility in the development of their financial management systems in order to pursue efficiencies. In addition, in some cases, departments and agencies have greater control over personnel matters than has been the norm, and this has also had implications for the pursuit of efficiencies in their budgeting and spending practices.

These reforms have been accompanied by greater efforts to specify objectives, to measure outputs, to clarify responsibilities, to assess management efficiency, and generally to improve information systems. It is in these ways that managerialism has come to the forefront in public sector management. In most cases, the emphasis on management encompasses an increased role for political heads and bureaucrats. The Canadian reform, for instance, is titled Increased Ministerial Authority and Accountability precisely to signify that the political head—the minister—is the chief executive officer of a department or agency (Aucoin and Bakvis 1988). The much heralded financial management initiative of the British government, introduced in 1982 and influential in similar developments elsewhere, was itself influenced by the initiative of one British minister to assert himself as the chief executive officer, or manager, of his department and to develop a management system to do so (Metcalfe and Richards 1987, 56–76).

The principal focus of these reforms is the public service. The rationale behind such reforms is that a concern for the management of financial resources—for achieving value for money and thus efficiency in the operations of government—cannot be restricted to either the political level of government or even the senior echelons of the bureaucracy. Rather, it must extend to managers down the line, given that decisions on both requests and spending occur at all levels of management. If highly centralized systems cannot cope with the volume and complexity of such decisions, some decentralization of authority is required. The recognition of this reality has meant initiatives to formally delegate authority to officials coupled with mechanisms to delineate responsibility and accountability. The increased discretion and flexibility noted above have been the means to these ends.

Although the present reforms have encompassed a comprehensive concern for public management in all its respects, the driving force behind them clearly has been the perceived need for restraint and the consequent demand to provide the same, or greater, level of public service with relatively fewer resources, given that most political regimes have not been willing or able to substantially cut back on public services themselves. These reforms have sought to make managers manage for results—that is, to provide the desired outputs and to do so with increased efficiency. Greater discretion and flexibility have been deemed to be essential for at least two reasons. First, greater discretion to reallocate funds within approved departmental/agency budgets enables managers to pursue their own priorities. They thus have an incentive to achieve efficiencies in their operations, because efficiencies in all or some activities produce the budgetary room for them to maneuver. This is especially the case when savings remain with the department or agency that secures them. Second, greater flexibility in terms of financial management, including the use of personnel resources, removes some of the "constraints to productive management" (Canada 1983) previously imposed by central corporate management agencies. In so doing, this may serve to reduce bureaucratic resistance to restraint: "More managerial flexibility can be an explicit quid pro quo for giving agencies less money" (Schick 1988, 531).

These management reforms are of recent origin; in most countries they are only now being implemented. Whether they will bring about the desired changes is still to be determined. Restraint has perhaps made managers more conscious of the limited supply of resources and of the need to husband them more carefully. But bureaucratic cultures are not easily transformed. This has been acknowledged in industrialized democracies, promoting a greater sense of corporate culture to offset the fragmentation of government bureaucracies with their tendencies to act as a conglomerate of highly independent, and therefore budget-maximizing, agencies. Restraint has also been an explicit objective of the management development centers and programs instituted in virtually all of these political systems. These same centers and programs, and the philosophies on which they are based, have also been designed or reoriented to promote a greater concern for the management of resources, financial and personnel, among top management, and those who aspire to the same, compared to the traditional preoccupations of senior bureaucrats with matters of public policy.

In ways that are sometimes explicit and sometimes implicit, these reforms are addressed to Niskanen's budget-maximizing bureaucrat thesis. Three dimensions are worthy of note. First, these reforms seek to force bureaucrats to focus on their management responsibilities by making clear that there is an important distinction between policy and management. Although bureaucrats may advise on the former, the latter is not to be left only to specialists in financial or personnel administration and to middle managers, who administer the actual programs of government agencies. At the same time, policy is to be directed by political officials—hence the centralization of power over strategic policy that is now to coexist with a greater decentralization of management—the "tight-loose fit" of centralization-decentralization prescribed by Peters and Waterman (1982). Under this kind of regime, bureaucrats from the top down are expected to focus on ways to deploy scarce resources efficiently.

Given that the management reform schemes now under way have been designed primarily by senior bureaucrats—albeit in many cases in response to political pressures and external influences—the effects of increased political control are clear. The days of budget maximizing as a positive measure of a bureaucrat's performance are numbered, if not over. In this sense, the normative culture has changed. Budgets are to expand only when in line with strategic political priorities, as determined by politicians and supported by political advisers. Otherwise, bureaucrats are to conserve, particularly to make room for new strategic political priorities. The reassertion of this traditional political/bureaucratic, or policy/management dichotomy, accordingly, is meant to reduce the legitimacy and thus the capacity of bureaucrats, as specialist managers of government organizations, to act as interpreters of the public interest in determining the resources to be devoted to an agency's mission. The critical question, however, is whether bureaucrats have been, or can be, restrained in these respects as a result of changes in the culture of governance. The evidence suggests that bureaucratic self-restraint has become a norm of some significance (Metcalfe and Richards 1987; Manion 1988; Halligan 1989).

Changes in culture are unlikely to come about, or at least not to have much effect on behavior, unless they are coupled with changes in organizational structures. The second dimension of management reform, namely increased decentralization of authority to line agencies and the reduction of central corporate controls over them, has been undertaken to provide greater incentives to pursue efficiency and to remove disincentives to the same end, respectively. These measures, accordingly, are focused directly on the matter of bureaucratic efficiency. They serve notice that governments have recognized that efficiencies are unlikely to be pursued by managers of government operations when these same managers are merely administrators, with little in the way of authority over their operations and restricted by centrally devised rules and regulations governing the departmental use of resources committed to their operations. Transforming these officials into managers constitutes an acknowlegement of the fact that efficiencics cannot be effected merely by top-down prescriptions nor by universally applied formulas. Indeed, it is increasingly recognized that, to the degree that line officials are treated as administrators of programs and systemwide administrative policies, there is every incentive for them to engage in budget maximization and other forms of pathological behavior to compensate for their lack of authority and discretion.

These measures, however, do contain ways by which the exercise of line managerial authority and discretion are meant to be assessed by central political authorities and their corporate support agencies. These include increased attention to clarifying agency and program objectives, delineating expected outputs, pinpointing managerial responsibilities, and improving information and reporting systems. However, increased efficiency is not simply the result of decentralization and deregulation. At the same time, decentralization and deregulation are necessary for the achievement of efficiencies, because they alter the incentives under which bureaucrats operate. In this sense, these changes constitute an acknowledgement that previous structures tended to foster budget maximization by bureaucrats.

The third dimension of these management reforms is that they are meant to enhance the capacities of political authorities and their corporate support staff to hold the managers of line agencies accountable for the degree to which organizational outputs are provided in an efficient manner. The enhancement of accountability regimes has been central to management reform in all governments, for it is critical to effective political control of the bureaucracy in terms of determining the appropriate levels of public service output in relation to the resources required for it. Only with improved accountability can politicians and their corporate support staff assess whether programs are being efficiently managed and whether budgetary requests are appropriate.

This dimension of government budgeting is its Achilles' heel with respect to the criterion of efficiency. It is not so much a question of whether politicians have the specialized knowledge or informational capacity to control the budget-maximizing tendencies of bureaucrats (or of guardians to do the same vis-à-vis spenders, whether political or bureaucratic), but rather whether the management of government operations can be subjected to analyses that ascertain the degree to which efficiency has been accomplished. This is especially the case if outcomes or results, as opposed to outputs, are being assessed. But even the assessment of outputs poses methodological problems that are not easily overcome.

What constitutes efficiency is, in many respects, a matter of judgment and not precise measurement according to some absolute criterion. This is well demonstrated by the fact that, in both the private and public sectors—and notwithstanding the presumed capacity of the former to be better able to determine efficiency—the favored measures to improve efficiency begin with reductions in administrative overhead, including personnel. The major difference in the behavior of the two sectors lies largely in the fact that managers in the private sector may have a personal interest in efficiency if they are financial shareholders in the corporations they manage. Public managers, and private sector managers with no financial interests in their corporations, have only their professional reputations at stake. The next step to management reform in Britain (hiving off separate executive agencies with clearly identified authority and accountability) is in recognition of this fact (Jenkins, Caines, and Jackson 1988). Those with managerial responsibilities for these new agencies are meant to have a personal stake in their performance, given that their operations are to be conducted in isolation from the organizational interdependencies that characterize so much of public administration and that have served to diffuse accountability for administrative behavior.

The bottom line of public sector management, namely accountable management, remains an elusive goal precisely because governments pursue a diversity of policy objectives, many of which are only indirectly, if at all, related to the prescribed outputs of a particular agency (Plumptre 1988). Although public sector managers may have become more conscious of the need to provide an account of their performance to their political and bureaucratic superiors, such accounts and their evaluation must contain a significant measure of judgment, political and professional. It is in this sense that accountable management regimes cannot eliminate the possibility that bureaucrats will seek to maximize their budgets. Enhanced mechanisms for extracting accounts, however, do improve the chances that the most pathological instances of the same will be reduced.

Conclusions

The politics and management of restraint over the past decade and more demonstrate how difficult it is to pursue efficiency in public management. Although governments may be led by politicians ideologically committed to restraint, and public opinion may be supportive in principle, there exist numerous constituencies that can be counted on to oppose specific measures of restraint. Such opposition tends to weaken the resolve of most politicians and, thus, their collective discipline, given that the maintenance of political power usually ranks higher in the goals of politicians and their political advisers than the accomplishment of ideological commitments. The basic dynamic of governance for restraint in this respect is between guardians and spenders at the level of political decision making in the budgetary process. Bureaucrats, whether career public servants or political appointees, are very much subordinate officials in this dynamic; their effect on basic budgetary decisions is marginal and has become more so with the centralization of power that has characterized efforts at restraining expenditures.

Efforts at restraint have not led to major innovations in budgeting as technical exercises. Rather, the measures employed to effect the restraint that has occurred have relied upon existing budgetary processes. In all of this it has been recognized that the analytical promises of earlier reform techniques have not materialized: the accounting may be performed in different fashion, but the essential political judgments are still required. In this respect, moreover, it is now acknowledged almost everywhere that more information on the budget requests and spending practices of line agencies does not in itself place politicians, their political advisers, or even corporate support agencies in a position where judgments are rendered any easier.

This is the case with regard to both budgetary trade-offs between programs and expenditures for individual programs. Whether bureaucrats or their political superiors in spending agencies seek to maximize their budgets in ways that are inefficient, either from the perspective of the total budget or in terms of what they actually need for their prescribed activities, is thus largely a matter of judgment. Cuts to administrative overhead and discretionary expenditures have characterized the efforts of governments to cope with restraint. Central budget decision makers and their advisers perceive inefficiencies in budgeting and spending, but there are limits to what they can do in the way of microbudgeting to remove these inefficiencies.

The most significant changes perhaps are those that aim to reform public management in the pursuit of efficiency. Administrative decentralization and delegation, as well as administrative deregulation, have come to the fore as the means of improving management in government operations. In some large part, these reform initiatives are predicated upon the assumption that managers, especially those down the line in complex organizations, constitute the critical points at which efficiencies can be effected. Greater managerial discretion has been coupled with increased efforts to secure accountability, but the crucial point is that the challenge of efficiency has been turned over largely to managers. Whether this managerial revolution will produce the desired result is an open question. From the perspective of the budget-maximizing bureaucrat thesis, however, it would appear that governments have decided that professional pride and integrity, coupled with professional peer pressure, will offset the temptation of bureaucrats to maximize their budgets in ways that do not serve the central corporate objectives of restraint and efficiency.

REFERENCES

Aberbach, Joel D., and Bert A. Rockman. 1988. Image I revisited: Executive and political roles. *Governance* 1(1): 1–25.

Aucoin, Peter. 1988. The Mulroney government, 1984–88: Priorities, positional policy and power. In Gollner and Salee 1988, 335–56.

———. 1989. Administrative reform in public management: Paradigms, principles, paradoxes and pendulums. *Governance* 3(2): 115–37.

Aucoin, Peter, and Herman Bakvis. 1988. *The Centralization-decentralization conundrum: Organization and management in the Canadian government.* Halifax: Institute for Research on Public Policy.

Bakvis, Herman. 1988. Regional ministers, national policy and the administrative state in Canada. *Canadian Journal of Political Science* 21:(3): 539–67.

Bulmer, Martin. 1988. Social science expertise and executive-bureaucratic politics in Britain. *Governance* 1(1): 26–49.

Canada, 1983. Office of the Auditor General. *Report to the House of Commons for the fiscal year ended 31 March 1983.* Ottawa: Minister of Supply and Services, 53–87.

———. 1986. Task force on program review. *Introduction to the process of program review.* Ottawa: Minister of Supply and Services.

Campbell, Colin. 1983. *Governments under stress: Political executives and key bureaucrats in Washington, London and Ottawa.* Toronto: Univ. of Toronto Press.

———. 1988a. The search for coordination and control: When and how are central agencies the answer? In Campbell and Peters 1988a, 55–78.

———. 1988b. Mulroney's broker politics: The ultimate in politicized incompetence? In Gollner and Salee 1988, 309–34.

Campbell, Colin, and B. Guy Peters, eds. 1988a. *Organizing governance and governing organizations.* Pittsburgh, Pa.: Univ. of Pittsburgh Press.

————. 1988b. The politics/administration dichotomy: Death or merely change? *Governance* 1(1): 79–99.

Derlien, Hans-Ulich. 1989. Genesis and structure of evaluation efforts in comparative perspective. In *Program evaluation and the management of government: Patterns and prospects across eight nations,* ed. Ray Rist. New York: Transaction Books.

Gollner, Andrew B., and Daniel Salee, eds. 1988. *Canada under Mulroney: An end of term report.* Montreal: Vehicule Press.

Halligan, John. 1989. The Australian public service reform program. In *Hawke's second government: Australian commonwealth administration, 1984– 87,* ed. R. Wettenhall and J. Nethercote. Canberra, Aus.: RAIPA/ CCAE.

Hansen, Michael G., and Charles H. Levine. 1988. The centralization-decentralization tug-of-war in the new executive branch. In Campbell and Peters 1988a, 255–82.

Hood, Christopher, Andrew Dunsire, and Lynne Thomson. 1988. Rolling back the state: Thatcherism, Fraserism and bureaucracy. *Governance* 1(3): 243–70.

Ingraham, Patricia W. 1987. Building bridges or burning them? The president, the appointees, and the bureaucracy. *Public Administration Review* 47(5): 425–35.

Jenkins, K., K. Caines, and A. Jackson. *Improving management in government: The next steps.* London: HMSO.

Johnston, Richard. 1986. *Public opinion and public policy in Canada.* Toronto: Univ. of Toronto Press.

Kemp, D. A. 1986. The recent evolution of central policy control mechanisms in parliamentary systems. *International Political Science Review* 7(1): 56–66.

Kooiman, Jan, and Kjell A. Eliassen, eds. 1987. *Managing public organizations: Lessons from contemporary european experience.* London: Sage.

Levine, Charles H. 1986. The federal government in the year 2000: Administrative legacies of the Reagan years. *Public Administration Review* 46(3): 195–206.

Manion, John L. 1988. New challenges in public administration. *Canadian Public Administration* 31(2): 234–46.

Maslove, Allan M., Michael J. Prince, and G. Bruce Doern. 1986. *Federal and Provincial Budgeting.* Toronto: Univ. of Toronto Press.

Metcalfe, Les, and Sue Richards. 1987. *Improving public management.* London: Sage.

Niskanen, William A. 1971. *Representative government and bureaucracy.* Chicago: Aldine Atherton.

Peters, B. Guy. 1989. *The politics of bureaucracy.* New York: Longman.

Peters, Thomas J., and Robert H. Waterman, Jr. 1982. *In search of excellence.* New York: Harper & Row.

Plumptre, Timothy W. 1988. *Beyond the bottom line: Management in government.* Halifax: Institute for Research on Public Policy.

Savoie, Donald J. 1990. *The politics of public spending in Canada.* Toronto: Univ. of Toronto Press.

Schick, Allen. 1988. Micro-budgeting adaptations to fiscal stress in industrial democracies. *Public Administration Review* 48(1): 523–33.

Sutherland, Sharon L., and G. Bruce Doern. 1986. *Bureaucracy in Canada: Control and reform.* Toronto: Univ. of Toronto Press.

Veilleux, Gerard, and Donald J. Savoie. 1988. Kafka's castle: The treasury board of Canada revisited. *Canadian Public Administration* 31(4): 517–38.

Wilson, V. Seymour. 1988. What legacy? The Nielsen task force program review. In *How Ottawa spends, 1988–89: The conservatives heading into the stretch,* ed. Katherine A, Graham, 23–48. Ottawa: Carleton Univ. Press.

6

D. RODERICK KIEWIET

Bureaucrats and Budgetary Outcomes: Quantitative Analyses

Niskanen's Model of Bureaucracy and Representative Government

The expansion of the public sector in advanced industrial democracies is one of the most important political developments of the last hundred years. Government bureaus throughout the world now provide trillions of dollars annually in services that previously were supplied either privately or not at all—from parking ramps to pollution control, health care to housing, and rockets to rock concerts. At the beginning of this long period of growth in the public sector, many observers welcomed it as the happy consequence of increasing affluence and the desire for social progress (Wagner 1958). It appeared to them that government, in response to popular demand, was simply shouldering its responsibility for the welfare of the citizenry from cradle to grave. By the 1970s, however, the public sector in many Western democracies accounted for over half of the GNP. By this time, the growth of government had provoked a great deal of alarm—especially among public choice theorists (Buchanan 1977). After regressing government growth rates on a battery of income, wealth, and population variables, Borcherding (1977) concludes that only about half of the growth in the public sector can be accounted for by increases in popular demand.

In much of the reaction against government growth there is the intimation that bureaucrats are somehow responsible, but in the

143

same crude sense that lawyers are blamed for expensive court settlements, or doctors for the high cost of medical care. The achievement of Niskanen's (1971) *Bureaucracy and Representative Government* is the explication of a formal theory linking budgetary outcomes to the maximizing behavior of bureaucrats. Niskanen argues that several components of a bureau manager's utility function increase with the size of the bureau's budget, and that the manager therefore seeks to maximize it. Some research has been done on the empirical merits of this claim, but the assumption that bureaucrats seek to maximize their budgets has the same quality as the analogous propositions that firms maximize profits and that congressmen maximize their probability of being reelected. They are not strictly true, but they are close enough approximations to what we experience as the real world that no alternative assumptions are as compelling.

Niskanen posits further that a government bureau and the popularly elected legislative sponsor that provides its budget are both in a monopoly position. The sponsor faces no competition from other possible bidders for the bureaus' services, and the bureau faces no competition from alternative suppliers of its services. A priori, the only prediction that follows from the presence of a bilateral monopoly is that outcomes lie along the protagonists' contract curve. Niskanen asserts, however, that differences in the two sides' incentives, together with the asymmetric way information is revealed in the bargaining situation, puts the bureau at a tremendous strategic advantage. While the legislative sponsor remains virtually ignorant of the bureau's costs of service provision, the bureau chief knows precisely how much the sponsor is willing to pay for any quantity of output. The bureau can thus act as a discriminating monopolist and make take-it-or-leave-it offers that the budget setter just barely prefers to receiving nothing at all. It follows directly that bureaucratic production is oversupplied and, to the extent it is in the bureau's interest to do so, it is supplied inefficiently.

This chapter examines quantitative research into several aspects of Niskanen's work, reviewing the literature in six broad areas of inquiry. The first two pertain to analyses that bear on the central oversupply and inefficiency hypotheses, respectively. It should be noted that in most cases the hypotheses tested are Niskanenesque; they are consistent with the general thrust of his model but are not equilibrium predictions that are formally derived from it. The remaining sections review programs of research that do focus on comparative statics implications derived from his model. The research reviewed in the third section concerns the effect of competition upon bureaucratic budgetary behavior. Studies in this area examine the straightforward prediction that bureaus facing competition from other public entities are forced to behave competitively and are no longer able to maximize their budgets. The fourth section assesses research on the budgetary consequences of legislative oversight. To the extent legislators are able to conduct better oversight, or are able to do so at lower cost, their enhanced bargaining position should result in bureaus obtaining smaller budgets. The fifth section examines studies that concern the effect of budgetary outcomes upon elections. If budgets exceed popular demand, as Niskanen's model implies, then electoral support for the incumbent party should vary negatively with government growth. The sixth section assesses research on the budget-maximization hypothesis in nonlegislative settings—more specifically, to referendum voting on budgetary proposals. Under direct democracy, bureaucratic officials often possess proposal powers that are far more monopolistic than those possessed by agencies confronting a legislative sponsor. For this reason, Niskanen's model can be tested more directly in such settings than in the context of representative government, to which it was originally applied.

The Oversupply Hypothesis

Several studies investigate the relationship between bureaucratic professionalism—typically measured by the percentage of government employees afforded civil service protection—and the amount of spending by federal, state, and local governments in a variety of policy areas. Although Niskanen does not explicitly derive any comparative statics results from variations in the nature of the bureaucracy, it is in keeping with the spirit of his work to hypothesize that careerist bureaucrats, subject to neither removal nor arbitrary harassment by their legislative sponsors, can extract more money from them. This literature grew mainly out of a desire by political scientists to refute the findings of Dye (1966) and Sharkansky (1967), who report that the policy outputs of states and localities are much more highly correlated with environmental variables such as population and economic growth than with political variables such as the extent of party competition. Many political scientists were disturbed by these findings, which suggest that what they study has little to do with public policy decisions. Bureaucratic professionalism is thus one of any number of political variables that might matter in explaining policy variation.

Not surprisingly, most efforts in this area tend to be large fishing expeditions, as Boyne (1985) points out in his exhaustive review of this literature. One study, for example, begins with forty-two independent variables and narrows them down to the best six. As a consequence, Boyne concludes: "Many of the results for individual variables appear capricious, contingent upon the statistical technique and bundle of other variables pressed into service" (501). Whatever the case, these studies frequently fail to find any effects on policy outputs associated with bureaucratic professionalism. Lineberry (1969), for instance, reports that this variable does not even covary with the amount of municipalities' expenditures on planning, which is perhaps the most bureaucratically treasured activity of them all. Interestingly, bureaucratic professionalism— at least as measured by extent of civil service coverage—correlates at a much higher level with the degree of redistributiveness arising from the interaction of revenue and expenditure policies than it does with actual spending (Fry and Winters 1970; Booms and Halldorson 1973).

In assessing this literature, it is also important to realize that a positive relationship between bureaucratic professionalism and amount of expenditures provides evidence for the oversupply hypothesis that is circumstantial in nature and, as such, consistent with a number of alternative explanations. Such a finding may indeed reflect a Niskanenesque effect of more highly trained, committed bureaucrats obtaining bigger budgets than their more amateurish, patronage appointee counterparts. But it could also be that the various bureaucracies being scrutinized produce outputs at precisely the level preferred by the median voter in the jurisdiction; supplying more goods and services simply requires employing more highly trained, professional bureaucrats.

A set of similar studies investigate the plausible notion that strong bureaus should achieve higher budget and staffing levels than weak bureaus and, alternatively, that strong bureaus should be more resistant to unfavorable shifts in demands, such as those generated by the election of conservative politicians to the sponsoring authority. Positing further that the best indicator of bureaucratic strength during a particular stretch of time is bureaucratic strength at the beginning of the period, their estimation strategy consists of regressing bureau expenditures or staff levels in one period on expenditures or staff levels in a previous period. In two studies of this type, Nicholson and Topham (1971; 1975) report that expenditures on housing and highways by county boroughs in England and Wales between 1962 and 1968 were positively related to expenditure levels of the recent past. In a similar analysis of staffing levels in the Local Authorities of London, however, Storey (1980) reports that growth in the number of staff employed between 1970 and 1976 was unrelated to absolute staff size in 1970.

In all likelihood this mixed pattern of results arises from differences in specification. The former studies regress levels on previous levels, while the latter regresses *changes* on previous levels. In either case, ordinary least squares regressions incorporating lagged endogenous variables on the right-hand side are not going to tell us anything about the oversupply hypothesis. As Boyne (1987) points out, "Previous policy outputs are likely to have been the product of the same gamut of forces as current policy outputs. Therefore, while bureaucratic power may be contained somewhere in the impetus variable, its extent is unknown" (82). Boyne goes on to address these shortcomings in an analysis of staffing levels in three different samples of English and Welsh boroughs and metropolitan districts. His strategy is to first regress staffing variables on several political and socioeconomic variables. The residuals derived from these equations, he argues, are indirect indicators of bureaucratic power in that they are not accounted for by the battery of independent variables. He then regresses change in staffing levels over the next two or three years on the same inde-

pendent variables plus the bureaucratic power residuals. He finds
that the effects of the latter are, if anything, in the opposite direction to that predicted. I suspect that his results primarily reflect a
regression to the mean phenomenon. Those local governments
that for one reason or another had atypically large staffs in 1980
tended to pick up fewer employees over the next few years, and
vice versa.

Whatever the case, the main shortcoming of Boyne's analysis is
one shared by other studies that use the residual from one equation
as the dependent variable in another—it is difficult to determine
how closely it approximates the underlying variable of interest, if at
all. It may be composed of nothing more than measurement error.
When there turns out to be no relationship in the expected direction
with an explanatory variable, Tufte's (1978, 5) dictum—"The absence of evidence is not convincing evidence of absence"—becomes
especially apropos.

One of the many things that governments supply is scientific
research, either in-house or in the form of grants to the scientific
community. Niskanen's model implies that investment in research, like everything else supplied by government bureaucracies,
is oversupplied. There are no precise predictions about how excessive supply would be, but it seems clear that the return to bureaucratically supplied research investment should be quite modest—
especially compared to the payoffs that obtain in the private sector,
where investment in research and development must meet a market test. This is the reasoning of Ruttan (1980), who estimates the
rate of return in public sector agricultural research. His results, in
conjunction with those of dozens of other studies, lead him to
conclude that annual rates of return from these public expenditures
range between 30 and 60 percent. If so, scientific research is one
bureaucratic output that would seem to be woefully undersupplied
and would thus constitute an important exception to the oversupply hypothesis.

Pasour and Johnson (1982) argue that Ruttan's work is beset by
several serious problems. Among other things, they assert that his
and other studies in this genre are characterized by a sampling bias
in favor of highly visible, successful programs, by failures to fully
account for all costs, and by large underestimates of shifts in sup-

ply and demand. Ruttan (1982) disputes their claims, some in a more convincing fashion than others. Rather than attempt to sort out the econometric issues involved, I think it is best to step back and consider the putative finding of 30–60 percent annual rates of return to investment in agricultural research. If research sponsored by government bureaus generated payoffs of this magnitude, the scientists employed by Ciba–Geigy or Monsanta could presumably achieve similar results. If so, I see little that would prevent a massive flow of capital to the firms involved in this research, a flow that would presumably continue until research, both public and private, again yielded a normal rate of return.

On the other hand, there are reasons to accept Ruttan's estimates of extraordinary rates of return to government-sponsored research as at least plausible. In many sectors of the economy, individual firms engaged in research may appropriate only a small fraction of the total social return; in the case of pharmaceuticals and computers, for example, close substitutes are developed so quickly that patent protection is almost a moot point. Government bureaus may tend to concentrate research efforts where rates of return are very high but where private firms are discouraged from investing because they appropriate too small a share of total profits. Competition from government and universities can itself discourage otherwise profitable private investment (Davis and Groth 1974). It is obvious that a proper assessment of findings in this area requires consideration of factors that take us far afield of the budgetary issues we are concerned about. Whatever the merits of the enterprise, estimating rates of return to government-sponsored research is thus not a fruitful approach to take in testing the oversupply hypothesis.

As indicated earlier, the hypotheses considered by the various studies discussed so far are Niskanenesque; while consistent with the spirit of his model, they fail to specify precisely the point at which a particular policy outputs is oversupplied. How do we know whether a lot of expenditures is too much? A crucial insight in this regard is that of McGuire (1981), who reasons that if a bureau were able to behave as a discriminating monopolist, it would be able to extract everything the sponsor was willing to pay at all levels of feasible output. Total benefit therefore equals total cost. This has an important implication: "Since quantity increases with a decrease in cost, and since budget is always equal to total benefit of the quantity produced, *total budget unambiguously rises with a decrease in the cost of output.* The percentage increase in quantity 'purchased' exceeds the percentage fall in unit cost. Demand always *appears* to be elastic" (315). From this, McGuire derives the explicit prediction that observed elasticities for bureaucratic production should always be less than −1.[1]

To examine this hypothesis, he reviews the findings of several studies that reportedly estimate the budgetary response of state and local governments to federal matching grants. Grants of this nature are tantamount to cuts in the price of services provided by local buraucracies. In McGuire's view, the hypothesis receives little support; most estimates of the elasticities of demand for public services are inelastic, as are other estimates of the derived demand for labor. In a similar study, Wyckoff (1988) tests the identical hypothesis concerning observed elasticities with revenue-sharing data from 115 small municipal governments in Michigan. Wyckoff finds some support for the hypothesis, in that the elasticity of demand he estimates for capital expenditures is less than −1, but for current expenditures it is only −.34.

Why are these results, especially McGuire's, not more supportive? Perhaps it is because the underlying model is flawed, but there are many other possibilities. One major problem with McGuire's analysis is that none of the observations of elasticities he collects from previous studies are actually price elasticities derived, as in the Wyckoff study, from data on federal grants. The Borcherding and Deacon (1972) study he reports actually computes a measure of marginal tax price. Another study, that by Bergstrom and Goodman (1973), employs a measure of tax share, defined as the tax bill on the median value house divided by total property tax revenue for the municipality (284). Such a variable registers, among other things, the extent to which local public goods supplied to residential home owners are subsidized by taxes on business and commercial interests or by other sources of revenue.

As Borcherding and Deacon point out, estimating elasticities in this manner requires making some strong assumptions, but there is probably no alternative method of estimation that is feasible in this context.[2] Despite these problems, the study whose operationalization of the tax price variable I most prefer (Borcherding and Deacon 1972) is also most supportive of the elasticity hypothesis. Ignoring the results for higher education and highways, which both receive large amounts of federal funding, estimates of elasticities in four of the seven service areas are less than −1 and the estimate of another (police) is −.9. Given the data and estimation problems involved, combined with the more positive results from Wyckoff's direct test, I would say that the hypothesis McGuire and Wyckoff derive from the Niskanen model fares reasonably well.

The Inefficiency Hypothesis

Niskanen (1975) cites several studies that find government bureaus to have significantly higher production costs than those incurred by private firms in providing essentially the same goods and services. These include fire services (Ahlbrandt 1973), airlines (Davies 1971), electricity production (De Alessi 1974), and garbage collection (Spann 1977). The most impressive figures I have come across are for education in Los Angeles (Shapiro and Korenstein 1989).[3] There are doubtless many more studies that make the same comparisons and arrive at similar conclusions.

Rather than review the data and methodology of these studies at length, I instead want to make only a couple of observations. First, the distinction between private production by a firm and public production by a bureau is often too facile. In the case of household refuse collection, for instance, several researchers have estimated that private firms perform the job at least cost than municipal sanitation departments, but only when they have been awarded a monopoly in a competitive bidding arrangement. The most costly alternative is to rely solely on private firms competing in an open-market situation, as no firm is able to realize the economies of density that obtain in picking up refuse (Kemper and Quigley 1976; Stevens 1978; Dubin and Navarro 1988). In short, the best responses to cases of market failure typically involve some combination of private provision and public authority.

Second the inefficiency of government bureaus compared to private firms, no matter how gross it might be, provides evidence for the inefficiency hypothesis that is at best circumstantial. Bureaucratic inefficiency may indeed result from the bureaucrats' quest for 'discretionary' income. But it may also be exactly what the legislative sponsor wants. An extreme argument in this regard is that legislators rejoice in the existence of poorly managed government bureaucracies, in that the resultant snafus provide opportunities for electorally rewarding interventions on behalf of their constituents; because bureaus must go to Congress for their budgets and program authorizations, a call from a congressman's office can be counted on to get things straightened out quickly (Fiorina 1977; Fiorina and Noll 1978). As Fiorina puts it, "In a very real sense each congressman is a monopoly supplier of bureaucratic unsticking services for his district" (43).

Less cynical and more plausible is the hypothesis that the extra jobs created by the inefficient operation of bureaus are valued by the individuals who hold them, and such individuals would presumably be unhappy with office seekers who proposed eliminating their positions. More generally, waste, fraud, and abuse are very much in the eye of the beholder. Virtually all the programs the Grace Commission (Congressional Budget Office 1984) attacked as wasteful and inefficient were of obvious benefit to a major interest group. In short, the origin of bureaucratic waste and inefficiency need not be the bureaucracy.

Multiple Jurisdictions and Bureaucratic Competition

In Niskanen's model, a government bureau faces no competition from alternative suppliers of its services. The most straightforward remedy for monopoly, of course, is competition. Although one can envision competition between bureaus within a single jurisdiction, the situation that is typically analyzed is one in which there are multiple, distinct city governments in the same urban area. The most common manifestation of this configuration in the United States is that of a central city surrounded by dozens of suburbs. There are, for example, over eighty separate municipal entities in Los Angeles County, and many dozens more in adjacent counties. In such situations, bureaus are still monopoly suppliers of public services within each jurisdiction, but individual citizens can "vote with their feet" by moving to a different jurisdiction where the level, mix, and cost of public services conforms more closely to their tastes. The classic statement of this thesis is that of Tiebout (1956). Among the many assumptions upon which his model hinges, that of costless mobility is the most important. As he puts it, "Moving or failing to move replaces the usual market test of willingness to buy a good and reveals the consumer-voter's demand for public goods" (420).

As this quotation clearly indicates, Tiebout sees his model as illuminating a solution to the nettlesome problem of demand revelation for public goods. As in the case of market competition, however, the quasi-market pressures that he portrays should also act to discipline government bureaus and to induce them to engage in less oversupply. Bureaus may indeed be capable of extracting everything a city council is willing to pay for its services, only to find that large numbers of people formerly living in their jurisdiction have moved to other jurisdictions where different (presumably lower) levels of the same services are provided at lower cost.

There are a couple of studies that subject the hypothesis that bureaucratic competition results in smaller budgets to empirical scrutiny. In an analysis of expenditure data from forty-eight urban areas in the South, Sjoquist (1982) reports that per capita expenditures in central cities fell markedly as the number of separate municipal jurisdictions in the greater metropolitan areas increased. In a considerably more comprehensive study, Schneider (1989) examines this hypothesis with a pooled cross-sectional sample of 839 suburban municipalities in thirty-nine standard metropolitan statistical areas for the years 1972, 1977, and 1982. Schneider regresses real per capita local expenditures, which he interprets as the amount of inputs into the bureaucratic production process and thus an indicator of the "exactive power of monopoly bureaucrats" (616), into a large battery of demand-related variables and two different measures of competition: (1) the total number of municipalities in the SMSA, and (2) the number of other municipal governments located on the border of each municipality. The coefficients of both indicators are in the predicted direction and statistically significant, leading Schneider to conclude that "an expanded set of alternate providers in the local market for public goods limits the size of local government by restricting successful rent seeking by bureacrats" (624).

Such findings provide impressive support for the Niskanen model, in that there are eminently plausible counterhypotheses that predict exactly the opposite pattern of results. Municipal reform advocates have long seen fragmentation and overlap as the source of inefficiency, duplication of administrative expenses and other forms of overhead, and lack of coordination. By this view, the consequence of too many competing governments is higher and more wasteful expenditures, which can only be trimmed by merging and consolidating jurisdictions. Second, Aaron (1969) notes that in the provision of public goods, the tax share of each individual falls as new residents enter the jurisdiction. Because of this, municipal governments have incentives to increase expenditures so long as they are more than offset by increases in population. Third, Baird and Landon (1972) conjecture that, to the extent individuals do sort themselves into different municipalities in the manner postulated by Tiebout, finer sorting implies more homogeneity of tastes for public goods within each jurisdiction. Greater homogeneity in turn implies greater perceived benefits and more widespread support for expenditures. Thus they too hypothesize that the greater the number of jurisdictions within a metropolitan area, the higher the level of local public goods expenditures.

Conversely, the bureaucratic competition hypothesis is not the only possible explanation for the inverse correlation between the number of jurisdictions and the level of local public expenditures. A pattern such as this also arises readily as the noncooperative solution to a fiscal prisoners' dilemma. Consider the case of a city that supplies public services at precisely the level preferred by the median voter. In this turns out to be relatively higher than in neighboring cities, citizens of surrounding jurisdictions can free ride, as in the case of suburbanites and central cities (Bradford and Oates 1974). Even worse, to the extent the provision of such services has (progressively) redistributive consequences, those with preferences for lower taxes and expenditures may move to those surrounding communities. While wealthy individuals and business flee, those who remain in the community now have an even higher demand for public services, but must now pay for them out of a diminished tax base. Facing this sort of threat from its neighbors, a "rational fiscal strategy" (Buchanan 1971) dictates providing incentives for the rich to move in and for the poor to move out, and to thus adopt policies that are regressively redistributive. Such policies may involve restrictions on lot size and land use, but almost always include very low expenditures on public services.[4] Indeed, Sjoquist (1982) interprets his results as showing that lower local expenditures result from greater intercity competition for tax base, rather than from greater competition among government bureaus.

The alternative hypothesis of tax base maximization is especially compelling once one realizes that a major reason why cities are created in the first place is to avoid redistributive spending. In his study of municipal incorporations in Los Angeles County, Miller (1981) identifies several municipalities, which he calls "minimal cities," that before passage of Proposition 13 in 1978 provided only the services that they were able to pay for without levying property taxes. The expenditure data Miller analyzes clearly indicate that between 1950 and 1970 the fiscal dilemma dynamic had the predictable effort of making the rich cities in Los Angeles County richer and the poor cities poorer, while giving all of them incentives to limit taxes and expenditures. In short, the evidence in this area of research is strongly consistent with the implications of Niskanen's model, but an observationally equivalent pattern of results is implied by an alternative hypothesis—tax base maximization—that is at least as plausible.

Fortunately, there is another sort of institutional arrangement in which the tax base maximization and bureaucratic competition hypotheses are not so deeply confounded. Similar expenditure-restraining effects have been posited for the presence of independent taxing and service provision districts that provide a specific service, such as education, street lighting, and sanitation. When a single, general purpose bureau or municipal government is the source of *all* public services, it can further exploit its monopoly position by requiring individuals within its jurisdiction to purchase an entire package of services. Referred to as *full-line forcing* in economics (Burstein 1960), the theoretical implications of service provision by one multipurpose bureau versus many single-purpose jurisdictions are worked out most thoroughly by MacKay and Weaver (1981). Overlapping, single-purpose jurisdictions such as independent school districts make consumer-voters better off, by this argument, by allowing them to select different levels of different services, even if all are supplied by monopolistic bureaus.

The expenditure-restraining effects of overlapping, single-purpose jurisdictions have been detected in a couple of careful, well-crafted studies. In their analysis of 164 counties in sixteen sourthern and border states, Wagner and Weber (1975) find that in counties with reasonably large populations (>150,000 in 1970), educational expenditures are lower when there are independent school districts than when public education is supplied by the county in conjunction with other services and funded out of general revenue. Strong support for this hypothesis also comes from DiLorenzo's (1981) analysis of some quasi-experimental policy innovations. He finds that restrictions on the creation of single-purpose districts, although ostensibly motivated by the desire to lower overall administrative costs, nonetheless led to significant increases in local expenditures in Oregon and California. Again, these findings are especially persuasive in that they would not seem to arise from the presence of a fiscal prisoners' dilemma.

Legislative Oversight

It is the bureau's overwhelming advantage in information vis-à-vis the sponsor, according to Niskanen, that transforms the bargaining situation from one of bilateral monopoly to one in which the bureau acts as a discriminating monopolist.[5] This implies that the more information the legislative sponsors can obtain about the bureau's cost of production, the stronger their bargaining position is, and thus the smaller the portion of surplus that the bureau should be able to expropriate. This has been the point of departure for a number of theoretical studies (Breton and Wintrobe 1975;

Miller and Moe 1983; Conybeare 1984; Banks 1989). Congressional scholars have also focused a great deal of attention on the problem of monitoring bureaucratic behavior, an activity that they refer to as *oversight*. The consensus of this literature is that congressmen engage in very little of it (Ogul 1976), although Aberbach (1990) presents evidence suggesting that oversight hearings are far more frequent today than they were a few decades ago.

The only study of which I am aware that examines this implication quantitatively is that of Crain et al. (1985). They posit that the extent to which the sponsor can acquire information about bureaucratic operations depends upon the division of labor within the legislature. A finer division of labor allows individual legislators to monitor particular bureaus more closely, thus fostering more efficient service provision. If so, the greater the division of labor and specialization—proxied by the number of committees and subcommittees—the smaller the size of the government sector. But they also speculate that the relationship might run in the opposite direction: "The degree of legislative specialization may be in response to demand-side forces, such as interest groups, and may therefore impinge positively on the size of the government. That is, more committees allow legislators to mirror interest groups and their concerns better, and hence lead to more rather than less government" (311).

Utilizing state-level data, they regress the number of state government employees (per capita) on the number of committees in the state legislature (also per capita), per capita state income, and a few other terms included as controls. Although it appears that the effect is decreasing at the margin, their results come down strongly on the side of the second hypothesis: the number of committees in the state legislature is positively related to the number of state government employees.

There are many problems with this analysis. Let us first assume that there is in fact a reliable, positive relationship between the size of state government and the number of committees in the legislature. Legislators in these states may be giving the voters precisely the government goods and services that they demand. Where this results in relatively larger bureaus or larger numbers of bureaus, the legislators simply set up more committees to perform a larger monitoring task. More fundamentally, though, I see no reason why the number of committees in a legislature need bear any relationship to the quantity and quality of the monitoring to which bureaucratic activity is subjected. I would argue instead that what really matters is not the number of committees but rather the realtive importance of oversight committees versus those composed primarily of program advocates. Nor do I see why the ability of interest groups to impinge on the legislative process should depend upon the sheer number of committees. It should also be kept in mind that not all committees that exist on paper actually exist. The Legislative Reorganization Act of 1946 slashed the number of committees in the U.S. Congress, but most of those eliminated had been moribund for decades.

It is also the case that Congress has delegated much of the work of oversight to agencies such as the General Accounting Office, the General Services Administration, and the Office of Management and Budget. Most state governments have developed analogous auditing and oversight capabilities. To be sure, these watchdog agencies may not do an exemplary job, but this has nothing to do with the number of committees in the legislature. Finally, as McCubbins and Schwartz (1984) point out, a vast amount of bureaucratic oversight is performed by affected third parties. Even if legislators spend little time or effort reviewing the activities of a bureau, they become terribly interested when their constituents complain to them about bureaucratic incompetence or high-handedness. McCubbins and Schwartz refer to this, fittingly enough, as *fire alarm oversight,* as opposed to *police patrol oversight.*

Any future research efforts in this area should be more carefully considered. One potentially fruitful approach is to consider the relative amounts of time that bureau chiefs and legislators have spent in their positions. Heclo (1977), for example, shows that both senior civil servants and senior members of congressional committees typically spend decades in their positions. The career life of the political appointees who ostensibly manage the agencies, however, is under two years. Until there is more progress in this area, however, empirical examination of the Niskanen model will be stymied. This is because the budgetary data we observe are always the joint product of the bureau and the legislature. Lacking knowledge about the information each side possesses or about the relative strength of their bargaining positions, we can infer little from budgetary outcomes—no matter how bloated a bureau's budget may seem or how inefficiently it appears to operate. What we observe may indeed be the product of a bureau wielding monopoly proposal power. But it may also reflect the choices made by a fully informed group of legislators, or something in between.

Public Sector Growth and Election Outcomes

Another major implication of the Niskanen model is that government expenditures exceed the level preferred by the median voter. Rational voters should be aware that spending by the government has to be funded one way or another—if not by taxes, then by asset-destroying inflation or by growth-inhibiting borrowing. If so, support for the incumbent party should be negatively related to the rate of growth in government expenditures. Of course, an appeal to the preferences of the median voter in the context of the multiple electoral districts and multidimensional issues over which elections are fought is pretty optimistic from a social choice point of view (Plott 1967; Austen-Smith 1987). But with this caveat in mind, we can proceed to review some studies that bear on this hypothesis.

The large loss of seats by the Democrats in the 1966 midterm elections, following enactment of several major pieces of Great Society social legislation in the preceding Congress, led many observers to conclude that the electorate had reacted negatively to a too rapid and too extensive commitment of federal expenditures. Political observers also speculated that some incumbent governors went down to defeat that year as a consequence of spending by their respective states having increased too rapidly. In Pomper's (1970) correlational analysis of data from non-southern states, however, there appears to be no relationship between the electoral fortunes of incumbent governors and the growth of state government spending. Noting that state spending is heavily influenced by national trends and other exogenous forces, Pomper concludes that voters are probably behaving sensibly by not punishing governors for outcomes over which they have little control.

His reasoning suggests that hypotheses concerning elections and the rate of government growth are better tested at the national level. This is exactly what Niskanen (1975) does. In one equation, he regresses vote share for the party of the incumbent president in elections between 1896 and 1972 on change in real per capita federal expenditures and, in a second equation, on change in real per capita federal revenues. Similar to other analyses of this type (Kramer 1971; Fair 1978), his equations also specified, as independent variables, change in per capita national product and dummies for war years. Niskanen reports that coefficients of both the expenditures and revenue terms are in the predicted direction, statistically significant, and that the same overall pattern of results obtains in estimations run separately upon different types of elections.

A problem with both Pomper's and Niskanen's analyses is that they focus on the electoral fortunes of executives, when, according to Niskanen's model, it is the legislative sponsors who are to blame for failing to restrain expenditures. Both studies implicitly assume either that the effects of legislative action on government growth are uncorrelated with the effects of executive action, or that rather than try to sort out who is to blame, displeased voters turn against the first target they see. The problem of identifying those responsible for undesired policy outcomes, of course, is a real one. Divided control of the executive and legislative branches makes things fuzzy enough. According to many congressional scholars, various institutional features of Congress and of the procedures it follows further obscure policy-making responsibility (Fiorina 1977).

Niskanen also omits from his equations measures for price inflation and unemployment, which other researchers generally find to adversely affect the incumbent party's performance at the polls. Due to the countercyclical nature of major entitlement programs, federal expenditures automatically increase along with unemployment. Price inflation drives up the rate of both expenditure growth and revenue growth. Niskanen's fiscal variables, in short, are correlated with omitted variables that strongly affect voting in presidential elections. To be sure, there is a plausible case to be made that the problem of spurious correlation works in the opposite direction, that is, the economic voting analyses are flawed for failing to specify expenditure or revenue variables. Economists have long wondered why people appear to be averse to inflation per se. The fact that it drives up taxes—in *real* terms, if the structure of taxes is progressive—would be a very good reason. Unfortunately, there are a very limited number of observations in even the longest running electoral time series. Combined with the presence of multicollinearity and other econometric problems, it is doubtful that the independent effects of fiscal and economic variables upon national election outcomes can be reliably estimated.

Bureaucratic Agenda Setting in Budgetary Referenda

Niskanen's model is more one of legislative failure than of bureaucracy chicanery. Although ostensibly there to enact the electorate's preferred policies, the legislative sponsors of government bureaus accede to budgetary demands that exceed what the voters prefer. Many bureaus at the state and local level, however, must appeal directly to the voters for their budgets in periodic (often annual) referenda. In other cases, state and local governments, constitutionally constrained to balance their annual budgets, must seek approval of the voters for additional spending in the form of bonded indebtedness.

The classic studies of budgetary referenda are those by Romer and Rosenthal (1979a, 1979b; 1982). Although the data they analyze are drawn only from local school districts in Oregon, about half the states in the United States (including California, Illinois, Michigan, and New York) fund some portion of their budgets for primary and secondary education through referenda. In the Oregon elections, voters are presented a proposed annual budget that is formulated, for all intents and purposes, by the district superintendent. If the proposal is rejected, the state constitution sets spending at the level of the budget for 1916 with an allowance for 6 percent annual growth. For old districts that have lost enrollment since 1916, this is not much of a threat. For the large majority of

Oregon school districts that were founded after 1916, however, the reversionary spending level is either zero or a figure below which the school can operate. If a school can continue to operate at the reversionary level, the superintendent typically identifies popular expenditures, for example, new football uniforms, that will have to be deferred if the proposal is turned down.

In the Romer and Rosenthal setter model, the school superintendent maximizes the district's budget by making a spending proposal that the median voter just barely prefers to the reversionary level. The lower the reversionary level, the higher the budget the bureaucratic setter is able to extract from the voters. Key features of these referenda—bureaucrats with monopoly proposal power and a harsh reversionary spending level—closely approximate the assumptions of Niskanen's model; as Romer and Rosenthal observe: "Direct democracy situations would appear more consistent with the monopoly assumptions than would the Congressional legislative context to which Niskanen [1971] first applied his model" (1979a, 564).[6]

Most of Romer and Rosenthal's findings are strongly supportive of their hypotheses. They estimate that the budget of a district with a reversion just below the level required to keep operating would be nearly 17 percent higher than the budget of a district just above that level (1982, 569). On the other hand, they fail to detect the expected linear effect associated with the magnitude of the reversion. In other words, once the threat of the school closing is accounted for, lower reversions do not lead to higher budgets. This suggests that school administrators are not maximizing their budgets, but there are other possible explanations for this negative finding; shortcomings of the data, uncertainty on the part of the administrator, and such. I suspect, however, that the sharp discontinuity associated with the reversion threat is real. In other words, voters respond to a proposal primarily in terms of whether or not its rejection would shut down the schools. As long as the school doors stay open, administrators are unable to capitalize on variation in the reversionary level.

Some of the strongest support for the setter model comes from those districts whose administrators chose to forgo a referendum and to instead operate at the reversionary level. Not surprisingly, these were pre-1916 districts with declining enrollments (most notably Portland) and thus very high reversionary levels. As Romer and Rosenthal point out, if administrators in such districts had sought budgets in line with the preferences of the median voter, most of them would have requested levies below the reversionary level. Certainly such districts could have operated on budgets substantially below their reversionary levels and still have outspent other districts of comparable economic standing. This did not happen. Despite considerable variation in their reversionary levels, from 1970 through 1977 these districts budgeted virtually every penny ($437.9 million out of a possible $438.2 million) to which they were legally entitled (1979a, 584).

There are doubtless other types of budgetary referenda that Romer and Rosenthal's setter model does not describe very accurately. Fort (1988), for example, reports that the setter model compares unfavorably to the median voter model in explaining the outcomes of nonrepeated bond issues for rural hospital construction. Still, their findings have many important ramifications. First, they call into question estimated demand functions for public goods that are based on the assumption that the median voter is pivotal (e.g., Bergstrom and Goodman 1973). Such models fit the data very well, but as Romer and Rosenthal (1979b) demonstrate, their explanatory power is misleading; models that posit the pivotal voter to be anywhere between the twentieth and eightieth percentile yield virtually identical R^2s, but dramatically different coefficients!

Second, once it is recognized that local administrators exercise proposal power in budgetary referenda, other, seemingly anomalous, results start to make sense. Olmsted, Roberts, and Denzau (1988), for instance, report that in 1975 the state of Missouri reassessed property values in conjunction with a tax rate rollback. In a large majority of cases (73 percent) where the rate rollback occurred, voters approved tax increases the following year that more than compensated for the rollback. They also report that between 1978 and 1980, 195 Missouri school districts reduced or eliminated their debt service taxes. Because this is tantamount to a pure income increase, it should not have generated approval for any significant tax increases for current operations. Yet voters in most of these districts subsequently approved increases in their taxes for current operations by amounts that were larger than the prior reduction.

According to Olmsted, Roberts, and Denzau, the behavior of voters in these tax referenda was "seemingly at odds with a consistent rational choice analysis." They observe, however, that it is lack of access to the agenda that was most likely responsible: "Even if voters were well informed, they might be unable to prevent the increase in spending. Voters can defeat proposed tax increases, but they cannot force school boards to reduce taxes" (4). In short, even though the proposals that were approved departed from what theory would imply about median preferences, most voters in these Missouri school districts probably perceived these proposed increases to be quite reasonable, given that far more ambitious proposals could have been offered.

To be sure, these tax referenda occurred during a period of relatively high inflation. It is possible that the upward adjustment in taxes may not have even maintained real expenditures in many districts. It is also possible that the pivotal voters in these districts favored increased spending on education and were willing to pay for it—especially if a disproportionate number of those voting in such elections were spending advocates. The median voter would thus prefer spending in excess of that preferred by the median individual. If so, the outcomes Olmsted, Roberts, and Denzau find surprising, instead of reflecting budget-maximizing behavior on the part of bureaucrats, are actually due to the unrepresentative nature of the electorate. Available evidence, however, suggests that this is not the case. Although some groups havè higher turnout rates in some types of elections (for example, individuals who have school-age children are more likely to vote in school elections), turnout in budgetary referenda appears to be largely uncorrelated with demand for expenditures (Rubinfeld and Thomas 1980; Schroeder and Sjoquist 1978).

Finally, the setter model also provides, as Olmsted, Roberts, and Denzau point out, an explanation for the celebrated flypaper effect. According to economic theory, a nonmatching grant to a state or locality is equivalent to an increase in aggregate personal income of the same amount. Writing a check to a local jurisdiction, or checks totaling the same amount to the citizens therein, should therefore have identical effects upon the jurisdiction's spending on local public goods. A recurrent finding of the empirical literature is that this is far from the case. The increase in public spending associated with a dollar increase in personal income is usually estimated to be around ten cents, while a dollar in unmatched aid generates about a 45 percent increase in local public spending! In other words, money sticks where it hits—hence the term flypaper effect. As researchers working in this area have noted, these differential effects are hardly surprising when agenda control is taken into account: "The obvious reason for this phenomenon . . . is that bureaucrats and politicians find it easier to avoid cutting taxes when the government receives revenue-sharing monies than they do to raise taxes when some exogenous event raises the income of the community" (Courant, Gramlich, and Rubinfeld 1979, 6).[7]

Direct democracy would thus seem to constitute one of the more efficient mechanisms ever designed for extracting revenue. But what about the celebrated referendums that have limited or rolled back taxes? The passage of many state-level tax-cutting initiatives in the late 1970s (Proposition 13 in California, Proposition 2 ½ in Massachusetts, and similar measures in dozens of other states) suggests that direct democracy gives voters an ultimate safeguard against bureaucratic encroachment. Perhaps so, but intelligent bureaucrats and politicians can readily avoid these occurrences. Given the collective action problems involved, highly unusual circumstances are required to galvanize the volunteer workers and contributors needed to put such initiatives on the ballot and get them enacted. In California in 1978, for example, many homeowners had recently received reassessments that were so large that they could no longer afford to live in their present homes. At the same time, Governor Jerry Brown and the California state legislature allowed a surplus of over $5 billion to pile up in the treasury. Although voters were perhaps incorrect in believing that they could get, as Sears and Citrin (1982) put it, "something for nothing," they were accurate in perceiving that this surplus could be used (as it was) to compensate for property tax rollbacks. Barring mistakes and miscalculations of this magnitude, then, tax revolts on the order of Proposition 13 are not likely to get under way.

Conclusion

How well does Niskanen's bureaucratic budget-maximization model stand up to the scrutiny it has received from the various programs of quantitative research reviewed in this chapter? In answering this question, we must remember that much of the research examines hypotheses that are merely Niskanenesque; while in keeping with the spirit of his model, they are not formally derived from it. Another recurrent problem is that the findings of many studies that purport to be direct tests of his hypotheses are consistent with any number of alternative hypotheses. Third, an inherent problem in examining the central oversupply and inefficiency hypotheses directly is that what we observe to be the bureau's output is the product of the bureau's interaction with its political sponsor. Politicians (and, directly or indirectly, many of the voters who elect them) may desire as much or more waste and inefficiency as bureau chiefs. Finally, in my view, it is simply not feasible to quantitatively evaluate the effectiveness of legislative oversight or to attempt to gauge the extent of informational asymmetries between bureau and legislature.

Despite these many problems in observation and analysis, I would say that Niskanen's model has fared at least as well as any other model in political economy of comparable generality. The oversupply hypotehsis, at least when distilled into the prediction that demand for bureaucratically supplied services should always appear to be elastic, gamers some support in the studies that perform the cleanest tests, that is, Wyckoff (1988) and Bergstrom and Goodman (1973). That no competing models predict the same phenomenon makes such findings considerably more compelling than they might otherwise be. Second, virtually every study that has ever compared the operations of public bureaus with those of private firms providing identical services has found data to support the inefficiency hypothesis. Third, the finding that local public expenditures are lower in the presence of bureaucratic competition appears to be robust. In the case of multiple adjacent municipalities, this pattern also emerges as the product of strategies designed to preserve and to expand the tax base. However, studies of overlapping, single-purpose jurisdictions find similar expenditure-restraining effects that are not so readily explained as the noncooperative solution to a fiscal prisoners' dilemma.

The most persuasive evidence for Niskanen's model comes from its application to nonlegislative settings, where certain institutional features determine the strategic positions of bureaucrats and voters in budgetary referendums. Romer and Rosenthal find several important pieces of evidence that bear out implications of their setter model. As Niskanen observes in chapter 1 of this volume, "These extraordinarily careful empirical studies are probably the strongest evidence for my general theory of the behavior of bureaus." In recent years, congressional scholars have made substantial progress in understanding how major structural and procedural features of a legislature—for example, voting rules, committee systems, and party leadership—shape policy decisions (for a thorough review see Krehbiel 1988). It would be highly profitable to now focus on how different bargaining institutions structure the strategic interaction between politician and bureaucrat.

NOTES

1. More specifically, McGuire points out that equilibria in the Niskanen model are at the intersection of the average benefit curve and average cost curve, and that the average benefit curve is always elastic. If $B(Q)$ is total benefit, average benefit is $B(Q)/Q$. The elasticity of $B(Q)/Q$ is $B(Q)/B'(Q)Q - B(Q)$, which is always less than -1 when marginal benefit, $B'(Q)$, is falling. Actually, Patinkin (1963) had made the same observation about all-or-nothing demand curves many years earlier.

2. Omitting prices for public goods (as well as for other private goods) requires Borcherding and Deacon (1972) to assume that the cross-effects of other public services are negligible and that the price of private goods is the same across units—in the case of their study, states in the United States in 1962 (893).

3. Only about a quarter of the Los Angeles Unified School District's employees are classroom teachers. Less than half of the $3.5 billion budget is earmarked for teachers' salaries (a figure that *includes* on-site administrators), books, materials, cafeteria, and physical plant. According to

the authors, the district has one off-campus administrator for every 382 students, while the school system run by the Archdiocese of Los Angeles has one external administrator for every 6,375 students.

4. This is not a logical necessity, however, as municipalities can also make expenditures that are regressively redistributive. Miller (1981), for example, identifies communities in southern California that issued bonds to finance high-income housing.

5. The implications of Niskanen's model concerning budgetary outcomes flow from the assumption that the bureaucrat has monopoly proposal power. The assertion that this derives from informational asymmetries serves to motivate and to defend this assumption. Formal models of bureaucratic budget bargaining that explicitly incorporate various forms of asymmetric information, but remove the assumption of monopoly proposal power, obtain results that are somewhat different from Niskanen's (see Bendor, Taylor, and van Gaalen 1987; Banks 1989).

6. Congress avoids being presented take-it-or-leave-it spending proposals through a number of mechanisms. Most notably, when funding bills for federal agencies are not passed before expiration of the current fiscal year, Congress immediately passes a continuing resolution that maintains funding at the level of the previous year or at the level specified in either the House or Senate bill, if it is lower. This reversionary spending formula affects the relative bargaining positions of the Congress and president (Kiewiet and McCubbins 1988). More important, however, it prevents any actor in the annual funding process from using as a threat the possibility of spending actually coming to a halt.

7. By ruling out the option for tax cuts, the study by Wyckoff (1988) implicitly relies upon a similar line of reasoning. Other explanations of the flypaper effect are typically based upon the view that voters misperceive actual tax and expenditure levels. If local administrators exercise agenda control, however, even perfectly informed voters make suboptimal choices. And there is some evidence that voters are aware that the cards are stacked against them. In 1970, 71 percent of Missouri voters voted against a constitutional amendment that would have changed the requirement for approval of local tax increases from two-thirds to a simple majority. In the view of Olmsted, Roberts, and Denzau (1988), majority support for a nonmajoritarian constitutional provision reflects a desire to offset other institutional features, that is, agenda control, that generate excessive spending (15). If only upwardly biased spending proposals are submitted to the voters, a two-thirds requirement might bring spending and taxes closer to median preferred levels than simple majority rule!

REFERENCES

Aaron, Henry. 1969. Local public expenditures and the migration effect. *Western Economic Journal* 7:385–90.

Aberbach, Joel. 1990. *Keeping a watchful eye: The politics of congressional oversight.* Washington, D.C.: Brookings.

Ahlbrandt, Roger. 1973. Efficiency in the provision of fire services. *Public Choice* 16:1–16.

Austen-Smith, David. 1987, Parties, districts, and the spatial theory of elections. *Social Choice and Welfare* 4:9–24.

Baird, Robert, and John Landon. 1972. Political fragmentation, income distribution, and the demand for government services. *Nebraska Journal of Economics and Business* 11:171–84.

Banks, Jeffrey. 1989. Agency budgets, cost information, and auditing. *American Journal of Political Science* 33:670–99.

Bendor, Jonathan, Serge Taylor, and Roland van Gaalen. 1987. Politicians, bureaucrats, and asymmetric information. *American Political Science Review* 31:796–828.

Bergstrom, Theodore, and Robert Goodman. 1973. Private demands for public goods *American Economic Review* 63:280–96.

Booms, Bernard, and James Halldorson. 1973. The politics of redistribution: A reformulation. *American Political Science Review* 67:924–33.

Borcherding, Thomas. 1977. The sources of growth of public expenditures in the United States, 1902–1970. In *Budgets and bureaucrats: The sources of government growth,* ed. Thomas Borcherding. Durham, N.C.: Duke Univ. Press.

Borcherding, Thomas, and Robert Deacon. 1972. The demand for the services of non-federal governments. *American Economic Review* 62:891–901.

Boyne, George. 1985. Theory, methodology and results in political science—the case of output studies. *British Journal of Political Science* 15:473–515.

———. 1987. Bureaucratic power and public policies: A test of the rational staff maximization hypothesis. *Political Studies* 35:79–104.

Bradford, David, and Wallace Oates. 1974. Suburban exploitation of central cities and governmental structure. In *Redistribution through public choice,* ed. Harold Hochman and George Peterson. New York: Columbia Univ. Press.

Breton, Albert, and Ronald Wintrobe. 1975. The equilibrium size of a budget-maximizing bureau: A note on Niskanen's theory of bureaucracy. *Journal of Political Economy* 83:195–207.

Buchanan, James. 1971. Principles of urban fiscal strategy. *Public Choice* 11:1–16.

————. 1977. Why does government grow? In *Budgets and bureaucrats: The sources of government growth,* ed. Thomas Borcherding. Durham, N.C.: Duke University Press.

Burstein, M. L. 1960. A theory of full-line forcing. *Northwestern University Law Review* 55:62–95.

Congressional Budget Office and General Accounting Office. 1984. *Analysis of the Grace Commission's major proposals for cost control.* Washington, D.C.: Government Printing Office.

Conybeare, John. 1984. Bureaucracy, monopoly and competition: A critical analysis of the budgetary maximizing model of bureaucracy. *American Journal of Political Science* 28:479–502.

Courant, Paul, Edward Gramlich, and Daniel Rubinfeld. 1979. The stimulative effects of intergovernmental grants: Or why money sticks where it hits. In *Fiscal federalism and grants in aid,* ed. Peter Miezkowski and William Oakland. Washington, D.C.: Urban Institute.

Crain, Mark, Robert Tollison, Brian Goff, and Diek Carlson. 1985. Legislator specialization and the size of government. *Public Choice* 46: 311–15.

Davies, David. 1971. The efficiency of public versus private firms: The case of Australia's two airlines. *Journal of Law and Economics* 14:149–65.

Davis, Lance, and Susan Groth. 1974. Institutional structure and technological change. In *Government policies and technological innovation.* Vol. 2, *State-of-the-art surveys,* PB244572/AS. Washington, D.C.: National Technical Information Service, National Science Foundation.

De Alessi, Louis. 1974. An economic analysis of government ownership and regulation: Theory and the evidence from the electric power industry. *Public Choice* 19:1–42.

DiLorenzo, Thomas. 1981. The expenditure effects of restricting competition in local public service industries: The case of special districts. *Public Choice* 37:569–78.

Dubin, Jeffrey, and Peter Navarro. 1988. How markets for impure public goods organize: The case of household refuse collection. *Journal of Law, Economics, and Organization* 4:217–41.

Dye, Thomas. 1966. *Politics, economics and the public.* Chicago: Rand McNally.

Fair, Ray. 1978. The effect of economic events on votes for president. *Review of Economics and Statistics* 60:159–73.

Fiorina, Morris. 1977. *Congress: Keystone of the Washington establishment.* New Haven, Conn.: Yale Univ. Press.

Fiorina, Morris, and Roger Noll. 1978. Voters, legislators and bureaucracy: Institutional design in the public sector. *American Economic Review* 68:256–60.

Fort, Rodney. 1988. The median voter, setters, and non-repeated construction bond issues. *Public Choice* 56:213–31.

Fry, Brian, and Richard Winters. 1970. The politics of redistribution. *American Political Science Review* 64:508–22.

Heclo, Hugh. 1977. *A government of strangers.* Washington, D.C.: Brookings.

Kemper, Peter, and John Quigley. 1976. *The economics of refuse collection.* Cambridge, Mass.: Ballinger.

Kiewiet, D. Roderick, and Mathew McCubbins. 1988. Presidential influence on congressional appropriations decisions. *American Journal of Political Science* 32:713–36.

Kramer, Gerald H. 1971. Short-term fluctuations in U.S. voting behavior, 1896–1964. *American Political Science Review* 65:131–43.

Krehbiel, Keith. 1988. Spatial models of legislative choice. *Legislative Studies Quarterly* 13:259–320.

Lineberry, Robert. 1969. Community structure and planning commitment: A note on the correlates of agency expenditures. *Social Science Quarterly* 50:723–30.

McCubbins, Mathew, and Thomas Schwartz. 1984. Congressional oversight overlooked: Police patrols versus fire alarms. *American Journal of Political Science* 28:165–79.

McGuire, Thomas. 1981. Budget maximizing governmental agencies: An empirical test. *Public Choice* 36:313–22.

Mackay, Robert, and Carolyn Weaver. 1981. Agenda control by budget maximizers in a multi-bureau setting. *Public Choice* 37: 447–72.

Miller, Gary. 1981. *Cities by contract: The politics of municipal incorporation.* Cambridge, Mass.: MIT Press.

Miller, Gary, and Terry Moe. 1983. Bureaucrats, legislators and the size of government. *American Political Science Review* 77:297–322.

Nicholson, R. J., and N. Topham. 1971. The determinants of investment in housing by local authorities: An econometric approach. *Journal of the Royal Statistical society,* series A, 34:273–303.

———. 1975. Urban road provision in England and Wales, 1962–1968. *Politics and Policy* 4:3–29.

Niskanen, William. 1971. *Bureaucracy and representative government.* Chicago: Aldine Atherton.

———. 1975. Bureaucrats and politicians. *Journal of Law and Economics* 18:617–44.

Ogul, Morris. 1976. *Congress oversees the bureaucracy*. Pittsburgh, Pa.: Univ. of Pittsburgh Press.

Olmsted, George, Judith Roberts, and Arthur Denzau. 1988. We voted for this? Institutions and educational spending. Political Economy Working Paper 128. St. Louis, Mo.: Washington University.

Pasour, E. C., and Marc Johnson. 1982. Bureaucratic productivity: The case of agricultural research revisited. *Public Choice* 39:301–17.

Patinkin, Don. 1963. Demand curves and consumer's surplus. In *Measurement in economics: Studies in mathematical economics and econometrics in honor of Yehuda Grunfeld,* ed. Carl Christ et al. Stanford, Calif.: Stanford Univ. Press.

Plott, Charles. 1967. A notion of equilibrium and its possibility under majority rule. *American Economic Review* 57:787–806.

Pomper, Gerald. 1970. *Elections in America: Control and influence in democratic politics*. New York: Dodd, Mead.

Romer, Thomas, and Howard Rosenthal. 1979a. Bureaucrats versus voters: On the political economy of resource allocation by direct democracy. *Quarterly Journal of Economics* 93:563–87.

———. 1979b. The elusive median voter. *Journal of Public Economics* 12:143–70.

———. 1982. Median voters or budget maximizers: Evidence from school expenditure referenda. *Economic Inquiry* 20:556–78.

Rubinfeld, Daniel, and Randall Thomas. 1980. On the economics of voter turnout in local school elections. *Public Choice* 35:315–31.

Ruttan, Vernon. 1980. Bureaucratic productivity: The case of agricultural research. *Public Choice* 35: 529–47.

———. 1982. Bureaucratic productivity: The case of agricultural research revisited—A rejoinder. *Public Choice* 39:319–29.

Schneider, Mark. 1989. Intergovernmental competition, budget-maximizing bureaucrats, and the level of suburban competition. *American Journal of Political Science* 33:612–28.

Schroeder, Larry, and David Sjoquist. 1978. The rational voter: An analysis of two Atlanta referenda on rapid transit. *Public Choice* 33:27–44.

Sears, David, and Jack Citrin. 1982. *Tax revolt: Something for nothing in California*. Cambridge, Mass.: Harvard Univ. Press.

Shapiro, Daniel, and Julie Korenstein. 1989. Bureaucracy is the heavy in L.A. schools. *Los Angeles Times,* 19 January.

Sharkansky, Ira. 1967. Economic and political correlates of state government expenditures: General tendencies and deviant cases. *Mid-Western Journal of Political Science* 11:173–92.

Sjoquist, David. 1982. The effect of the number of local governments on central city expenditures. *National Tax Journal* 35:79–88.

Spann, Robert. 1977. Public versus private provision of government services. In *Budgets and bureaucrats: The sources of government growth,* ed. Thomas Borcharding. Durham, N.C.: Duke Univ. Press.

Stevens, Barbara. 1978. Scale, market structure, and the cost of refuse collection. *Review of Economics and Statistics* 60:438–48.

Storey, D. 1980. The economics of bureaus: The case of London boroughs 1970–76. *Applied Economics* 12:223–34.

Tiebout, Charles. 1956. A pure theory of local expenditures. *Journal of Political Economy* 64:416–24.

Tufte, Edward. 1978. *Political control of the economy.* Princeton, N.J.: Princeton Univ. Press.

Wagner, Adolf. 1958. The nature of the fiscal economy. Reprinted in *Classics in the theory of public finance,* ed. Richard Musgrave and Alan Peacock. London: Macmillan. Wagner's work was originally published in 1883.

Wagner, Richard, and Warren Weber. 1975. Competition, monopoly, and the organization of government in metropolitan areas. *Journal of Law and Economics* 18:661–84.

Wyckoff, Paul. 1988. A bureaucratic theory of flypaper effects. *Journal of Urban Economics* 23:115–29.

7

ANDREW DUNSIRE

Bureaucrats and
Conservative Governments

It might be argued that a conservative government, committed to cutbacks in spending and staffing and to reducing the size of the state, will reward bureaucrats who *minimize* budgets and that, therefore, the budget-maximizing strategy is not a sound one for a self-regarding bureaucrat under a conservative government. This is the argument that is explored in this chapter, with empirical data from the United Kingdom in the decade 1975 to 1985.

This would seem to be a uniquely—or at least an unusually—good site and time for exploring this proposition. At the beginning of that period, a Labour government was in power, with both sides of industry—management and labor—well organized and involved in macroeconomic decision making through tripartite structures of neocorporatism such as the National Economic Development Council. In the middle of the period, a Conservative government came to office pledged to reduce the size of the state. We should thus have an eminently suitable test site for examining the proposition. If self-interested bureaucrats maximize budgets in all circumstances, corresponding behavior patterns will remain constant throughout the decade; if under Conservative governments they minimize budgets, we expect to find a change of behavior in or around 1979–1980—provided, that is, the Conservative government of Margaret Thatcher counts for the purpose of the proposition as a conservative one, and that James Callaghan's Labour government counts as nonconservative.

175

It is a definitional matter of some significance. The previous Conservative government under Edward Heath (1970–1974) would probably not be counted conservative, in this sense, throughout its term, although it started out to roll back the state; nor would the Conservative government of Harold Macmillan (1957–1963). The Labour government of James Callaghan (1976–1979) was frequently taunted as being more conservative than socialist, but more to the point, it found itself, under financial disciplines imposed by the International Monetary Fund in 1976, cutting public expenditure quite drastically—by much more, in fact, than did Margaret Thatcher's government over a similar length of time: by 7.43 percent, as against a *gain* of 6.86 percent, at constant prices, under Thatcher (*Appropriation Accounts*).

By contrast, Thatcher appeared to welcome the characterization of her regime as revolutionary and radical—dedicated to overthrowing a whole era of welfarism: although committed to rolling back the state, *conservative* as an epithet hardly seems appropriate. And if we are to measure by results, then the Labour government of Clement Attlee from 1945 to 1951 reduced the size of the civil service by almost twice as much as did Margaret Thatcher over a similar period—by 33.6 percent, as against 18.2 percent (*Civil Service Statistics 1988*)—and invented the term *bonfire of controls*. Admittedly, this latter is an unfair comparison, since Attlee was dismantling the war machine.

Let me therefore tackle the problem in two parts. Reducing the size of the state as a policy may be either voluntary or involuntary. Enforced retrenchment may reduce the size of the state, though the government is not conservative. The question is whether the Niskanen model of the budget-maximizing bureaucrat explains behavior during retrenchment just as well as it does during expansion (budget maximizing being deemed equivalent to budget preservation, or keeping the budget as high as it can be). We examine this proposition regarding the whole decade 1975 to 1985 as one of retrenchment and cutback.

Then we distinguish between mere cutbacks, on the one hand, and rolling back the state as an ideological platform, on the other, and look at the Thatcher period in particular. The proposition to be tested there is that the behavior of bureaucrats in such an era is better explained by a *budget-minimizing* model than a *budget-maximizing* one. Bureaucrats will aim to reduce budgets and will benefit from doing so—rather than from increasing them. The assumption that all bureaucrats are looking for benefits for themselves is not, however, the only one in the literature.

Disinterested and Self-Regarding Bureaucrats

The debate about the nature of bureaucrats is as old as bureaucracy. Plato's idea of the elite guardians, who should have no property of their own in order to avoid self-interest, is at one extreme. Rousseau (1973) offered a more general analysis of the problem. He argued that it is the nature of man to pursue his own interest; the father in a family, a small businessman, a monarch, would be acting quite naturally in seeking their own betterment. Public servants, by contrast, embody three kinds of interest: their individual interest, their corporate interest, and the interest of the public they serve. And whereas in perfect government the individual interest of the public servant should be "at zero," the corporate interest very subordinate, and the public interest the "sole guide" of all the rest, in the natural order of things the public interest tends to be the weakest, the corporate interest comes next, and the interest of the individual public servant predominates (213–14).

Hegel offered an idealized view of public servants as the "universal class." Compared with farmers and industrialists, for example, they were educated to seek only the general interest, and their private interests were satisfied in the awareness of the greatness of their tasks and by their guaranteed middle-class standard of living (Hegel 1942, 193). This view of the permanent civil service in Britain informed the Northcote-Trevelyan Report of 1853; and John Stuart Mill in 1861 wrote of trained and skilled officials, "governors by profession," subject to a besetting flaw of "routine" but—if properly selected and held to account by representative government—offering the advantage of disinterested expertise where expertise was needed (1910, 245–47). Schaffer refers to the nineteenth-century "public service bargain," by which bureaucrats offered "anonymity, some sacrifice of political rights, and proficient performance, in return for permanent careers, honours and a six-hour working day" (1973, 252). The essence of this model of the perfect bureaucrat was incorporated in the twentieth century in Max Weber's ideal type (1948).

The alternative stereotype came from Rousseau through Adam Smith, who appeared to believe, in his 1776 critique of the East India Company, that self-interested behavior in civil servants is inculcated by "the system," rather than being merely "natural." The country they govern is owned by their masters, the company, which cannot but have some regard, therefore, for its welfare; but it does not belong to the servants of the company, who therefore support their own interest "with rigorous severity: I mean not to throw any odious imputation upon the general character of the servants of the East India Company, and much less upon that of any particular person. It is the system of government, the situation in which they are placed, that I mean to censure" (Smith 1812, 507). Ninety years later, Walter Bagehot (a banker and the editor of *The Economist*) did not distinguish between *nature* and *system:*

> Not only does a bureaucracy . . . tend to under-government, in point of quality; it tends to over-government in point of quantity. The trained official hates the rude, untrained public. He thinks that they are stupid, ignorant, reckless—that they cannot tell their own interest—that they should have the leave of the office before they do anything. . . . A bureaucracy is sure to think that its duty is to augment official power, official business, or official members, rather than to leave free the energies of mankind. (Bagehot 1964, 197)

The Adam Smith/Bagehot view was formalized and developed by, preeminently, Downs (1967) and Niskanen (1971).

Of course, the two views are not necessarily incompatible; as in Rousseau, the disinterested bureaucrat may reflect aspiration— what *should* be the case—while the self-regarding bureaucrat mirrors reality—what human nature *is* like in such situations. There are, in fact, many models of bureaucrat in the literature, besides these two. The evangelistic bureaucrat or crusader uses public office neither as mere servant of political masters nor as nest-featherer, but as a vehicle for attaining a political aim of his or her own (Davies 1972; Frederickson 1971; Thompson 1975). The "corruption" literature provides another raft of typologies (Rogow and Lasswell 1963; Heidenheimer 1970). Aberbach et al. (1981) describe four types of relationship between the political and the bureaucratic milieus.

Perhaps the truth is that every bureaucrat cares about some mix of private desires, social goals, and public policies, and has divided loyalties. The disinterested and self-regarding stereotypes merely represent two of the poles, between which any real-life position may be found. Nevertheless, these are the poles we are concerned with here, and the stereotypes enable us to devise and test alternative hypotheses about how bureaucrats behave in a period of cutbacks.

Cutbacks and Budget Preservation

In a period of politically ordained retrenchment of public spending and cutbacks in government staffing, the basic aim of Weberian disinterested bureaucrats, we assume, is to bring about effective cuts quickly. The basic aim of bureaucrats at the other end of the spectrum—the Adam Smith-type, or self-regarding, bureaucrats (equating generally with the Niskanen model)—is to avoid or avert reductions in their own budget or complement, to minimize their own injury.

The early literature on cutbacks tends to assume a self-regarding bureaucrat who would resist cuts by wool-pulling: "A major strategy in resisting cuts is to make them in such a way that they have to be put back" (Wildavsky 1964, 102). The psychological climate of the spending cutbacks of the 1960s and early 1970s in Britain also was that cuts could be survived and that good times would come again: you should offer "fairy gold" or "paper cuts" (cuts in growth, or in planned expenditure), employ "creative accounting" (hiving-off staff into subordinate agencies), use "bleeding stump" ploys (cut where it shows), let the squeakiest wheel go without the oil, and so on. Later, as the real-world fiscal crisis developed, the literature discounted such cosmetic reactions and discovered distinctions between types of real cuts: between "incremental" and "quantum" cuts, for example (Levine 1978; Glassberg 1978), or between equal misery and priorities (Hartley 1981, 143), or between percentage cuts all around and selective cuts (Wright 1981, 13).

As long as cutbacks could be regarded as a storm that would pass, perhaps no civil servant (or minister for that matter) would make a real sacrifice in budget or in staff if the appearance of a sacrifice would serve. However, when cuts really do have to begin to bite, we have argued in recent publications (Hood, Huby, and Dunsire 1984; Hood, Dunsire, and Huby 1988; Dunsire and Hood 1989), these types of cuts correspond to positions on the spectrum of bureaucratic orientations. A Weberian official's first reaction when faced with the necessity of imposing cuts is to prune back by a small amount all around; selective cutting appeals more to the Adam Smith tendency.

To the Weberian, percentage cuts are more effective and quicker, because by preserving parity of esteem among those cut (the equal misery effect), they minimize recalcitrance and disruption. They may even seem more rational, transferring the real decisions nearer to the operating level, whose least harm judgments will be better informed than those of top bureaucrats (Levine 1978, 322). It may also seem rational to cut back everything a little in order to keep the basic fabric in being for as long as possible.

However, if imposing equal misery is unacceptable, because it does not minimize one's own injury, ways must be found of imposing all the required cutbacks on others. The literature agrees that cutbacks seem to bring out the worst in self-regarding bureaucrats. So we find authors using mean phrases like "exploit the exploitable" (Levine 1978, 320), "beggar thy neighbour" (Glennerster 1981, 191), "hitting at enemies and weaklings" (Hood and Wright 1981, 202), and the like. "It seems absolutely human and understandable," said a former Downing Street policy adviser, "that if cuts are imposed, those who decide where the cuts should be implemented decide 'they should be on anybody else but us' " (Dr. Bernard Donoughue in *The Times,* 2 April 1980, quoted in Hood and Wright 1981, 201).

However, there may be a time element involved. Percentage cuts are a type of incremental cut. Others are freezes on recruitment and promotion, cash limits on expenditures, deferral of maintenance and new capital formation, and the like. These incremental (or more accurately, decremental) cuts, according to Beck Jørgensen (1987a; 1987b), are quick to find, they are easy to put into effect, and they minimize conflict. But after a while, Jørgensen says, two things begin to be noticed: first, the amount saved from the cuts begins to drop off quite rapidly, and second, the effects of piecemeal unplanned cuts, postponements, and freezes begin to send in their bill, in minor collapses of many sorts in bureaucratic structure and workings.

Lack of maintenance, for example, brings its nemesis; the buildup of detrimental effects means not only that a cheap return to the status quo is less and less possible but that the current situation cannot be sustained. People begin to appreciate that decremental cutting is wasteful. Even Weberian officials, if cutback pressures continue, must eventually turn to planned and selective cuts.

Accordingly, the argument will only discriminate between bureaucratic orientations, if at all, in the early stages of real cutbacks. The hypothesis to be tested against the data is therefore: (1) *If, during the early stage of retrenchment, bureaucrats are predominantly self-regarding, the types of cutback imposed in Britain in 1975–1985 will be selective rather than imposing "equal misery all round."*

The differing orientations of bureaucrats toward the Weberian pole or the Adam Smith pole should, however, emerge in the bases of selectivity used. For instance, does cutting spending or cutting staff best suit the aims of each? For the Weberian, this means judging which brings the more immediate and certain savings. Leaving aside all recalcitrance and self-interest, the logic of budget making (annual allocations, upward of 80 percent already committed, etc.) indicates that it really is difficult to find significant savings in selective cutting of the current budget, or even of next year's. Budgets have a long lead time. One can offer cash limits and closer control of discretionary expenditures; but outcomes will take a long time to become apparent.

Staff cutting, by contrast, can in principle begin to have effect the day after the decision, because natural wastage (deaths, retirements, resignations) occurs throughout the year with closely predictable incidence, and a ban on replacements, even if selective, will produce returns within months. So the Weberian may opt to cut staff before budget for quicker results.

The reputation of self-regarding bureaucrats, however, is that they will always choose the most staff-intensive way of doing anything (Breton 1974). A larger staff means status, rank, and power. Accordingly, the Adam Smith bureaucrat will cut spending before cutting staff. This produces a second hypothesis: (2) *If, in retrenchment, bureaucrats are predominantly self-regarding, spending will be cut before staffing.* Spending, we assume, will nonetheless have to be cut at some time—if not first, then second. When selecting which items of spending to cut, there are again choices to be made: for example, between economic categories, that is, between current and capital spending; between spending on goods and services (including salaries) and on transfer payments; and between central government spending and spending by other public bodies.

The choice between current and capital spending is a cruel one for the public-service-oriented bureaucrat, because it is a choice between short-term and long-term considerations. In the short term, it is often feasible to postpone capital expenditure without immediately imperiling service quality, so that a Weberian official faced with the need for quickly apparent spending cuts might cut capital expenditures in order to save current outputs of service. But in the long term, not renewing capital formation will have repercussions on service quality anyway. We might therefore expect a hesitation to cut all capital spending, in Weberian officials, but that short termism will win, as in most political crises.

For the self-regarding bureaucrat there is no dilemma; salaries come out of current spending, which is therefore preserved at the expense of capital spending. All in all, therefore, we could predict that, whatever kind of bureaucrat is making the choices, the following holds: (3) *Capital spending will be cut more than current.*

As between different items of current spending, a hard-pressed but disinterested official looking for quick and effective savings may choose to cut first what he has most control over. Transfer payments (e.g., welfare benefits) are often demand led; loans, subsidies, and grants are policy determined; and neither is easily adjustable. The quickest effect may therefore be obtainable by cutting back on purchases of goods and services, and this is what we can expect if an official with Weberian orientation is in charge.

But in British national accounts, *goods and services* includes salaries of staff. A self-regarding bureaucrat may therefore be expected to cut the "money-moving" or transfer-payments expenditures before cutting purchases. So the hypothesis is as follows: (4) *If in retrenchment bureaucrats are self-regarding, spending on grants and transfers will be cut rather than spending on goods and services (including staff salaries).*

By and large, the same applies between spending authorities. Control over local authority and public corporation spending is relatively remote, compared with control over central departments' expenditure. We might therefore expect that under cutbacks by Weberian officials, spending by central government would go down earlier and more than spending by other types of authority.

But the expectation about Adam Smith bureaucrats is clearly the opposite; they will slash the other authorities' budgets before their own, if they can: (5) *If in retrenchment bureaucrats are self-regarding, local and other bodies' spending will be cut before central spending.*

What about cuts in staffing? We must distinguish here between staff savings, measured in numbers, and budget savings on staff, measured in money; we will deal only with the former. How will the disinterested bureaucrat react to demands for staff cuts? Which groups of personnel are likely to be cut first, on an objective, impersonal analysis of the balance between speedy results and least harm to services?

The main source of relatively painless staff cutting (avoiding time-consuming quasi-legal procedures) is nonreplacement of natural wastage. Clearly, the groups with the largest incidence of natural wastage are the most vulnerable, and significant numbers will come from the largest groups—those at the base of the pyramid. So we can predict that under a Weberian-oriented official numbers of blue-collar workers and lower grades of white-collar workers will decrease more than other groups. Such groups are also the most vulnerable to automation and computerization and other measures to increase efficiency, and the jobs they do are the most amenable to contracting out. All in all, it seems a safe bet that at the hands of the Weberian official the lower ranks will suffer more than the middle ranks.

The upper ranks, however, should have a relatively high incidence of age retirement, and they are also the levels with greatest job mobility. They might be expected to suffer more proportionately, even if the numbers are small. Finally, if staff lost by natural wastage have to be replaced, it might seem rational to appoint a temporary or part-time staff, who can be let go even more easily if further cutbacks are required; so we might expect the proportions of these groups to increase, at least at first.

By contrast, "anybody but ourselves" perhaps sufficiently tells us what Adam Smith bureaucrats can be expected to do in selective staff cutting. Top brass as self-regarding staff cutters will ensure that the burden falls on the middle and lower ranks rather than on themselves. Mandarins, as generalists, will similarly see to it that it is the specialist and technical occupational groups that bear the brunt; white-collar workers will take the cuts out of the blue-collar workers, part-time staff will be the first to go—and so on. If in retrenchment bureaucrats are self-regarding, the hypotheses about staff cuts are therefore as follows: (6) *blue-collar, lower-, and middle-grade workers will be cut more than top echelons; (7) specialists will be cut more than generalists; and (8) part-time staff will be cut more than full-time staff.*

This logic gives us eight hypotheses to test against the facts of the decade of cutbacks in the United Kingdom between 1975 and 1985. What, then, actually happened? To present the findings from our survey in the form of tables of data would take up a great deal of space, though they are of course available (see Dunsire and Hood 1989). I shall therefore only summarize the results here.

As can be seen from figure 7.1, during the decade 1975–1985 as a whole, staffing was cut much more than spending. After an initial rise, staffing fell steadily from an initial 701,000 (or from its peak of just under 750,000) to just under 600,000; while after an initial fall, spending (deflated) rose from an initial £74 billion (or trough of £67 billion) to £78 billion. Partly as a function of this difference between spending and staffing fortunes, the distribution of cuts among thirty six departments of central government showed misery more widely spread in staffing than in spending. The average number of departments per year showing a decrease in spending was 16.44; in staffing, 24.22.

FIGURE 7.1
Central Government Gross Actual Expenditure and
Total Civil Service Staff, 1 April 1971 to 1 April 1985

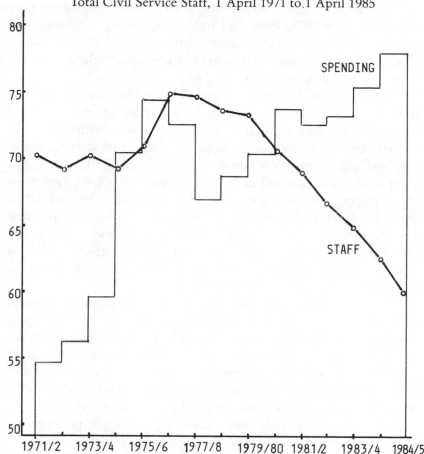

Sources: *Appropriation Accounts; Annual Abstract of Statistics.*
Note: Vertical scale, spending is in £billion; staffing is in thousands. Totals
include industrial plus nonindustrial staff. Gross domestic product deflator, 1980
= 100.

But there is some support for the idea that, when pressure is first
applied, the initial response is to cut widely by a little. In the
Callaghan years (1975–1978), the emphasis was on IMF-required
spending cuts, and those are the years of most widespread spending cuts (twenty four, twenty five, and twenty three departments

cut). After 1979, in the early Thatcher years, the emphasis was on quick staffing reductions, and these were the years of the most widespread staff cuts (twenty six, thirty one, and twenty nine departments, in 1979, 1981, and 1982—1980 being something of a puzzle, with only twenty departments cut in staff, the lowest Thatcher figure, while nineteen departments, the highest Thatcher figure, were cut in spending).

The finding on the first hypothesis is not, therefore, absolutely clear. There are several indications of Weberian tendencies toward equal misery in the early years of each government, with two-thirds of departments being cut in both spending and staffing under Callaghan, and two-thirds being cut in staffing under Thatcher. But there were always a number of departments that showed increases while others were being cut—an indication of selectivity, or Adam Smith tendencies. Only one, however, received no cuts in spending (the Department of Health and Social Security), and all but one (a tiny department, the Registers of Scotland) were cut in staff in at least two years. On balance, the point probably should go to the Weberians; misery was relatively equal.

The second hypothesis concerns the choice between cutting staff and cutting spending. It is true that initially, in the IMF years, spending went down immediately and heavily, while totals of staff rose (see figure 7.1). This would indicate Adam Smith influence and a tendency to be self-regarding, according to our reasoning. But over the decade as a whole, spending went up while staffing went down by a considerable amount: a finding that supports a Weberian influence, and disinterestedness. Counting the respective numbers of years, the point should probably again go to the Weberians.

The suggestion in the third hypothesis—that capital spending will be cut before current spending whatever the proclivities of bureaucrats—is amply supported; capital spending went down in 1976 and kept on going down (until 1981), whereas current spending went up in 1976, blipped briefly in 1977, but then resumed a steady climb. The 1985 figure (deflated) for current expenditure is 129 percent of the 1975 figure, whereas the 1985 figure (deflated) for capital expenditure is only 40 percent of the 1975 figure.

The fourth hypothesis suggests that Weberian-oriented bureaucrats will cut spending on goods and services before spending on transfer payments on the grounds that controls on purchases of goods and services (including salaries) are quicker acting and more effective than controls on transfer payments; self-regarding bureaucrats will do the opposite. Spending on goods and services did go down in 1976 and 1977, while transfer payments went up as a proportion of total government expenditure. Thereafter, goods and services (which include bureaucrats' salaries) increased but slightly from the initial 43 percent, varying around 45 percent of total expenditure and never higher than 46 percent; transfer payments, beginning at 27 percent of total government expenditure, never slackened their steady climb to 35 percent in 1985. In terms of our (admittedly simple) logic, the point must again go to the Weberians.

The fifth hypothesis predicts that if bureaucrats are Weberian oriented, central spending will go down while local spending will go up—because control over central spending will be better than control over local spending; if bureaucrats are self-regarding, the opposite will happen. The opposite did happen, and the self-regarding hypothesis is sustained. Whether in capital or current expenditure or in spending on goods and services or transfer payments, the central government's share of total government spending went up throughout the period. This is one for the Adam Smith school of thought.

On staffing cuts (hypothesis six), the figures show that staff cuts only began to bite seriously in 1977. From that date to 1985, the percentage reductions were as under:

Top brass (the three highest grades)	19.04
Lower ranks (the three lowest white-collar grades)	10.39
Middle grades (those between)	7.23
Blue-collar workers	34.02

Thus blue-collar workers undoubtedly bore the brunt of the staff cuts (in absolute numbers, falling from 177,000 to 101,000). On the other hand, these years were but part of a long-term decline in public sector blue-collar work (mainly in royal dockyards and ordnance factories); industrial civil servants had numbered 615,000 in 1945.

For the rest, the logic of the wastage rate (the Weberian-oriented bureaucrat's basis for selective staff cutting) was a good predictor of what happened. Top brass certainly did not preserve themselves at the expense of all others, as would have been expected had they been self-regarding; indeed, they were the first cut (in 1976) and the most heavily cut of all in percentage terms (dropping from 870 to 687 in the decade). Lower grade white-collar civil servants were cut first in 1977, falling from 444,000 to 398,000. The middle grades were the survivors: they continued to *grow* until 1980 and suffered less than any other group, whatever time period we measure. As a proportion of the total civil service, the middle grades continued to increase (from 13.53 percent in 1977 to 14.90 percent in 1985).

This conforms to what may appear to be a general "law of bureaucratic slimming": during cutbacks, the middle tends to expand at the expense of the top and the base. A similar finding was noted for police agencies, city administrators, and the federal government service in the United States (Martin 1983, 51–54). There appears to be a linkage between turnover rates, promotion rates, and average length of service in a grade. If promotion criteria are unchanged, a grade or group of grades with low turnover will tend to swell and to age in comparison with others. The effect will be exacerbated if promotion out of that grade is limited.

On the sixth hypothesis, therefore, the evidence favors the Weberian rather than the self-regarding assumption. The same turns out to be true for the seventh and eighth hypotheses. The proportion of generalists did not increase at the expense of specialists, and the proportions of part-time staff were considerably higher at the end of the period than at the beginning (from 3.0 to 4.1 percent). So there is nothing in the idea that the stereotypical mandarin will take it out on all other types of staff before himself.

It seems, therefore, that the stereotype of *homo bureauensis* as self-regarding does not do as well as a predictor of outcomes than the rather less popular and more prosaic disinterested-public-servant expectations. For some of the predictions, the Weberian stereotype wins on points only, in boxing terms. In only one case (central versus local spending) did the evidence clearly point to an Adam Smith orientation in central bureaucrats. Thus, insofar as the Niskanen model of the budget-maximizing bureaucrat is captured by our model of the Adam Smith, self-regarding bureaucrat in times of retrenchment, the data invalidate the Niskanen model.

There are several possible explanations. First, we may not have been looking at the right kind of data. We restricted ourselves to already gathered, unobtrusive figures, whereas a more qualitative type of inquiry into attitudes and practices could conceivably produce different results. Second, many observers have pointed to some well-known differences between bureaucratic milieus in Britain and in the United States: the latter is much more decentralized and business oriented in any case, the former much more tightly controlled, with the higher ranks socialized into an ethos that stresses service standards and places higher value on administrative operations that are lean than on bureaucratic bloat (Self 1972; Kogan 1973; Young 1974). Some would say that the self-regarding British civil servant is more likely to *avoid* budgetary and other expansion if he can, as being irreconcilable with the "on-the-job leisure" from which the bureaucrat may also derive utility (Leibenstein 1976, 95–117; Jackson 1982, 133; Peacock 1983, 128).

An important and more general line of argument is Dunleavy's (1985) critique of the Downs/Niskanen model, using the same analytic method but with different assumptions; showing that not all bureaucrats have identical utility functions, that strategies can be strung out on a spectrum of advantages from the highly personal to the collective, and that the definition of which budget is being maximized (broadly, *core*—or staffing and internal maintenance only—or *bureau,* meaning core plus external spending on services—or *program,* meaning core and bureau plus external funding, or "money-moving") is very significant. Dunleavy's conclusion is that bureau chiefs, in contrast to lower level bureaucrats, derive little benefit from many kinds of budgetary expansion; if they are self-interested, they may aim to shape their bureaus in ways that make these bureaus smaller, containing less executive work, and thus more high-status staff and budgets that are more discretionary. The figures we used are too crude for us to be able to test this version of the self-regarding bureaucrat theory, though it is notable that it is consonant with Niskanen's latest statement of his own model (see chapter 1, this volume).

We have tested the Niskanen budget-maximizing bureaucrat

model against an alternative public-service-oriented bureaucrat model, using empirical observations of a decade of British government, all of which might be deemed conservative in the sense of being a decade of retrenchment. By and large, the evidence contradicts the Niskanen model. But there is another (perhaps the main) sense in which *conservative* is used, to mean not merely responding to fiscal pressures by cutbacks but to mean intent on "rolling back the state" as a matter of principle. Here the relevant alternative to the Niskanen budget-maximizing model is a budget-*minimizing* one. We explore this proposition with evidence from the Thatcher period in the United Kingdom.

Rolling Back the State and Budget Minimizing

The thesis is that conservative governments, governments committed to rolling back the state, will reward bureaucrats who minimize budgets, that is, who seek to reduce their budgets year by year rather than raise them; and that therefore self-regarding bureaucrats under such governments will follow a budget-minimizing strategy, not a budget-maximizing one. The crudest test of this with the U.K. data would be to see whether total spending went down markedly after 1979, at Margaret Thatcher's accession: (9) *If budget-minimizing strategy is being followed, total spending under a conservative government will go down.* But we know, of course, from figure 7.1, that total spending went up. This is compatible with the budget-maximizing hypothesis, but hardly with a budget-minimizing one.

However, there is more than a suggestion in the budget-maximizing bureaucrat literature that the real aim of self-regarding bureaucrats in maximizing budgets is to maximize establishment, or staffing: it is extra staff that is said to bring more prestige, promotion, and power. Under conservative rule, then, by the alternative hypothesis, it will be fewer staff, success in staff cutting, that will be rewarded. (10) *If budget-minimizing strategy is being followed, total staffing under a conservative government will go down.* Figure 7.1 gives us the data on this also: and indeed, total establishment did go down famously under the Conservatives. So the budget-minimizing hypothesis is not ruled out on staffing.

Total spending and total staffing figures are, of course, only aggregates of departmental spending and staffing, and may well mask quite varied results, department by department. But the budget-minimizing hypothesis would be upheld, strongly or weakly, if a majority of departments showed decreases in either spending or staffing over the conservative period. (11) *If budget-minimizing strategy is being followed, more individual departments will show decreases in spending and staffing than show increases.* Table 7.1 presents, not the absolute figures, but the percentage change in the figures for staffing and spending in the twenty four largest central government departments (more than 1,000 staff) between 1975/1976 and 1979/1980, and between 1980/1981 and 1984/1985. We can see that, first, the decrease in staffing in the Conservative period was very widely shared, only three departments showing increases. Second, despite the large increase in spending overall, fewer than half of the departments showed any increase at all over the five-year period, and of those, most were among the larger departments. So far as it goes, the departmental breakdown of the totals for staffing and spending in the 1980 to 1985 period strengthens the budget-minimizing hypothesis rather than the straight Niskanen one: of forty-eight figures, thirty-four are decreases, and only fourteen are increases. If budget minimizing was going on, because that is what was being rewarded by a Conservative government, can we trace the incentives? What were the rewards?

Perhaps the explanation of the discrepancy between total staffing decreases and total spending increases is simple; maybe success in reducing staffing was being rewarded by increases in budget. Share of total budget is a well-known indicator of departmental clout, and increased spending need not always go on increased staffing—departments that spend the same differ greatly in the extent to which their budgets are staff heavy. (12) *Under a Conservative government, staff minimization is rewarded by budgetary increase.* If this principle was working, we should expect in table 7.1 to see the columns for staffing and spending in the later period negatively correlated. The higher the minus figure in the staffing change column, the higher the plus figure in the spending change column, and vice versa. Unfortunately for that hypothesis, it turns out otherwise. The correlation is positive, quite strongly so, during 1980 to 1985 (*r*

TABLE 7.1

Percentage Change in Departmental Staff and Spending,
Twenty-four Departments, Two Five-Year Periods

Department	Rank Order by Staff Size	1975/1976–1979/1980[a]		1980/1981–1984/1985[b]	
		Staff	Spending	Staff	Spending
Employment[c]	4	+45.15	+39.26	+11.16	+56.92
Land Registry	14	+19.92	+23.30	+14.46	+51.99
Home Office	6	+10.71	+14.34	+4.88	+10.71
Lord Chancellor's[d]	11	+4.39	+18.15	−1.22	+67.26
Welsh Office	18	+104.72	+42.10	−14.14	+52.33
Inland Revenue	3	+15.72	+1.37	−10.69	+26.21
Customs & Excise	7	+6.52	+5.04	−7.26	+15.12
Health & Social Security	2	+12.61	+33.95	−5.38	+9.81
Foreign & Commonwealth Office	12	−5.27	+29.57	−4.78	+21.61
Energy	22	+7.71	−52.57	−14.05	+21.04
Defence	1	−6.73	+1.70	−16.06	+6.44
Export Credits Guarantee	20	+11.89	−77.92	−7.78	−37.15
Overseas Development	21	+2.16	+17.58	−10.00	−9.16
Scottish Office	10	+10.59	+14.25	−6.02	−11.35
Northern Ireland Office	24	−0.89	+56.55	−14.61	−5.62
Central Office of Information	23	−9.50	+20.48	−18.44	−5.95
Education & Science[e]	17	−6.17	+16.16	−7.71	−17.17
Trade & Industry[f]	8	−4.19	+87.59	−22.07	−46.59
Treasury, Cabinet, Civil Service	15	−1.70	+11.91	−18.65	−78.37
National Savings	13	−20.74	−13.00	−22.14	−13.43
Environment and Transport	5	−4.54	−8.10	−21.21	−24.32
Agriculture, Fisheries, & Food	9	−7.57	−56.15	−13.48	−24.54
Population Censuses & Survey	19	−7.93	−16.14	−17.73	−25.54
Ordnance Survey	16	−20.86	−19.75	−18.45	−59.60

Sources: Spending figures are from annual supply estimates; staffing figures are from annual *Civil Service Statistics*.

a. Labour majority.

b. Conservative majority.

c. Includes Manpower Services Commission (MSC); Advisory, Conciliation and Arbitration Service (ACAS); Health and Safety Council (HSC); and Health and Safety Executive (HSE).

d. Includes public trustee.

e. Includes arts and libraries but excludes museums.

f. Includes Department of Industry (DI); Department of Trade and Industry (DTI); Department of Trade (DTr); and Department of Prices.

= 0.65). If results are the outcomes of incentives, the Conservatives rewarded staff increases with increased budgets, and not staff cuts. This is contrary to the budget-minimizing hypothesis.

Maybe, then, success in cutting staff, under the conservative regime, was rewarded by higher salaries in some way. That would clearly be the simplest and most direct reward for approved conduct. (13) *Under a Conservative government, staff minimization is rewarded by salary increase.* It is the case that in the first four years of this period, 1975 to 1979, under the Labour government, civil service staff numbers overall increased (+ 4.9 percent), but wages and salaries costs were cut (− 3.6 percent); whereas the Conservatives, in the four years 1980 to 1984, cut civil service staff numbers (− 8.0 percent) but increased wages and salaries costs (+ 5.1)—a larger amount of money went to a smaller number of people (*Sources:* Annual Abstract of Statistics, and U.K. National Accounts 1984.)

This is also suggested if we take only the top salaries—those of permanent secretaries, deputy secretaries, and under secretaries, grades 1 to 3. Their maximum salary scales did not go up at all in 1976, 1977, and 1978, although the retail price index climbed thirty points (1975 = 100; 1976, 116.5; 1978, 146.2). Between 1980 and 1984, however, permanent secretaries' scales went up by 45.8 percent, deputy secretaries' by 48.9 percent, and under secretaries' by 49.6 percent, against a rise in the RPI of 43.4 percent. Civil service wages and salary costs as a whole increased by 45.8 percent in the same period (*Sources: Civil Service Yearbook,* and *Economic Trends* (annual)). So on this governmentwide level, the budget-minimizing proposition is sustained: under the Conservative government, salary budgets went up as staff complement went down. Let us see whether it is also sustained on a departmental breakdown.

Different departments reduced staff at very different rates; and departments do vary greatly in their average salary costs (total salary estimates divided by total number of staff). For example, in 1981, the Department of National Savings was the lowest, with an average salary of £5,559, while that in the Department of Energy was £10,595 (table 7.2). If salary increases were being used as rewards for success in meeting the government's objectives in staff

TABLE 7.2
Average Staff and Salary Estimates, 1981/1982 and 1984/1985, Twenty-three Departments

Department	1981/82			1984/85			% Change 1981/1982–1984/1985	
	Staff	Salary Total	(£) Average	Staff	Salary Total	(£) Average	Staff	Salary
Employment[a]	57,952	440,646	7,604	56,636	420,036	7,416	-2.27	-2.47
Land Registry	5,630	34,491	6,126	6,785	50,024	7,373	+20.50	+20.36
Home Office	35,200	370,846	10,535	36,137	476,347	13,182	+2.66	+25.13
Lord Chancellor's[b]	10,000	69,821	6,982	10,160	80,738	7,947	+1.60	+13.82
Welsh Office	2,330	19,083	8,910	2,201	20,605	9,364	-5.54	+14.33
Inland Revenue	74,990	513,394	6,846	70,025	565,901	8,081	-6.62	+18.04
Customs & Excise	26,643	219,667	8,245	25,250	240,491	9,524	-5.23	+15.51
Health & Social Security	100,350	655,790	6,535	90,305	685,114	7,587	-10.01	+16.10
Foreign & Commonwealth Office	9,536	90,654	9,506	9,405	137,478	14,617	-1.37	+53.77
Energy	1,189	12,598	10,595	1,100	13,514	12,285	-7.48	+15.95
Defence	206,650	1,538,916	7,447	180,306	1,597,953	8,862	-12.75	+19.00
Export Credits Guarantee	1,885	14,679	7,787	1,840	16,626	9,036	-2.39	+16.04

Overseas Development	2,110	19,968	9,463	1,677	17,598	10,494	−20.52	+10.89
Scottish Office	12,663	110,297	8,710	11,915	116,998	9,819	−5.91	+12.73
Northern Ireland Office	214	2,898	13,542	198	2,259	11,410	−7.48	−15.74
Education & Science	2,495	24,909	9,984	2,437	28,957	11,882	−2.32	+19.01
Trade & Industry	15,665	134,549	8,589	12,746	130,154	10,211	−18.63	+18.88
Treasury, Cabinet, Civil Service	4,782	45,365	9,487	5,408	55,819	10,322	+13.09	+8.80
National Savings	9,874	54,894	5,559	8,038	51,637	6,424	−18.59	+15.56
Environment & Transport	53,012	399,304	7,532	46,302	420,386	9,079	−12.66	+20.54
Agriculture, Fisheries, & Food	12,903	111,972	8,673	11,472	112,203	9,781	−11.09	+12.71
Censuses & Surveys	2,638	22,186	8,413	2,144	16,853	7,860	−18.73	−6.54
Ordnance Survey	3,289	23,332	7,094	2,882	24,269	8,422	−12.37	+18.72
Total	691,880	5,001,785	7,223	616,904	5,335,400	8,649	−10.85	+19.64

Source: H. M. Treasury, *Supply Estimates: Chief Secretary's Memorandum on the Estimates*, table 8.

a. Includes Manpower Services Commission (MSC); Advisory, Conciliation and Arbitration Service (ACAS); Health and Safety Council (HSC); and Health and Safety Executive (HSE).

b. Includes public trustee.

c. Includes Department of Industry (DI); Department of Trade and Industry (DTI); Department of Trade (DTr); and Department of Prices.

cutting, then this ought to show up in differential increases in salaries for departments that do more cutting when the global figures are broken down. If departments with a higher than average cut in staff over these years were rewarded with a higher than average increase in average salaries, then columns seven and eight ought to correlate negatively—the biggest minuses on staff change ought to match the biggest pluses on salary change.

In fact, there is no significant relationship at all between the two columns, and what relationship there is is positive, not negative ($r = 0.16$). So it does not, after all, look as if salaries were being used as rewards for budget minimizing. This result was checked against a table (not reproduced here) showing the strength of cuts, whether in spending or in staffing, for these same departments over the years 1980 to 1984. Again, no relationship between salary change and cuts emerged. The salary increases of these years were perhaps what you might expect on a straight Niskanen model but were not supportive of the budget-minimizing thesis, in its staff-minimizing version.

Perhaps, then, the self-regarding and successful budget-minimizing bureaucrat in a Conservative regime is rewarded with promotion? In a very centralized civil service, like the British one, staff salaries are still more centrally negotiated and so less amenable to discretionary choice than is the promotion system. Let us test the hypothesis that (14) *under a conservative government, staff minimization is rewarded by accelerated promotion*. We have, however, no numerical data covering promotions on which to test this hypothesis. But there was plenty of anecdotal evidence on this point under Margaret Thatcher: it was commonplace of weekend journalism for many years that she took a much closer personal interest in the appointments to vacancies at the most senior level of the civil service than had been the practice of her predecessors. Pundits named names of people promoted over the heads of other people, or who were brought up rapidly from obscurity to the top, and of others edged into premature retirement. And certainly, in her decade of office, Thatcher had the opportunity to replace practically every permanent secretary and deputy secretary.

Commentators have made much of her celebrated inquiry, "Is he one of us?"—a phrase that may have been misinterpreted, even at the highest level. A former head of the civil service (Lord Bancroft), a former permanent secretary of the treasury (Sir Douglas Wass), and a former political adviser at Number 10 Downing Street (Sir John Hoskyns) have made speeches and written books expressing the opinion that top civil servants have been put in an impossible position and predicting the creation of a cadre of political mandarins, coming in and going out with their ministers on the French or United States pattern, as a possible solution (Wass 1984; Wass et al. 1986; Hoskyns 1984). Some notable prosecutions over civil service leaks have led to a debate about civil service and ministerial responsibilities (Robinson et al. 1987; Marshall 1988). On the other hand, an independent investigation by the Royal Institute of Public Administration concluded that rumors about politicization are groundless (RIPA 1987).

What is said to have happened is that Thatcher, faced with two candidates for a permanent secretaryship, chose the one with the more can do approach, the better executive track record, and the more managerialist or value-for-money outlook. She was looking for people who would carry forward the Thatcher revolution in British government and society, generally, and not hinder it; who would be cost conscious, and see staffing as a businessperson sees it, a cost to be whittled down. In other words, she wanted those who would be budget minimizers, rather than budget maximizers on the Niskanen model.

This movement to managerialize the civil service antedates Thatcher by a long way, but it certainly intensified after her arrival. If bureaucrats were rewarded by promotion under her regime, it was probably for their zeal in this regard—what in current terms would be called greater efficiency, rather than better public service.

In the absence of numerical data on promotions, there are some other numerical indicators that might be relevant. The top salaries review body recommended in 1985, that the pay of some top civil servants be related to their performance, and this was first introduced for staff in grades 2 and 3 in October 1987. Since April 1988, over 80,000 civil servants are in grades covered by performance-related pay (Cabinet Office 1987; H. C. Deb quoted in Chapman 1988b, 27).

Top posts were fewer toward the end of the 1975 to 1985 period
than at the beginning; in a declining total, the proportion of staff in
grades 1 to 3 went down, not up (from 0.17 percent to 0.14 percent). Yet in more recent years, the government either has been
unable, or has not waited, to find enough promotable men and
women within the civil service ranks and has increasingly re-
cruited people from outside for top posts. Richard Chapman has
drawn attention to the scale of this "inward secondment": between
1979 and 1985, some 70 appointments were made from outside the
civil service at grade 3 and above; and the average number of all
such posts in those years was 751. In eight months, from 1 May
1986 to 31 December 1986 (after new regulations were introduced), the Civil Service Commission approved 52 inward secondments in total, as against 78 recruits by the normal competi-
tions to the basic grade of "fast-stream generalists" in the full year
1986 (Civil Service Commission, quoted in Chapman 1988a, 3).
One may conclude that roughly as many civil service managers in
that year entered in midcareer, possibly for relatively short terms,
as entered by the traditional methods of recruiting people destined
for top posts. Insofar as this information can be interpreted in
relation to the rival hypotheses we are discussing, it might seem
that not enough career civil servants are budget minimizing
enough to be rewarded with promotion into top jobs.

Of the six hypotheses tested by data for the decade 1975 to 1985
in the United Kingdom, exploring the proposition that, under a
Conservative roll-back-the-state regime, self-regarding bureaucrats strive to minimize rather than maximize budgets, one was
falsified and two were upheld. Under the "conservative" regime in
the United Kingdom between 1979 and 1985, total spending did
not go down, but total staffing did—markedly. When the figures
are disaggregated by department, the result also favors a budget-
minimizing thesis: both departmental spending and departmental
staffing decreased between 1980 and 1985 in more departments
than it increased.

However, when we took the facts of staff reductions and tried to
identify the rewards that might be motivating such apparently
budget-minimizing behavior on the part of self-regarding bureau-

crats, we had less success. Staff cutting was associated with budget increase overall, but the correlation disappeared (and even went the other way) when a more detailed analysis at the departmental level was undertaken. The same happened with salary increase: plausible positive relationships at overall level were replaced with negative correlations on the departmental analysis. Thus, although the figures of staff cuts themselves suggest that staff minimizing was happening, it is difficult to see what was in it for the self-regarding bureaucrat—unless it was promotion.

There is some persuasive logic relating cutback performance with promotion success. The inculcation of a managerialist ethos, of which the minimization of both money and labor inputs is a cardinal tenet, was intensified by specific higher management training schemes after 1979; and there is some anecdotal evidence, from both supporters and opponents, that a good track record in this regard was a strong recommendation for promotion to and within the top ranks under Margaret Thatcher. The evidence of top posts being filled increasingly by inward secondment of noncareer managers, rather than by promotion of existing civil servants, is equivocal. It would strengthen the hypothesis by implying that more civil servants would have been promoted if more of them had been more managerial.

The tentative conclusion, therefore, is that the main hypothesis is supported: under a Conservative government, a staff-minimization strategy did apparently operate—something that would not ordinarily be considered compatible with the straight Niskanen model. But incontrovertible evidence is lacking that this bureaucratic strategy was a self-regarding one. It did not lead to bigger budgets, or more salary, or even more promotion opportunities (there were progressively fewer top posts to be promoted into). If the only sign of being self-regarding is that you seek promotion competitively by excelling in furthering the ends of your political masters, then it is harder to distinguish the self-regarding Adam Smith bureaucrat from the disinterested Weberian bureaucrat than we thought.

This ambiguity is built into the hypothesis itself. The essence of the Niskanen model is that the behavior of the self-regarding bu-

reaucrat is in conflict with the aims of the sponsor. Budget minimizing, when budget minimizing is what your sponsor wants, is
unNiskanenish conduct to start with.

Conclusion

This chapter has explored, on the basis of empirical evidence
drawn from a study of the U.K. central government in the decade
1975 to 1985, the applicability of the Niskanen model in explaining
the behavior of British bureaucrats by testing it against two rival
models. The significance of the site and the period is that succes-
sive governments were committed to reducing the size of the state,
the earlier (Labour) government because of fiscal crisis and international pressure, the later (Conservative) government from convic-
tions about rolling back the state.

First, the alternative to the hypothesis of a self-regarding,
budget-maximizing bureaucrat is that of the classic public-service-
oriented, disinterested, professional civil servant, in the context of
general retrenchment. Second, the alternative to the self-
regarding, budget-maximizing bureaucrat is the self-regarding,
budget-minimizing bureaucrat, in the context of ideological contraction of the state.

The conclusions are (1) that the public-service-oriented bureaucrat model better explains behavior at this site, at this period, than
does the self-regarding (or budget-maximizing) bureaucrat model;
to that extent, the Niskanen model is invalidated by this evidence;
and (2) that it is not clearly demonstrated that a Conservative
government rewards budget minimizing by bureaucrats and that,
therefore, a budget-minimizing strategy is superior to a budget-
maximizing one for a self-regarding bureaucrat; to that extent, the
Niskanen model is not invalidated by this evidence.

NOTE

The research reported in this essay is part of a larger project I carried
out with Christopher Hood. It was supported by the U.K. Economic and

Social Research Council (award E 00232018). I am grateful to Christopher Hood for his comments on an earlier draft.

REFERENCES

Aberbach, J. D., et al. 1981. *Bureaucrats and politicians in western democracies.* Cambridge, Mass: Harvard Univ. Press.

Bagehot, W. 1964. *The English constitution.* Ed. R. H. S. Crossman. London: C. A. Watts. Bagehot's work was originally published in 1867.

Breton, A. 1974. *The economic theory of representative government.* London: Macmillan.

Cabinet Office. Annual. *Civil service yearbook.* London: HMSO.

Cabinet Office, and MPO. 1987. *The challenge of change in the civil service: A report on the work of the Management and Personnel Office.* London: HM Treasury and Cabinet Office.

Central Statistical Office. Annual. *Annual abstract of statistics.* London: HMSO.

———. Monthly. *Economic trends.* London: HMSO.

———. Annual. *United Kingdom national accounts.* London: HMSO. The CSO Blue Book.

Chapman, R. A. 1988a. The British civil service: Inward secondments— cause for concern. *Public Policy and Administration* 3(2): 1–3.

———. 1988b. *The art of darkness: An inaugural lecture.* Durham, U.K.: Univ. of Durham.

Davies, J. G. 1972. *The evangelistic bureaucrat.* London: Tavistock.

Downs, A. 1967. *Inside bureaucracy.* Boston: Little, Brown.

Dunleavy, P. 1985. Bureaucrats, budgets and the growth of the state. *British Journal of Political Science* 15:299–328.

Dunsire, A., and C. C. Hood. 1989. *Cutback management in public bureaucracies: Popular theories and observed outcomes in Whitehall.* Cambridge: Cambridge Univ. Press.

Frederickson, H. G. 1971. Toward a new public administration. In *Toward a new public administration,* ed. F. Marini. Scranton, Pa.: Chandler.

Glassberg, A. 1978. Organizational responses to municipal budget decreases. *Public Administration Review* 38(4): 325–332.

Glennerster, H. 1981. Social service spending in a hostile environment. In Hood and Wright 1981, 174–96.

Hartley, K. 1981. Defence: A case study of spending cuts. In Hood and Wright 1981, 125–51.

Hegel, G. W. F. 1942. *The philosophy of right.* Trans. T. M. Knox. Oxford: Oxford Univ. Press. Hegel's work was originally published in 1821.

Heidenheimer, A., ed. 1970. *Political corruption*. New York: Holt, Rinehart, & Winston.

HM Treasury. Annual. *Appropriation accounts*. London: HMSO.

———. Government Statistical Service. Annual. *Civil service statistics*. London: HMSO.

———. Annual. *Supply estimates: Chief Secretary's memorandum on the estimates*. London: HMSO.

Hood, C. C., A. Dunsire, and M. Huby. 1988. Bureaucracies in retrenchment: Vulnerability theory and the case of UK central government departments, 1975–85. *Administration and Society* 20(3): 275–312.

Hood, C. C., M. Huby, and A. Dunsire. 1984. Bureaucrats and budgeting benefits: How do British central government ministries measure up? *Journal of Public Policy* 4(3): 163–79.

Hood, C. C., and M. Wright, eds. 1981. *Big government in hard times*. Oxford: Martin Robertson.

Hoskyns, J. 1984. Conservatism is not enough. *Political Quarterly* 55:3–16.

Jackson, P. M. 1982. *The political economy of bureaucracy*. Oxford: Philip Allan.

Jørgensen, T. Beck. 1987a. *Models of retrenchment behaviour*. Working Paper 24. Brussels: International Institute of Administrative Sciences.

———. 1987b. Financial management in the public sector. In *Managing public organizations: Lessons from contemporary European experience*, ed. J. Kooiman and K. A. Eliassen. London: Sage.

Kogan, M. 1973. *Comment on Niskanen's Bureaucracy, servant or master?* London: Institute of Economic Affairs.

Leibenstein, H. 1976. *Beyond economic man: A new foundation for microeconomics*. Cambridge, Mass: Harvard Univ. Press.

Levine, C. H. 1978. A symposium: Organizational decline and cutback management. *Public Administration Review* 38(4): 316–25.

Martin, S. 1983. *Managing without managers*. Beverly Hills, Calif: Sage.

Mill, J. S. 1910. *Considerations on representative government*. Ed. A. D. Lindsay. London: J. M. Dent. Mill's work was originally published in 1861.

Niskanen, W. A. 1971. *Bureaucracy and representative government*. Chicago: Aldine Atherton.

Peacock, A. T. 1983. Public X-inefficiency: Informational and constitutional constraints. In *Anatomy of government deficiencies*, ed. H. Hanusch, 125–38. Berlin/Heidelberg: Springer.

Robinson, A., R. Shepherd, F. F. Ridley, and G. W. Jones. 1987. Symposium on ministerial responsibility. *Public Administration* 65(1): 61–91.

Rogow, A., and H. Lasswell. 1963. *Power, corruption and rectitude.* Englewood Cliffs, N.J.: Prentice-Hall.

Rousseau, J.-J. 1973. *The social contract.* Trans. and ed. G. D. H. Cole. Rev. ed. London: J. M. Dent. Rousseau's work was originally published in 1762.

Royal Institute of Public Administration (RIPA). 1987. *Top jobs in Whitehall: Appointments and promotions in the senior civil service.* London: Royal Institute of Public Administration.

Schaffer, B. B. 1973. *The administrative factor.* London: Frank Cass.

Self, P. J. O. 1972. *Administrative theories and politics.* London: Allen and Unwin.

Smith, A. 1812. *An inquiry into the nature and causes of the wealth of nations.* 3 vols. London: Ward, Lock. Smith's work was originally published in 1776.

Thompson, V. A. 1975. *Without sympathy or enthusiasm.* University, Alabama: Univ. of Alabama Press.

Wass, D. 1984. *Government and the governed.* London: Allen and Unwin.

Wass, D., M. Elliott, and A. Barker, eds. 1986. *Policy analysis and constitutional issues.* London: Royal Institute of Public Administration.

Weber, M. 1948. Bureaucracy. In *From Max Weber: Essays in sociology,* trans. and ed. H. H. Gerth and C. W. Mills. London: Routledge and Kegan Paul. Weber's work was originally published in 1921.

Wildavsky, A. 1964. *The politics of the budgetary process.* Boston: Little, Brown.

Wright, M. 1981. Big government in hard times: The restraint of public expenditure. In Hood and Wright, 1981, 3–31.

Young, R. G. 1974. The administrative process as incrementalism. Part 3 of *Approaches to the study of public administration,* in Public administration, Block 2 D331, part of *Social sciences: A third level course.* Milton Keynes: Open Univ. Press.

8

ANDRÉ BLAIS,
DONALD E. BLAKE, AND
STÉPHANE DION

The Voting Behavior of Bureaucrats

According to the budget-maximizing bureaucrat model, bureaucrats systematically request larger budgets because it is in their interest to do so. From that perspective, it is also in their interest to deal with politicians who are positively disposed toward the growth of public expenditures. As a consequence, the bureaucrat has two sets of (convergent) interests. In his or her bureau, the bureaucrat will press for a larger budget; at the polls, he or she will support those candidates and parties standing for greater state intervention. If they are successful at the polls, their jobs will be easier: it will be easier to obtain a larger budget if the sponsor is committed rather to increase spending than to decrease it.

As public expenditures tend to increase when parties of the Left form the government (Castles 1982; Cameron 1978), one would expect bureaucrats to vote for parties of the Left. To the extent that public sector employees and their dependents come to form a large part of the electorate, the bureaucrats' vote could even play a major role in the electoral victories of the Left. The bureaucrats' vote could be one of the major causes of the growth of the state.

This is not to say that a budget-maximizing bureaucrat will always vote for a left-wing party. The voting decision involves many other dimensions. Moreover, budget-maximizing bureaucrats are concerned with the budget of their own bureau rather than with the overal budget of the state. Still, one may suppose that the greater the increase in the total budget of the state, the better are the chances that a given bureau will obtain a large increase. We should thus expect a leftist bias in the voting behavior of bureaucrats. The existence of a bias would not by itself prove the validity of the model, but it would be consistent with the idea of a bureaucrat in search of larger budgets.

This chapter determines whether public sector employees are more likely than private sector employees to support parties committed to greater state intervention. We examine surveys done in eleven countries over the last thirty-five years. The existence of a public/private sector cleavage of the sort predicted here (the public sector supporting parties of the Left) would be consistent with the budget-maximizing bureaucrat model, and the absence of such cleavage would tend to discredit the model. We also indicate what kind of political context is more conducive to the emergence of a public/private sector cleavage and examine potential variations in voting behavior within the public sector.

Public Choice and the Voting Behavior of Bureaucrats

Tullock (1970) was the first to suggest that bureaucrats have a bias toward those candidates and parties that favor the growth of public expenditures. In his review (Tullock 1972) of Niskanen's *Bureaucracy and Representative Government,* he notes that the pressure of bureaus to get larger budgets is reinforced by the demands of bureaucrats as voters. Later, Tullock (1974) and Buchanan and Tullock (1977) argue that "the votes of bureaucrats would be partially directed toward expanding the size of their agencies and partially toward raising their own salaries" (ibid., 148). On that basis, Tullock (1970, 126–27) asserts that public sector employees are in a conflict of interest position and should not have the right to vote.

Neither Tullock nor the other public choice authors who have dealt with this question (Bennett and Orzechowski 1983; Borcherding, Bush, and Spann 1977; Bush and Denzau 1977; Frey and Pommerehne 1982) present any evidence on the vote orientation of public sector employees. They have focused their attention on turnout instead. Many studies have shown that public sector employees are more likely to vote than their counterparts in the private sector (Bennett and Orzechowski 1983; Frey and Pommerehne 1982; Dupeux 1952; Lipset 1983; Martin 1933; Tingsten 1937; Wolfinger and Rosenstone 1980). In the United States, there is a substantial gap of fifteen to twenty percentage points in the turnout of the public and private sectors, and the difference cannot be explained away by other socioeconomic factors (Bennett and Orzechowski 1983; Wolfinger and Rosenstone 1980). The finding is interpreted as confirming the public choice hypothesis that bureaucrats are more likely to vote because they have more to gain, as the outcome of the election decides which party (or coalition) will be their boss (Downs 1957, 254). It is then inferred that "since many elections are decided by small margins, an intense minority such as government employees can exert an enormous impact on election outcomes" (Bennett and Orzechowski 1983, 274) or even that "one of the major reasons for this [the growth of the state] is that bureaucrats vote" (Tullock 1970, 126).

All this assumes, of course, that public sector employees vote differently from private sector ones. This is the crucial assumption, as Bush and Denzau (1977, 90) acknowledge. Yet the public choice literature has not produced any empirical evidence on this simple but basic question. This chapter intends to fill that gap. We determine whether or not bureaucrats are more likely to support parties of the Left, which tend to be more favorable toward state intervention. We determine whether the public sector effect exists and, if it exists, whether it emerges systematically in every country and in every election. We will check whether it disappears when other socioeconomic variables are controlled for, and whether it is general or limited to a particular subsector (teachers, for instance).

The literature on the public/private sector cleavage is thin. Lipset (1983, 230–232) identifies six basic social cleavages relevant to politics: class, religion, ethnicity, sex, age, and residence (urban/rural). The sectoral cleavage, which is our concern here, is absent from the list. Oddly enough, voting behavior research has largely ignored the state/market dichotomy. If we are to assess the validity of the public choice hypothesis about the voting behavior of bureaucrats, a review of the literature will not do it. We will have to dig out the evidence ourselves.

The Study

Our approach is simple. We used the surveys listed in the appendix to this chapter. We have data on forty-three elections held in eleven countries, over the last thirty-five years. The basic findings are reported in table 8.1. The first column shows the zero-order difference in support for parties of the Left between the public and the private sectors. For instance, if 55 percent of public sector employees vote for parties of the Left but only 50 percent of those in the private sector, the sectoral difference is +.05. The second and third columns indicate the specific impact of the sectoral variable in a multivariate regression analysis including other socioeconomic variables, those variables that other studies have found to be significant predictors of the vote. The list of control variables for each country is given in the appendix. A coefficient of +.05 means that, when all the other socioeconomic variables are controlled for, support of the Left is five percentage points higher in the public than in the private sector.

One control variable raises special problems: unionization. In many countries, the public sector is more unionized than the private sector (Rose 1985). It seems fair to assume that sector causes unionization, rather than the other way around. That being the case, controlling for union membership would conceal the indirect (but real) impact of the sectoral variable (through unionization). To the extent that the public sector induces unionization, the effect of the latter variable should be considered as an (indirect) product of the sectoral cleavage. The point is well made by Dunleavy: "Given the strong influence of sectoral locations on unionization, it seems legitimate to conclude that the unionization influence alignment reflects the influence of sectoral locations" (1980, 546). Likewise, in their comparative analysis of public and private schools, Chubb and Moe eschew any statistical control because "an institutional perspective suggests that all major variables are probably endogenous" (1988, 1071–72).

Table 8.1, therefore, presents the results for regressions excluding and including unionization as a control variable. The former indicates the total effect of sector, directly and indirectly through union membership. The latter indicates the direct sectoral impact

TABLE 8.1
The Public Sector Effect on the Left Vote

Country and Year of Election Survey	Initial Difference	Multivariate Analysis	
		Total Effect	Direct Effect
Great Britain			
1964	−.00	+.10 (2.25)★	+.07 (1.97)★
1966	+.03	+.10 (2.12)★	+.10 (2.86)★
1970	−.01	+.08 (1.62)	+.15 (3.43)★
1974 (February)	−.04	+.07 (1.43)	+.01 (0.39)
1974 (October)	+.04	+.09 (3.20)★	+.04 (1.55)
1979	+.04	+.03 (0.80)	−.01 (0.19)
1983	+.02	+.06 (3.75)★	+.06 (3.66)★
United States			
1960	− 00	−.03 (0.42)	+.03 (0.62)
1964	−.02	+.01 (0.33)	+.04 (1.13)
1968	+.06	+.03 (0.67)	−.01 (0.18)
1972	+.07	+.05 (1.40)	+.04 (1.33)
1976	+.00	+.02 (0.44)	+.01 (0.12)
1980	+.10	+.10 (2.25)★	+.08 (1.80)
1984	+.15	+.13 (2.82)★	+.11 (2.29)★
Canada			
1968	−.01	−.01 (0.25)	−.00 (0.21)
1974	+.00	+.04 (1.48)	+.03 (0.91)
1979	+.05	+.06 (2.55)★	+.04 (1.64)★
1980	+.06	+.08 (3.14)★	+.06 (2.29)★
1984	+.05	+.07 (3.01)★	+.06 (2.31)★
1988	+.02	+.04 (2.03)★	+.01 (0.30)
Germany			
1953	−.08	+.04 (0.96)	+.06 (1.19)
1961	+.01	+.11 (1.58)	
1965	−.05	−.13 (1.32)	−.02 (0.14)
1969	+.04	+.04 (0.41)	+.02 (0.26)
1972	−.17	−.05 (0.45)	−.04 (0.42)
1976	−.04	−.06 (1.14)	−.11 (1.88)
1980	−.06	−.03 (1.69)	−.07 (3.63)★

(continued)

TABLE 8.1   continued

Country and Year of Election Survey	Initial Difference	Multivariate Analysis	
		Total Effect	Direct Effect
Netherlands			
1971	+.07	+.09 (2.38)★	+.08 (2.08)★
1972	+.09	+.14 (2.95)★	+.13 (2.77)★
1977	+.01	+.05 (1.27)	+.02 (0.52)
1981	+.08	+.10 (2.58)★	+.10 (2.32)★
1982	+.09	+.06 (2.35)★	+.05 (2.05)★
Denmark			
1971	−.14	+.03 (0.84)	
1973	−.07	+.06 (1.04)	
1975	+.09	+.18 (4.47)★	
1979	+.11	+.14 (4.67)★	+.11 (3.80)★
1981	+.13	+.19 (4.58)★	+16 (3.81)★
France			
1958	+.23		
1967	−.04	+.06 (1.38)	−.02 (0.35)
Switzerland			
1972	−.06	+.04 (0.71)	+.00 (0.06)
Norway			
1981	+.02	+.06 (2.53)★	+.03 (1.07)
Australia			
1967	+.10	+.14 (3.44)★	+.08 (3.33)★
Japan			
1967	+.12	+.15 (2.80)★	+.08 (1.45)

Note: Figures in parentheses are t statistics.
★Significant at the .05 level (two-tailed test).

independent of unionization. The two sets of results must be considered. The total effect informs us about the overall scope of the sectoral cleavage. The direct effect constitutes the most crucial test of the model: the budget-maximizing bureaucrat model will be supported only if unionized public sector employees are different from their counterparts in the private sector. In short, including unionization as a control variable guarantees that there is a sectoral effect and that the sectoral effect is not explained entirely by unionization.

The results reported in table 8.1 are based on ordinary least squares regression. While logit or probit is technically more appropriate for the dichotomous dependent variables analyzed here, we opted for regressions for reasons of cost and ease of presentation. In previous work (Blais, Blake, and Dion 1990), we found that the findings are not sensitive to the statistical technique utilized.

We have run many more regressions than those reported in table 8.1 and have checked the possibility of class interaction effects; that is, whether a sectoral effect emerges only among the middle class. We have also paid particular attention to the behavior of teachers, a group that may be more leftist than other groups of the public sector. Finally, we have looked at specific parties that bureaucrats may find particularly attractive or repulsive. We note these more complex patterns (not indicated in the table) whenever appropriate.

For each of the eleven countries, we start with a review of the literature, then analyze the major results as reported in table 8.1 and point out more complex cleavages within the public sector and the party system. We finally reassess the public choice hypothesis in the light of the evidence assembled.

Findings

Great Britain

Dunleavy (1980) was the first to examine the impact of sectoral location on political alignment in Britain. He cites evidence from surveys that, by 1974, "public employees were rather more likely to perceive Labor as better in terms of fair wages, pensions or unemployment than comparable privately employed voters" (ibid., 536). Using log-linear analysis, he finds no independent effect of sector on party choice. He argues, however, that sector has an indirect effect through unionization and class. For the same election, Alt and Turner (1982) show that there is a cleavage, but only among voters of middle-class background. Among those whose families had been middle class, 71 percent of the private sector voters supported the

Conservative party, compared to 44 percent of public sector employees. No difference was found among those of working-class background. They also note substantial differences between sectors on perceptions of the best party for the respondent's own income, but only small ones on poverty and health services questions, which "suggests that one should look at the sector-vote connection in instrumental rather than expressive terms" (ibid., 248). For the 1983 election, Whiteley (1986) reports that Labour vote was ten percentage points higher in the public than in the private sector, but the gap is reduced to five percentage points when other social attributes are controlled for. Heath, Jowell, and Curtice (1985) indicate that the gap holds only for the upper occupational class.

Our analysis makes use of a larger number of election studies and a larger number of independent variables. If we simply examine voting behavior by sector, there does not appear to be any sectoral cleavage: the differences between the two sectors are minor and inconsistent (see table 8.1). However, multivariate analysis incorporating the socioeconomic variables normally used to explain British voting behavior (Whiteley 1986) as well as occupational sector provides a convincing demonstration of the importance of the public/private sector cleavage. The coefficient of the public sector variable has the expected sign in every election and reaches statistical significance in four instances. The average coefficient is .08, which means that, everything else being equal, support for Labour is eight percentage points higher in the public sector. This is a substantial difference, which is only slightly affected by the inclusion of unionization: the average coefficient is .06.

We explored possible within-sector differences by using variables to distinguish public administration, armed forces, teacher, and medical categories from the public sector as a whole. The results were generally not impressive. In the 1974 elections, when the public sector variable was not itself statistically significant, there was some evidence of above average Labour support among the medical category (the coefficients and t-ratios for this variable in February and October were, respectively, $b = .16$, $t = 1.79$, and $b = .20$, $t = 2.77$) and in 1970, evidence of less than average support among the teaching category ($b = -.17$, $t = -1.65$). In 1983, it proved possible to distinguish between public sector employees on the basis of whether they were employed by government agencies, who constitute about two-thirds of the public sector in that sample or in the nationalized industries. Doing so provides evidence that the government category is less pro-Labour than the nationalized sector. The coefficient for government is $+.02$, compared to $+.09$ ($t = 3.41$) for the nationalized sector, which may reflect reactions to the Thatcher government's privatization program. (We found no evidence of a class/sector interaction effect suggestive of greater support for Labour among middle-class public sector workers. In fact, the only significant interaction with social class appeared in 1970, suggesting that working-class public sector workers had a higher level of support for Labour than did their middle-class counterparts.)

There is thus undoubtedly a sectoral effect in British voting behavior. Public sector employees are more likely to support the Labour party. The effect is consistent over time and is not confined to any particular subgroup.

United States

In the United States, hardly any attention has been paid to a potential sectoral cleavage in voting behavior. Meier (1975) and Goodsell (1985, 84) report no difference in the party identification of public and private sector employees. There is evidence, however, of differential voting on tax limitation referendums (Citrin and Green 1985; Gramlich and Rubinfeld 1982; Ladd and Wilson 1982; Leavy 1975). In Michigan, for instance, 58 percent of state and local employees voted against the 1978 Headlee amendment, which imposed a mild limitation on state and local taxing and spending, compared to 39 percent in the rest of the electorate (Gramlich and Rubinfeld 1982, 520).

Our analysis utilizes the American National Election studies. Table 8.1 portrays initial differences in presidential voting with a pro-Democratic preference on the part of public sector members emerging first in 1968 (six percentage points) and then increasing from seven percentage points in 1972 to fifteen points in 1984. The 1976 election, however, shows no such bias. The picture is less clear for congressional voting, which has been analyzed in detail elsewhere (Blais, Blake, and Dion 1990).

Regression analysis, which uses as control variables the best predictors of pro-Democratic preference identified by Stanley, Bianco, and Niemi (1986), shows that only the 1980 and 1984 elections exhibit a sectoral effect when other determinants of voting are controlled for. However, the sign of the public sector coefficient is as predicted for six out of seven elections. If we restrict ourselves to elections held in the 1970s and 1980s, the average coefficient is .08 when unionization is excluded and .06 when it is included, which is identical to what we observed in Britain.

Dummy variables distinguishing between public administration and educational employees were also tested. In 1972, the public administration and educational worker variables had opposite signs, with public administration workers apparently less Democratic than private sector workers. In all other elections, however, coefficients for both variables had the same sign (indicating pro-Democratic) as the public sector coefficient itself.

We also ran regressions including a class/public sector interaction term. In 1980, significant interaction effects begin to appear that suggest that working-class/public sector respondents are no more pro-Democratic than the working class in general. Summing the coefficients yields a net pro-Democratic score of only .03 for public sector/working class. In 1984, the coefficient for the interaction variable also had a negative sign but was not statistically significant ($t = -1.41$). Hence, while the result is not conclusive, there is some suggestion that the pro-Democratic sympathies of public sector employees are stronger among those in the middle class.

Overall, the impact of the sectoral variable is modest in the United States, but this is no justification for ignoring it. Where the cleavage exists, it operates in the direction the public choice approach would have expected—greater public sector support for the more left-wing party. The effect is as substantial as that of gender, which suggests that it should be paid as much attention as the gender gap. For recent elections, it is also similar in magnitude to the one observed in Britain. Finally, there is some indication that the effect is greater within the middle class.

Canada

The literature on the public/private sector cleavage in Canada is thin. Only one study has examined the voting behavior of Canadian bureaucrats at the federal level (Johnston 1979). It indicates, for the 1968 election, identical levels of support for the major leftist party, the New Democratic party (NDP), in the two sectors (with the exception of teachers, who voted for the NDP at a greater rate), but slightly higher support for the Progressive Conservative party in the private (28 percent than in the public (25 percent) sector. At the provincial level, larger differences emerge. In British Columbia, the NDP vote in 1979 was eight percentage points higher in the public sector among blue-collar workers and ten percentage points higher among managers and professionals (Blake 1985, 99). In the latter group, the difference is even increased when other socioeconomic variables are taken into account (ibid., 109). In Quebec, the major leftist party, the Parti Québécois, received ten percentage points more votes in the public sector in the 1981 election, with the independent effect of the sectoral variable amounting to seven percentage points after controls (Blais and Nadeau 1984). That difference vanished in the 1985 election after the Parti Québécois substantially reduced public sector salaries, the bureaucratic sector preference then benefiting the left-wing NDP (Blais and Dion 1987).

Our analysis utilizes the Canadian election studies for 1968, 1974, 1979, 1980, 1984, and 1988. Table 8.1 (column 1) indicates that a sectoral cleavage began in 1979, with a consistent pro-NDP bias of five to six percentage points since then.

Regression analysis—using control variables from LeDuc (1980)—shows no sectoral effect in 1968. However, the public sector coefficient is positive in all elections held in the 1970s and 1980s, the average being a difference of six percentage points, an impact a bit smaller than in Britain and the United States. Including union membership in the analysis reduces the value of the public sector coefficient but still confirms a small impact of sector on NDP support in the three elections from 1979 to 1984. The most recent election (1988) did not produce a pro-NDP bias because public sector employees, who were more likely to oppose the proposed Free Trade Agreement with the United States, supported the Liberal party rather than the NDP (the two parties opposed the agreement).

Distinguishing between government employees and teachers has little effect. Both coefficients are positive, with the teacher coefficient slightly higher, and both are significant in those cases where the public sector coefficient by itself is significant. Finally, unlike the case in the United States, there is not even a hint of a class/sector interaction effect.

There is thus evidence of a sectoral cleavage in Canadian voting behavior, at least in recent elections. The direct effect of the sectoral variable is four percentage points (when unionization is included) if we restrict attention to elections held in the 1970s and 1980s.

Germany

We do not know of any study that has examined the impact of sectoral employment on voting behavior in Germany. Our analysis is based on surveys with respect to seven federal elections held between 1953 and 1980. In five elections, public sector employees were less likely to vote for the Social Democratic Party (SPD), the average difference being minus five percentage points, a result in conflict with the public choice hypothesis. However, when we control for other socioeconomic variables (using Urwin 1974), the average coefficients are $-.01$ and $-.03$, and they are systematically nonsignificant except for the 1980 election. A plausible reason why public sector employees appear to be less likely to vote for the SPD is that they come from the middle class, which is generally less supportive of that party. However, because our indicator of sector is the respondent's occupation (see the appendix) and the only occupations specific to the public sector are middle-class ones, it is impossible to test for potential class/sector interaction effects.

There is no evidence of a sectoral cleavage in Germany. As we shall see, among the countries with a longtime series of election studies available, this is the only one in which the public choice prediction is never borne out.

The Netherlands

The public/private sector cleavage has been ignored by Dutch electoral analysts. The social class cleavage, together with gender, age, and religion has long served as the principal factor distinguishing between supporters of the liberals and socialists, the main contenders for control of government coalitions (Andeweg 1982; Daalder 1987; Irwin 1982; Irwin and Dittrich 1984). Our analysis, based on Dutch election studies covering the elections of 1971, 1972, 1977, 1981, and 1982, suggests that the neglect is undeserved. Respondents in public sector occupations, defined as those classified as public service in the survey, exhibit a preference for the socialist party that averages seven percentage points.

Moreover, the sectoral cleavage has a significant effect on the vote in four of the five elections studied when the other important predictors of Dutch voting are controlled (Irwin 1982). In the one apparent exception, 1977, the sign of the public sector coefficient is positive as predicted. The average impact over the five elections is +.08 (when unionization is included). Sectoral differences are clearly important, eclipsing gender and age, which have received considerable attention in other studies of Dutch voting behavior.

There is some evidence of differences within the public sector linked to occupation and social class differences that vary over time. A test of differences between education, medical categories, and public administration—which includes those in government (nonmilitary) services but not government-owned industries—revealed that those in public administration were less likely to vote socialist than other public sector workers in 1972. Unfortunately, the information required to produce these classifications was not available in the later surveys.

The possibility of class/sector interactions was tested by adding a working-class/public sector term. There were no significant interactions in 1971 and 1972, but there were in 1977 and 1981. The sign of that coefficient in these cases is negative, indicating that it is in the middle class that the sectoral impact is being felt. It seems that the sectoral effect in the Netherlands in recent years is primarily a phenomenon of higher than expected support for the Left among middle-class public sector employees.

In short, there is strong support for the hypothesis that public sector employees are more likely to vote for parties of the Left in the Netherlands. It appears, however, that in recent elections, the effect is largely confined to the middle class.

Denmark

In Denmark, Andersen and Borre have examined the impact of sectoral employment on the vote. Andersen (1984) notes that the 1971 election produced no difference in the behavior of the two sectors, but a cleavage emerged thereafter. In 1981, 58 percent of nonmanual wage earners in the public sector supported socialist parties, compared to 31 percent for their private sector counterparts. Only among the military and police did the nonsocialists obtain a majority of public sector votes. The shift to the Left is spectacular among educational personnel, where the vote for socialist parties more than doubled between 1971 and 1979. There is also a difference within the working class, but it is a weaker one. Borre (1987) examined voting behavior in the 1987 election. Socialists parties obtained 58 percent of the vote in the public salariat, compared to 32 percent in the private salariat.

Our analysis confirms the discontinuity noted by Andersen. By 1975, a powerful sectoral effect, and one of the strongest in the table, had emerged. Moreover, the effect is only slightly diminished when union membership (available only for the 1979 and 1981 surveys) is added to the list of control variables.

France

In France, there seems to have been a long-standing pattern of a greater support for left-wing parties in the public sector. In 1924, according to Chevalier (1958, 554), civil servants played a crucial role in the electoral victory of the Cartel des Gauches. In the 1950s, surveys show support for the Socialist Party (SFIO) to be twice as high in the public sector as in the whole electorate (Kesler 1980, 100). In the 1973 legislative election, 64 percent of public sector employees voted for parties of the Left compared to 54 percent of private sector ones (ibid.). In the 1974 presidential election, François Mitterrand obtained 70 percent of second-ballot votes among public sector employees and 57 percent among private sector ones (ibid.). In the 1978 legislative elections, within the middle class, support for the Left was a little higher in the public (58 percent) than in the private sector (53 percent) (Lavau, Grundberg, and Mayer 1983, 370). The first ballot of the 1981 presidential elections gave François Mitterrand 35 percent of the votes among public sector employees and 27 percent among private sector ones (Hardouin 1983). Finally, 44 percent of the votes for the Left at the first ballot of the 1986 legislative elections came from the public sector, but only 25 percent in the case of the vote for parties of the Right (Jaffré 1986, 214).

The pattern in France appears to be consistent. However, these findings do not control for the impact of other socioeconomic variables. It may well be that public sector employees in France are less religious, and that this is the main reason why they support left-wing parties (see Kesler 1980, 102). Moreover, there is no way to tell whether leftist inclinations are to be found in all categories of bureaucrats, or are rather concentrated among teachers, who are old allies of the Socialist Party (Aubert, Ozouf, and Ozouf 1987; Bacot 1977; Kesler 1980, 106; Mayer and Schweisguth 1985).

We have only two surveys on French electoral behavior pertaining to the legislative elections of 1958 and 1967. In 1958, we observe a huge gap between the two sectors, the Left obtaining twenty-three percentage points more in the public sector. In 1967, the difference completely disappeared mostly because of the gains made by the Communist party in the private sector. The socialist vote, however, was ten percentage points higher in the public sector.

We could not proceed to a multivariate analysis in the case of the 1958 election because of the lack of data on most control variables. The results of the regression for the 1967 election are reported in table 8.1. Everything else being equal, public sector employees are slightly more favorable to parties of the Left only if we exclude unionization. There is no direct impact of sector on voting behavior. There is every reason to believe, however, that there was an effect in the 1958 election (as controls do not substantially affect the results in 1967).

The absence of a sectoral cleavage in France is surprising. The explanation probably lies mainly in the divisions within the Left. Support for the Left within the public sector does not extend to the Communist party. We have run a separate regression for the socialist vote in 1967 (with the same control variables including unionization), and the sectoral variable turns out to be positive though not quite significant ($b = +.06$, $t = 1.18$). However, we found that the socialist vote is basically confined to teachers; in the multivariate analysis, the probability of a leftist vote is twenty-five percentage points higher among teachers than in the private sector, whereas it is the same in the rest of the public sector.

The findings on France are ambiguous. On the one hand, it can be pointed out that there was no sectoral impact in 1967 and that only teachers behave differently. On the other hand, it can be argued that it is the socialist rather than the leftist vote that is relevant in France, as reactions to the Communist party involve many other considerations unrelated to the issue of the size of the state, and that there are strong reasons to believe that there was a sectoral effect in 1958. The French case does not clearly confirm nor disconfirm the public choice model.

Switzerland

For Switzerland, as for Germany, we do not know of any study that has examined the possibility of a sectoral cleavage in voting behavior. In the one survey available, public sector employees even prove to be less supportive of the Left. When we introduce the appropriate controls (Lijphart 1980), however, the coefficient of the sectoral variable is positive but clearly not significant. We must conclude that there is no sectoral effect in Switzerland.

Norway

Andersen (1984, 252) quotes a study (Valen 1981) that apparently highlights the greater propensity of public sector employees in Norway to vote for leftist parties. Lafferty and Knutsen (1984) also show that, in terms of ideology, the public sector is clearly more leftist than the private sector.

We were able to use one survey, conducted in 1982 for the class structure and class consciousness study, that contained questions pertaining to the 1981 national election. In that election, there was little difference in the behavior of the public and private sectors. Multivariate analysis, however, shows a small sectoral effect (three percentage points with unionization controlled). While there was no class/sector interaction, a complex occupational breakdown shows a clear pro-Left pattern only for managerial-technical workers. There is evidence of a small sectoral cleavage in Norway, especially among the middle class.

Australia

As far as we can tell, the potential impact of sectoral employment on voting behavior has never been studied in Australia. There is only one survey available—the one held in the federal election of 1967, which shows a ten percentage point difference in the relative propensity of the two sectors to vote Labour. When we control for other socioeconomic variables (Aitkin and Kahan 1974), the difference is eight percentage points, if we include union membership among the control variables. We also distinguished teachers from the rest of the public sector (government) and ran an additional regression with two public sector variables instead of one. Only the government coefficient came out positive and significant.

The Australian case thus provides strong support for the hypothesis that public sector employees are more prone to vote for parties of the Left. The sectoral cleavage is a crucial dimension of Australian voting behavior.

Japan

We have not seen any reference in the literature to a possible public/private sector cleavage in Japan. Yet there is ample evidence of such a cleavage in the one survey we have been able to use. There is an initial difference of twelve percentage points in leftist support between the two sectors, which shrinks to eight points after the introduction of control variables. Teachers are not more supportive of the Left than the rest of the public sector, but the sectoral effect is more substantial in the middle class. Japan is, therefore, a case that clearly confirms the public sector's greater propensity to support parties of the Left.

Conclusion

Table 8.1 summarizes our findings on bureaucrats' voting behavior in eleven countries. The hypothesis that public sector employees are more likely to support parties of the Left is clearly borne out in four countries: Britain, the Netherlands, Japan, and Australia. It is clearly disconfirmed in Germany and Switzerland. In Norway, there is a small, direct, but not statistically significant, sectoral effect. France is an ambiguous case; the sectoral variable is related only to socialist vote, not to leftist voting generally. Finally, in Canada, the United States, and Denmark, the sectoral cleavage emerges only in recent elections. It is now very important in Denmark. In no country is there evidence that public sector employees are less likely to vote for parties of the Left. Altogether, considering all elections, the hypothesis is confirmed in four cases (Britain, the Netherlands, Japan, and Australia), disconfirmed in two cases (Germany and Switzerland), and neither clearly confirmed nor disconfirmed in four other cases (France, Canada, the United States, and Denmark). The typical sectoral effect in the eleven countries examined is a five percentage point difference between public and private sector employees.

Do these findings support the budget-maximizing bureaucrat model? We believe that the answer is a qualified yes. Of course, many elections do not produce a sectoral cleavage. But there are many in which a sectoral effect emerges, and that effect, when it occurs, is consistently in the predicted direction. The effect tends to be modest, but that is to be expected. There are multiple determinants of voting behavior, and it would be unrealistic to suppose that any specific factor or consideration could have an overwhelming influence in all elections, in all countries, and in all time periods (Young et al. 1987). The bureaucrat is also influenced by gender, age, class, and religion (to take only socioeconomic variables).

It remains to be explained why the sectoral effect is strong in some instances, weak in others and nonexistent in still others. We would expect the sectoral cleavage to depend on the actual distance separating the Left from the Right, distance that may vary across elections as parties adopt new strategies, as well as on the relative salience of the debate on the size of the state on the political agenda (Blais, Blake, and Dion 1990). As the distance between the Left and the Right varies over time and across countries, the magnitude of the sectoral cleavage may increase or decrease (or even vanish). This is the avenue we intend to explore in our future work. It is the overall pattern that is the concern here, and that pattern is consistent with the assumption that bureaucrats tend to support parties that are more favorable to the growth of public expenditures.

This being said, the sectoral cleavage identified in our study is much smaller than public choice theorists seem to believe. The bureaucratic interest in larger budgets explains only a small fraction of electoral behavior. Indeed the theory is partial, as many theories in political science are. But the fact that it is only partially valid in no way entails that it should be treated as useless.

It could be argued that our analysis underestimates the strength of the sectoral cleavage. Our measure of sectoral employment is, in many cases, quite imperfect. In Germany and Switzerland, the two countries where the hypothesis is disconfirmed, we had to construct a sector variable from a list of occupations, given the absence of a direct question on sectoral employment (see appendix). Measurement error is bound to depress correlations. Likewise, in most cases we have been unable to distinguish the level of government involved within the public sector. It could be that in national elections the sectoral effect is larger among employees of the national government (for evidence of such a pattern in a provincial election, see Blais and Dion 1987). The work we have done so far, however, suggests that these problems are minor and do not substantially affect the results. In the United States, for instance, it is only for the 1984 election that we have direct information on the sectoral employment of the respondent; yet the results obtained for that election are not strongly at variance with those pertaining to earlier elections (Blais, Blake, and Dion 1990).

Finally, the findings reported here could reflect differences in the ideologies of the two sectors rather than divergences of interest. As Harrop and Miller (1987, 194) note: "Perhaps public sector employment only strengthens liberal values which originate elsewhere—in family background, higher education or a post-materialist ideology." And indeed, the public choice model is not alone when it predicts a potential correlation between public sector employment and prostate attitudes. Studies of the recruitment of civil servants indicate the existence of a selection bias: those who are more favorably disposed toward the state are more likely to look for and get a job in the public service (Aberbach, Putnam, and Rockman 1981, 77; Islam and Paquet 1975; Ponzer and Schmidt 1982; Rawls et al. 1975). Analysts of the new middle class contend that its greater liberalism, postmaterialism, and support for state intervention can be accounted for by its being in the nonmarket (state) sector; members of that class wish to expand society's nonmarket (state sector) "by 1) supporting values and political ideologies which favor noneconomic aspects of social life such as New-Left politics and postmaterialist values . . . and 2) encouraging the development of the public sector, the educational system, private welfare, philanthropic organizations, and cultural agencies" (Lamont 1986, 9). The attitudes of public sector employees are explored by Donald Blake in chapter 9 of this volume.

The evidence of a sectoral cleavage in voting behavior, therefore, does not unequivocally demonstrate the validity of the budget-maximizing bureaucrat model. It is simply consistent with it and tends to support it. Whether the pattern uncovered here is best explained by interests or values is a more difficult question and requires a close examination of specific elections, of the issues involved, and of party stands on these issues. This is the subject of another study. What we can conclude at this stage is that the available evidence on voting behavior of bureaucrats indicates that it would be unwise to reject the model. There is a sectoral cleavage, and that cleavage must be considered when it comes to understanding bureaucratic behavior.

APPENDIX

The surveys used in the study were made available by the Inter-University Consortium for Political and Social Research, the Danish Data

Archive, the Dutch Data Archive, and the co-investigators for the 1988 Canadian Election Study. Neither the archives nor the principal investigators are responsible for the analyses or interpretations presented here.

In all countries but Switzerland and Japan, the unit of analysis is the individual; in Switzerland and Japan, we relied on households in order to increase the number of cases. For each country, we included in the multivariate analysis those socioeconomic variables that previous studies had indicated were the most influential. Here are the variables and the major study that was used to select them:

- *Britain:* Homeownership, gender, class, occupation (Whiteley 1986).
- *United States:* race, religion, gender, region, class, union (Stanley Bianco, and Niemi, 1986).
- *Canada:* Region, religion, class, union membership, age, gender, community size (LeDuc 1984).
- *Germany:* Self-Employment, class, union membership, religion (Unwin 1974).
- *Netherlands:* Class, age, education, urbanization, gender, religion.
- *Denmark:* Education, income, urbanization, church attendance, age, gender, union membership (Andersen 1984).
- *France:* Homeownership, class, union membership, religion, income (Michelat and Simon 1985).
- *Switzerland:* Class, language, religion, union membership (Lijphart 1980).
- *Norway:* Class, income, education, union membership, (Lafferty and Knutsen 1984).
- *Australia:* Urbanization, education, union membership, country (birth), religion, class (Aitkin and Kahan 1974).
- *Japan:* Class, education, urbanization, age, gender, union membership (Flanagan 1984).

Information on the employment sector (obtained directly by asking respondents about sector) was available only for Britain (October 1974–1983), the Netherlands, France, Denmark, and Norway. For the United States, information obtained in that fashion was contained in the 1984 survey. For Canada, the employment sector was constructed by adding employees in health and education to the government employee category. In all other cases, we had to construct the sectoral variable by combining occupations such as public administration with those (especially health and education) that are found largely within the public sector. Whenever a list of industries was available, we also tried to include employees of nationalized industries in the public sector.

REFERENCES

Aberbach, Joel D., Robert D. Putnam, and Bert A. Rockman. 1981. *Bureaucrats and politicians in western democracies.* Cambridge, Mass.: Harvard Univ. Press.

Aitkin, Don, and Michael Kahan. 1974. Australia: Class politics in the new world. In *Electoral behavior: A comparative handbook,* ed. Richard Rose. New York: Free Press.

Alt, James, and Janet Turner. 1982. The case of the silk-stocking socialist and the calculating children of the middle class. *British Journal of Political Science* 12:239–48.

Andersen, Jorgen G. 1984. Decline of class voting in class voting? Social classes and party choice in Denmark in the 1970's. *European Journal of Political Research* 12:243–59.

Andeweg, Rudy G. 1982. *Dutch voters adrift: On explanations of electoral change: 1963–1977.* Leyden: Rudy Andeweg.

Aubert, Véronique, Jacques Ozouf, and Mona Ozouf. 1987. La tradition politique des instituteurs. *Pouvoirs* 42:53–65.

Bacot, Paul. 1977. Le comportement électoral des instituteurs: mitterrandistes et giscardiens. *Revue française de science politique.* 27:884–914.

Bennett, James T., and William O. Orzechowski. 1983. The voting behavior of bureaucrats: Some empirical evidence. *Public Choice* 41: 271–83.

Blais, André, Donald E. Blake, and Stéphane Dion. 1990. The public/private sector cleavage in North America. *Comparative Political Studies* 23: 381–403.

Blais, André, and Stéphane Dion. 1987. Les employés du secteur public sont-ils différents? *Revue française de science politique* 37:76–97.

Blais, André, and Richard Nadeau. 1984. L'appui au Parti québécois: évolution de la clientèle de 1970 à 1981. In *Comportement électoral au Québec,* ed. Jean Crête. Chicoutimi: Gaëtan Morin.

Blake, Donald E. 1985. *Two political worlds: Parties and voting in British Columbia.* Vancouver: Univ. of British Columbia Press.

Borcherding, Thomas E., Winston C. Bush, and Robert M. Spann. 1977. The effects on public spending of the divisibility of public outputs in consumption, bureaucratic power, and the size of the tax-sharing group. In *Budgets and bureaucrats: The sources of government growth,* ed. Thomas E. Borcherding. Durham, N.C.: Duke Univ. Press.

Borre, Ole. 1987. Some results from the Danish 1987 election. *Scandinavian Political Studies* 10:345–57.

Buchanan, James M., and Gordon Tullock. 1977. The expanding public sector: Wagner squared. *Public Choice* 31:147–50.

Bush, Winston C., and Arthur T. Denzau. 1977. The voting behavior of bureaucrats and public sector growth. In *Budgets and bureaucrats: The sources of government growth,* ed. Thomas E. Borcherding. Durham, N.C.: Duke Univ. Press.

Cameron, David. 1978. The expansion of the public economy: A comparative analysis. *American Political Science Review* 72: 1243–61.

Castles, Francis C. 1982. Introduction: Politics and public policy. In *The impact of parties: Politics and public policy in democratic capitalist states,* ed. Francis C. Castles. Beverly Hills, Calif.: Sage.

Chevalier, Jean-Jacques. 1958. *Histoire des institutions politiques de la France moderne (1789–1945).* Paris: Dalloz.

Chubb, John E., and Terry M. Moe. 1988. Politics, markets and the organization of schools. *American Political Science Review* 82:1065–87.

Citrin, Jack, and Donald P. Green. 1985. Policy and opinion in California after Proposition 13. *National Tax Journal* 38:15–25.

Daalder, Hans. 1987. The Dutch party system: From segmentation to polarization—and then? In *Party systems in Denmark, Austria, Switzerland, the Netherlands, and Belgium,* ed. Hans Daalder. London: Frances Pinter.

Downs, Anthony. 1957. *An economic theory of democracy.* New York: Harper.

Dunleavy, Patrick. 1980. The political implications of sectoral cleavages and the growth state employment, 2: Cleavage structure and political alignment. *Political Studies* 28:527–49.

Dupeux, Georges. 1952. Le problème des abstentions dans le département du Loir-et-Cher au début de la troisième République. *Revue française de science politique* 2:71–95.

Flanagan, Scott. 1984. Electoral change in Japan: A study of secular realignment. In *Electoral change in advanced industrial democracies: Realignment in dealignment,* ed. Russell J. Dalton, Scott C. Flanagan, and Paul Allen Beck. Princeton, N.J.: Princeton Univ. Press.

Frey, Bruno S., and Werner W. Pommerehne. 1982. How powerful are public bureaucrats as voters? *Public Choice* 38:253–62.

Goodsell, Charles T. 1985. *The case for bureaucracy: A public administration polemic.* Chatham N.J.: Chatham House.

Gramlich, Edward M., and Daniel C. Rubinfeld. 1982. Voting on public spending: Differences between public employees, transfer recipients, and private workers. *Journal of Policy Analysis and Management* 1:516–33.

Hardouin, Patrick. 1983. Le PS: un parti d'intellectuels? *Intervention* no. 5–6:66–76.

Harrop, Martin, and William L. Miller. 1987. *Elections and voters: A comparative introduction.* London: Macmillan.

Heath, Anthony, Roger Jowell, and John Curtice. 1985. *How britain votes.* Oxford: Pergamon.

Irwin, G. A. 1982. Patterns of voting behavior in the Netherlands. In *The economy and politics of the Netherlands since 1945,* ed. R. T. Griffiths. The Hague: Martinus Nijhoff.

Irwin, G. A., and Karl Dittrich. 1984. And the walls came tumbling down: Party dealignment in the Netherlands. In *Electoral change in advanced industrial democracies,* ed. Russell J. Dalton. Princeton, N.J.: Princeton Univ. Press.

Islam, Nasir, and Michel Paquet. 1975. Les étudiants et la fonction publique: une étude des perceptions, des valeurs progressionnelles et de l'attrait comparatif. *Administration publique du Canada* 18:38–54.

Jaffré, Jérome. 1986. Front national: la relève protestataire. In *Mars 1986: la drôle de défaite de la gauche,* ed. Elizabeth Dupoirier and Gérard Grundberg. Paris: Presses univ. de France.

Johnston, Richard. 1979. Bureaucrats and elections. In *Studies in public employment and compensation in Canada,* ed. Meyer We. Bucovetsky. Montreal: Institute for Research on Public Policy.

Kesler, Jean-François. 1980. *Sociologie des fonctionnaires.* Paris: Presses univ. de France.

Ladd, Helen F., and Julie B. Wilson. 1982. Why voters support tax limitations: Evidence from Massachusetts Proposition 2 ½. *National Tax Journal* 35:121–48.

Lafferty, William M., and Oddbjorn Knutsen. 1984. Leftist and rightist ideology in a social democratic state: An analysis of Norway in the midst of the conservative resurgence. *British Journal of Political Science* 14:345–67.

Lamont, Michèle. 1986. New middle class liberalism and autonomy from profit-making: The case of Québec. Paper presented at the annual meeting of the American Sociological Association, New York.

Lavau, Georges, Gérard Grundberg, and Norma Mayer. 1983. *L'univers politique des classes moyennes.* Paris: Presses de la Fondation nationale des sciences politiques.

LeDuc, Lawrence. 1984. Canada: The politics of stable dealignment. In *Electoral change in advanced industrial democracies,* ed. Russell J. Dalton, Scott C. Flanagan, and Paul Allen Beck. Princeton, N.J.: Princeton Univ. Press.

Levy, M. 1975. Voting in California's tax and expenditure limitation initiative. *National Tax Journal* 28:426–37.

Lijphart, Arend. 1980. Language, religion, class and party choice: Belgium, Canada, Switzerland and South Africa compared. In *Electoral participation: A comparative analysis,* ed. Richard Rose. Beverly Hills, Calif.: Sage.

Lipset, Seymour M. 1983. *Political man: The social basis of politics.* London: Heinemann.

Martin, Rosco C. 1933. The municipal electorate: A case study. *Southwestern Social Science Quarterly.*

Mayer, Nona, and Etienne Schweisguth. 1985. Classe, position sociale et vote. In *Explication du vote,* ed. Daniel Gaxie. Paris: Presses de la Fondation nationale des sciences politiques.

Meier, Kenneth John. 1975. Representative bureaucracy: An empirical analysis. *American Political Science Review* 69:526–46.

Michelat, Guy, and Michel Simon. 1985. Religion, classe sociale, patrimoine et comportement électoral: l'importance de la dimension symbolique. In *Explication du vote,* ed. Daniel Gaxie. Paris: Presses de la fondation nationale des sciences politiques.

Ponzer, Barry A., and Warren W. Schmidt. 1982. Determining managerial strategies in the public sector: What kind of people enter the public and private sector? *Human Resources Management* 18:35–43.

Rawls, James R., et al. 1975. A comparison of managers entering or reentering the profit and nonprofit sectors. *Academy of Management Journal* 18:616–23.

Rose, Richard. 1985. The significance of public employment. In *Public employment in western nations,* ed. Richard Rose. Cambridge: Cambridge Univ. Press.

Stanley, Harold W., William T. Bianco, and Richard G. Niemi. 1986. Partisanship and group support over time: A multivariate analysis. *American Political Science Review* 80: 969–76.

Tingsten, Herbert. 1937. *Political behavior: Studies in election statistics.* London: P. S. King and Son.

Tullock, Gordon. 1970. *Private wants, public means: An economic analysis of the desirable scope of government.* New York: Basic Books.

———. 1972. Book review. *Public Choice* 24:19–22.

———. 1974. Dynamic hypothesis on bureaucracy. *Public Choice* 19: 127–31.

Urwin, Derek W. 1974. Germany: Continuity and change in electoral politics. In *Electoral behavior: A comparative handbook,* ed. Richard Rose. New York: Free Press.

Valen, H. 1981. *Valg og politikk*. Oslo: NKS forlaget.

Waldo, Dwight. 1975. Political science: Tradition, discipline, profession, science, enterprise. In *Handbook of Political Science,* ed. Fred I. Greenstein and Nelson W. Polsby. Vol. 1. Reading, Pa.: Addison-Wesley.

Whiteley, Paul. 1986. Predicting the Labour vote in 1986: Social backgrounds versus subjective evaluations. *Political Studies* 34: 82–98.

Wolfinger, Raymond E., and Steven J. Rosenstone. 1980. *Who votes?* New Haven, Conn.: Yale Univ. Press.

Young, Jason, Eugene Borgida, John Sullivan, and John Aldrich. 1987. Personal agendas and the relationship between self-interest and voting behavior. *Social Psychology Quarterly* 50:64–71.

9

DONALD E. BLAKE

Policy Attitudes and Political Ideology in the Public Sector

As William Niskanen reminds us in his contribution to this volume, bureaucratic *behavior* is the central focus of his model of the budget-maximizing bureaucrat (Niskanen 1971). Moreover, that behavior can be explained by the distinctive characteristics of bureaus without reference to the personal characteristics of bureaucrats. In fact, while the assumption that bureaucrats act as if budget maximization was their goal yields testable propositions about budgetary outcomes, the adequacy of the theory does not depend on the empirical accuracy of that assumption.

Nevertheless, the urge to test the assumption is difficult to resist, especially since Niskanen himself speculates about the attitudes of bureaucrats. As he puts it, "Any form of organization, including bureaus, will differentially reward those whose capabilities *and attitudes* best serve the organization, and people will sort themselves out among forms of organization depending on their perceived reward" (ibid., 40, italics added). Since, according to the model, the rewards of bureaucracy go to budget maximizers, presumably bureaucrats will be more favorably disposed toward policy proposals and political ideologies that require state expansion. James Buchanan makes this explicit: "Clearly their interests lie in an expanding governmental sector, and especially one that expands the number of its employees" (1977, 15).

Despite the connotations of the word *bureaucrat,* the ambit of the Niskanen model is not confined to bureaucrats who hold senior

231

policy and management positions in central bureaucracies. Niskanen explicitly covers virtually the entire public sector, including government departments and agencies, organizations providing public services funded partially or completely by government, such as health care, education, and social welfare, and enterprises dependent on public funds for some part of their revenue (Niskanen 1971, 15).

In short, if "organizations differentially reward those whose capabilities and attitudes best serve the organization" (Niskanen 1971, 40), and the interests of public sector employees "lie in an expanding governmental sector" (Buchanan 1977, 15), we would expect to find more support for left-wing ideologies in general, and for increased public expenditures in particular, in the public sector than in the private sector. Moreover, this preference should be apparent at all levels of the public sector.

Existing empirical research on the subject includes two types of studies: those dealing with public/private sector differences on specific policy issues, including government spending, and those focusing on attitudes that are indirectly related to the question of state expansion and expenditure growth such as the left/right ideological dimension. Although relatively little research has been carried out, predictions about specific policy differences are borne out in Sweden and Norway. Sarlvik and Holmberg (1985) report that, in Sweden, state and local government employees disagree with the view that the public sector should be cut (the balance of opinion—percentage that disagrees minus percentage that agrees—is twenty-five and thirty-four percentage points, respectively). In Norway, Lafferty and Knutsen (1984) found significant differences between public and private sector workers on five of six measures of ideology, including an index of government regulation and self-placement on a left/right scale. The difference holds within each occupational group, but is greatest for high-level functionaries. In fact, "not only are public-sector 'bosses' more leftist than their private-sector counterparts, they are also more leftist than private sector workers" (ibid., 364). Attitudes toward social welfare constitute the only exception to this pattern.

The results are more ambiguous in other countries. In Britain, Lewis and Jackson (1985) note that the sectoral variable does not show consistent and significant differences for public expenditure preferences. In Quebec, bureaucrats are no more likely than private sector employees to oppose reductions in public expenditures (Blais and Dion 1987). In the United States, public sector employees are slightly more favorable to increased taxes on high incomes, but the difference is not statistically significant (Meier 1975, 541). Wuthnow and Shrum (1983) also indicate that support for redistributive spending varies positively with government employment among professional-technical workers and managers, but Brint (1984) reports no significant public sector effect among the determinants of support for increased spending on social programs, although younger public sector social and cultural specialists are more likely to have antibusiness attitudes (ibid., 48). Ladd (1979) found no differences between profit and nonprofit sectors on a new liberalism index, which included measures of ideological self-placement and attitudes toward government spending.

Lewis (1990) explored sectoral differences in attitudes toward government spending in eleven policy areas but found significant differences only for military spending and space exploration, with government employees favoring higher spending than the general public. Finally, Blais, Blake, and Dion (1990) found no evidence of a sectoral effect on attitudes toward the trade-off between tax cuts and government spending on services in the United States, once competing determinants were controlled, nor on a scale constructed to measure preferences for more or less government activity in Canada. The same study analyzed left/right self-placement in the 1980 and 1984 U.S. election studies and the 1979 and 1984 Canadian election studies but found a significant sectoral effect only once—in the 1984 Canadian election.

When it comes to issues most directly linked to bureaucratic interests—salaries and working conditions in the public sector— the sectoral cleavage is very stark. In Britain, the relative odds for public employees compared to private employees to prefer Labour rather than Conservatives as the party most likely to ensure a fair wage for themselves range from 1.38 to 24.00, depending on the occupational group (Dunleavy 1980, 537). In Quebec, only 10 percent of public sector employees who had suffered a wage cut imposed by the government agreed with the measure, compared to 51 percent of private sector employees (Blais and Dion 1987).

The most systematic cross-national study of the ideology of bureaucrats is that by Aberbach, Putnam, and Rockman (1981), who compare bureaucrats and politicians in the United States and several European countries on a number of ideological dimensions. Although a version of the public choice perspective— "bureaucrats have a vested interest in expanding the role of the state, and in claiming to offer cures for alleged social ills"—is offered as one of four initial hypotheses (ibid., 118), their evidence places European bureaucrats in the center or right of center. Only for the United States, and then only for career officials and not political appointees (appointed by the Nixon administration), were bureaucrats found to be left of center. However, they also found some differences within the bureaucracy, with U.S. and German bureaucrats in social welfare departments more left-wing than their counterparts in other departments (ibid., 162) and ministry bureaucrats in Sweden more left wing than those in boards and public corporations (ibid., 167). In chapter 4 of this volume, Colin Campbell and Donald Naulls also note the importance of the political appointee in bureaucracy. They found substantial differences in the motivations and role perceptions of Carter and Reagan appointees in the upper reaches of the U.S. administration, with the latter more likely to favor budget cuts.

Another study of elites, using 1977 data for Canada (Ornstein and Stevenson 1984), offers a somewhat broader basis of comparison across occupational sectors by examining business, labor, and state elites (a category that includes both politicians and bureaucrats) regarding attitudes toward the rights of labor, social welfare, and state economic intervention. They found that "business and labour leaders consistently occupy the right and left poles of the ideological continua, and the state elites occupy the middle ground" (ibid., 337). Although not a central concern of the authors, differences within the state elite, where they exist, generally indicate a greater preference by civil servants for the status quo and, among civil servants, greater support for state intervention by those at the federal rather than provincial or municipal levels. Using the same data supplemented by a mass sample survey, Ornstein (1986) confirms these findings and provides information that suggests that civil servants are located to the right of the general public on the three dimensions.

These studies represent a wide variety of theoretical and methodological approaches. The results of the elite studies are equivocal. Aberbach, Putnam, and Rockman (1981) reject the public choice hypothesis. Ornstein (1986) and Ornstein and Stevenson (1984) might also be used to refute it on the grounds that the bureaucratic elites they interviewed have predominantly a status quo orientation regarding labor rights, state economic intervention, and welfare. On the other hand, they are still found to the left of business leaders who occupy similarly high-level positions. Few of the mass-level studies are comparative, and even if they are, comparison is made difficult by differences between countries in the attitudinal measures available. Some studies employ few or no control variables, leaving open the possibility that apparent sectoral differences are the product of differences between sectors in other characteristics known to be linked to ideological differences such as social class position or education. Our ability to generalize is further constrained by differences in the time periods examined in different countries.

This chapter deals with some of these drawbacks in two ways. First, I examine data on policy attitudes over time in Great Britain, the Netherlands, and the United States. That choice was dictated principally by data availability, but happily includes two of the countries where the debate about the role and size of government has been most intense, one of which inspired the budget-maximizing model. Second, I look at data from four countries— Norway, Sweden, Canada, and the United States—for which identical measures of policy attitudes exist and that differ in ways that may help explain the differences between countries revealed by my literature review.

Attitude Cleavages in Great Britain, the Netherlands, and the United States

The lack of published longitudinal information about sectoral differences in political attitudes can be overcome to some extent by examining time-series data on Great Britain, the Netherlands, and the United States.[1] The three countries are the only ones for which repeated measures of attitudes toward the trade-off between taxes and services are available. All three countries also offer measures of left versus right self-placement. However, extensive data on attitudes toward spending cuts are available only for the United States and Great Britain. Finally, the British data offer an extended time series on attitudes toward nationalization.

Sectoral effects were tested in two stages. First, a simple difference of means test was applied to the relevant attitudinal measures, most of which were attitude scales.[2] Then, scale scores were treated as dependent variables in regression analysis that included the accepted predictors of partisanship in each country as additional control variables. The results are reported in table 9.1.

Wherever significant differences appear between public sector and private sector employees, they show the former to be more left wing, more supportive of government spending and nationalization policies, and more opposed to tax cuts.[3] However, these differences seem to be a relatively new phenomenon. In both Great Britain and the Netherlands, there is no evidence of the expected cleavage on ideological self-placement, or on the trade-off between tax cuts and increased spending, until the 1980s. This is also true for the British dimension with no gaps in the time series: nationalization versus privatization. The cleavage appears for the first time with the election of the Thatcher government. Sectoral differences on social spending did not appear until 1983.[4]

Between-country comparisons must be handled cautiously, because there are important differences in the way each dimension is measured in the three countries. Nevertheless, the United States appears to stand out as the country that shows little or no evidence of a sectoral cleavage in attitudes associated with the role and size of the state. It appeared for left/right self-placement in 1974, tax cuts versus improved services in 1984, and social spending in 1986.[5] However, the apparent sectoral effect disappeared when standard predictors of partisanship were controlled.

These results and the literature suggest that the expected cleavage for policy attitudes and values is time and country dependent.

TABLE 9.1
Public Versus Private Sector Attitudinal Cleavages in Great Britain, the Netherlands, and the United States

Country and Year	Zero-Order Cleavage	Cleavage After Controls
Left versus Right self-placement		
Great Britain		
1964	No	No
1966	No	No
1983	Yes	Yes
Netherlands		
1971	No	No
1972	No	No
1981	Yes	Yes
1982	Yes	Yes
United States		
1972	No	No
1974	Yes	No
1976	No	No
1984	No	No
1986	No	No
Cut taxes versus improve services		
Great Britain		
1963	No	No
1966	No	No
1970	No	No
1979	Yes	Yes
1983	Yes	Yes
Netherlands		
1971	No	No
1982	Yes	Yes
United States		
1980	No	No
1984	Yes	No
1986	No	No
Cut versus increase social spending		
Great Britain		
1974	No	No
1979	No	No
1983	Yes	Yes

(continued)

TABLE 9.1   continued

Country and Year	Zero–Order Cleavage	Cleavage After Controls
United States		
1982	No	No
1986	Yes	No
Nationalization versus privatization		
Great Britain		
1964	No	No
1966	No	No
1970	No	No
1974 (Feb.)	No	No
1974 (Oct.)	No	No
1979	Yes	Yes
1983	Yes	Yes

Note: Zero-order cleavages were tested using a difference-of-means test with each attitude scale. Cleavages after controls were tested by treating attitude scores as the dependent variables in multivariate regression analysis. The .05 significance level (two-tailed) was used in each case. See appendix for question wording and control variables. The 1979 sectoral cleavage on nationalization after controls in Great Britain appears only if union membership is excluded from the set of control variables.

This is also true of voting, as André Blais, Stéphane Dion, and I have shown in the previous chapter. Timing is apparently linked to growing support for neoconservative policy options in Western capitalist societies (Hibbs and Madsen 1981). I now turn to a different body of data in order to try to explain differences between countries.

Attitude Cleavages in Canada, Norway, Sweden, and the United States

The data come from the class structure and class consciousness surveys conducted in the early 1980s, a period during which sectoral cleavages in attitudes and voting are more noticeable. Although not identical, the survey instruments have a number of variables in common, which allowed me to construct identical measures of left versus right positioning in each country.[6] A comparison allows me to consider the significance of differences in the size of the public sector as well as differences in political context, especially the strength of left-wing parties. Thus, both Sweden and Norway have been dominated by social democratic parties, but the public sector in Sweden is much larger than in Norway, with total government outlays as a percentage of the GDP in 1985 of 64.5 percent, compared to 48.1 percent (OECD 1985). Socialist parties are weaker in Canada and virtually nonexistent in the United States, but Canada has a larger public sector (47.0 percent versus 36.7 percent). Finally, the rate of state growth also varies considerably across the four countries. From roughly similar starting points in 1960, government expenditures as a percentage of the GDP have grown by 33.5 percentage points in Sweden, 18.2 points in Norway, 17.1 points in Canada, but only 9.7 points in the United States (ibid.).

Since public sector growth is linked to an expanded social role for government and increased economic intervention (Rose 1985), we would expect public sectors in countries such as Sweden to contain a higher proportion of employees sympathetic to government activism than in countries such as the United States. While Canada and Norway have public sectors of similar size, Norway has been characterized as a "social democratic state," where "statist intervention in both the running and redistribution of the economy are demonstrably stronger than in other welfare states" (Lafferty and Knutsen 1984, 348). Conversely, Cameron, studying federal spending in Canada, reports that "the composition of governments—that is, whether Liberals or Conservatives rule— had virtually no effect on the scope of the public economy" (1986, 45–46). In other words, one might expect the public sector in Norway to contain more employees with leftist views than that sector in Canada, on the grounds that recruitment practices in Norway are likely to reflect the explicit state-building orientation of the Norwegian Labour party.[7]

An analysis of the most prominent election issues in the four countries since World War Two (Budge and Fairlie 1983) confirms the fact that issues involving socioeconomic redistribution, government control and planning, and free-enterprise economics form a higher proportion of the total in the Nordic democracies than in

North America, although they are somewhat more prominent in
U.S. elections than in Canadian elections.[8]

As before, I expect to find sectoral differences in political ideology, with public sector employees, on average, located to the left
of private sector ones. However, given the results above and those
of other mass-level studies, as well as my arguments about the
potential significance of differences in the size of the public economy, I anticipate sectoral differences to be more apparent in the
Nordic democracies than in Canada or the United States, and
sharpest of all in Sweden, which has by far the largest public sector
of the four. Finally, I expect differences between sectors to be more
pronounced at the top of the occupational hierarchy.

Analysis and Results

The authors reviewed in the first section acknowledge that ideological differences between the Left and the Right are rich and
varied; however, there is a consensus that they include differences
over trade union rights, the appropriate scope for government
intervention in the economy, and the redistribution of wealth in
society. The class consciousness and class structure surveys contain
several questions that deal with two of these three components.
Factor analysis was used to determine whether the structure of
opinion on these issues was sufficiently similar across the four
countries to justify creation of a left/right scale to be employed in
comparative analysis. As a result, attitudes toward corporate
power and selfishness, the profit motive, rights of workers, workers' control, and government ownership were combined to produce a left versus right dimension.[9]

The surveys did not contain any measures of support for social
egalitarianism or redistribution, but Lafferty and Knutsen (1984)
find this to be the only attitudinal dimension for which there are
no sectoral differences in Norway. Accordingly, the five items
were combined into a simple additive index, running from one
(extreme left) to five (extreme right). The five-item index proved
to be a powerful predictor of support for social democratic parties

in Sweden and Norway, for Democratic versus Republican party identification in the United States, and for Progressive Conservative and New Democratic party identifications in Canada.[10] The index items are only indirectly related to the issue of budget maximization, but it is unlikely that those critical of corporate power, free-enterprise ideology, and the treatment of labor would oppose expansion of the state. Indeed, proponents of the Niskanen model have no difficulty believing that the public sector contains a higher proportion of left wingers than the private sector (Breton 1974, 163; Buchanan 1977, 15).

A comparison of average scores shows that Americans regardless of sector) are, on average, to the right of Swedes, a result that is consistent with a report by Granberg (1987) about left/right self-placement in the two countries. Norwegians and Canadians fall in between. In each country, public sector workers are found to the left of private sector workers; however, only the differences in Norway are statistically significant, according to a test of difference of means.[11] Still, the direction of the differences is consistent with the public choice hypothesis in each country, justifying further analysis. The result for Norway is also gratifying since it confirms the results reported by Lafferty and Knutsen, even though my measure of ideology differs from theirs.

When left/right index scores are used as the dependent variable in regression models that include other potential determinants of ideological position and partisanship, the significance of occupational sector depends on the treatment of union membership (table 9.2). In all four countries, public sector workers are significantly more left wing than private sector workers in regressions that omit union membership. However, when union membership is included as a predictor of ideological position, the sectoral variable declines in magnitude and is significant only in Norway, although it has the expected sign elsewhere.

The expected between-country differences did not materialize, unless one is prepared to argue that only Norway truly exhibits a sectoral effect. While it is risky to compare coefficients across equations because of differences in the other independent variables used, in the models excluding union membership, the public sec-

TABLE 9.2
Sectoral Differences in Ideology, Four Countries

Independent Variable	Canada b_i	Canada b_i^a	Norway b_i	Norway b_i^a	Sweden b_i	Sweden b_i^a	United States b_i	United States b_i^a
Male	.02	.00	...	...	...	...	...	...
Working class	-.21*	-.23*	-.37*	-.38*	-.51*	-.65*	-.21*	-.25*
Education	.15*	.16*	.06*	.06*	.07	.06	.16*	.20*
Income	.06*	.05*	.03	.02	.09*	.07*	.05*	.04*
Age[b]	.05*	.05*	...	...	...	...	...	...
Catholic	-.15*	-.17*	...	...	...	...	-.08	-.07
Jewish	...	...	...	...	...	...	-.17	-.14
Noncharter language	.10*	.10*	...	...	...	...	...	...
Black	...	...	...	...	...	...	-.41*	-.43*
Union membership	-.32*	...	-.18*	...	-.69*	...	-.44*	...
Public sector employment	-.05	-.17*	-.11*	-.16*	-.02	-.15*	-.10	-.16*
(Constant)	2.08*	2.05*	2.67*	2.63*	2.70*	2.42*	2.56*	2.46*
R^2	.12	.09	.11	.10	.22	.14	.15	.11
N	1,825		1,248		704		779	

Note: Dependent variable is respondent score on left/right scale.
*Significant at .05 level (two-tailed).
a. Union membership omitted.
b. Multiplied by 100 to simplify table construction.

tor effects are similar in magnitude in all four countries. If we compare beta weights, subjective class position (the working class is more left wing) appears to have the greatest effect on attitudes in Norway and Sweden, whereas education (with higher education associated with more right-wing views) plays that role in Canada and in the United States. In all four countries, public sector betas are comparable in magnitude to those of the other significant independent variables.

As has been argued elsewhere (Blais, Blake, and Dion 1990; also see Dunleavy 1980, 546), a case can be made for considering occupational sector as determining union membership, justifying its omission from the model, since the public sector tends to be more highly unionized than the private sector in many countries. That is certainly true in Norway (union membership is 79.1 percent in the public sector and 51.5 percent in the private sector) and probably in Canada (59.8 percent unionized in the public sector and 23.4 percent in the private sector). However, unionization in the United States is rather low in both sectors (21.9 percent for the public sector and 15.6 percent for the private sector), whereas in Sweden, union membership is very high in all sectors (100 percent for government industries, 85.8 percent for government agencies, and 76.5 percent for the private sector.)[12] However, rather than attempt to disentangle the effects of the two variables, I proceeded with an analysis using a more refined breakdown of occupations.

A crude public/private sector dichotomy glosses over distinctions within sectors that might be associated with ideological position. For example, both public and private sectors contain members of the "new class of salaried professionals and technically trained managers" (Brint 1984, 30) who have been identified as sources of upper middle-class liberalism. We also have Lafferty and Knutsen's (1984) finding that the ideological gap between sectors in Norway is greatest at the top of the occupational hierarchy. It also seems reasonable from the public choice perspective, since higher-level employees are more likely to be involved in setting organizational goals.

In order to test these possibilities in all four countries, respondent occupations were broken down by the creation of dummy variables for professional, managerial and technical, clerical, white-collar service, unskilled service, and blue-collar categories. Where an occupational group crossed sectoral boundaries, additional dummy variables were created by multiplying the occupational dummy by the sector dummy variable.[13] Adding these variables to those used earlier as predictors of ideological position—except public sector, which is replaced by its occupational components—produced the results in table 9.3. Again, two versions of the model are presented for each country, one of which excludes union membership. Sectoral effects exist whenever the public version of a given occupational group has a statistically significant coefficient. Unlike those reported in table 9.2, the results are basically the same whether union membership is included or not.

The figures in table 9.3 indicate that, in three of the four countries, the expected sectoral effect exists only for those in upper-status occupational categories.[14] The picture is clearest in Canada and Norway, where both professional and managerial/technical categories in the public sector differ significantly from their private sector counterparts. For example, the estimated net coefficient for public sector professionals in Canada is −.24 (that is, .36 − .60), compared to .60 for private sector professionals. For managerial and technical employees in the public sector, the net effect is positive (.16), but substantially less than that for the private sector (.53). In Norway, the sectoral effect extends down to clerical and secretarial grades. Below that there is apparently no effect of the expected kind in either country. In fact, in Norway, public blue-collar workers are significantly *more* right wing than their private sector counterparts.[15]

In Sweden the story for professional categories seems roughly similar, although the relevant coefficients do not reach statistical significance.[16] However, managerial and technical categories appear to be significantly more right wing than other groups regardless of sector. Strictly speaking, public sector clerical and secretarial workers are the only group that is significantly more left wing than its private sector counterpart, and only if union membership is ignored. In the United States, the managerial and technical group also stands out as more right wing than others. However,

Table 9.3
Sectoral Differences in Ideology by Occupation and Country

Independent Variable	Canada b_i	Canada b^a	Norway b_i	Norway b_i^a	Sweden b_i	Sweden b_i^a	United States b_i	United States b_i^a
Professional	.33*	.36*	.56*	.55*	.41	.46	.09	.15
Public professional	-.39*	-.60*	-.67*	-.70*	-.40	-.51	.00	-.11
Managerial & technical	.49*	.53*	.49*	.50*	.39*	.45*	.53*	.61*
Public managerial & technical	-.26*	-.37*	-.34*	-.39*	.07	-.07	-.25	-.26
Clerical/secretarial	.06	.10	.25*	.28*	.24	.31	-.10	-.04
Public clerical/secretarial	.01	-.14	-.22	-.29*	-.29	-.46*	-.07	-.13
White-collar	-.22	-.31	.68	.79	.19	.25	.18	.14
Public white-collar	.26	.18	-.60	-.72	...	...	...	...
Unskilled	-.22	-.18	-.19	-.10	.00	.09	-.27*	-.22
Public unskilled	-.05	-.22	-.08	-.10	-.04	-.11	.37	.33
Blue-collar	.07	.00	-.04	-.04	-.01	-.02	-.08	-.14
Public blue-collar	.08	.00	.28*	.26	.16	.12	-.08	-.03
Union	-.29*		-.18*		-.52*		-.39*	
(Constant)	2.15*	2.11*	2.73*	2.67*	2.51*	2.18*	2.79	2.75*
R^2	.15	.13	.15	.14	.22	.19	.20	.17
N	1,825		1,248		638		789	

Note: Regression coefficients were obtained by adding occupation variables to the models in table 9.2, omitting "public sector." Coefficients for control variables were omitted to simplify presentation.

*Significant at .05 level (two-tailed).

a. Union membership omitted.

while the signs of the public sector interaction terms for this category hint at greater leftism in the public sector, they are not statistically significant in either model.[17]

Conclusion

These results offer some support for the hypothesis that public sector workers have more left-wing views than those in private sector employment. Their credibility is enhanced by examination of time-series data in three countries and by a four-country comparison using the same measure of ideological position. However, the differences between countries and over time suggest that there are contextual differences that must be examined before the public choice hypothesis can claim wider support. Sectoral differences in policy attitudes related to the role of the state seem to be a relatively recent phenomenon, one linked to the increased importance of size of state issues in public debate. As for between-country differences, it was anticipated that public sector size and the character of the party system would be two of the differences in context that might affect the importance of the sectoral cleavage. However, that proved to be only partially correct.

The size of the public sector, by itself, does not seem to be significant. Even though the United States, with the smallest public sector and slowest rate of state growth of the four, shows little evidence of sectoral effects when occupations within sectors are broken down, they are more apparent in Norway and Canada than in Sweden, which has the largest and fastest growing public sector.

The similarity of results for Canada and Norway—and again, Sweden's peculiarity—also suggest that a long history of left-right conflict dominated by social democratic parties is neither necessary nor sufficient for the emergence of ideological cleavages between employment sectors. The case of the United States is instructive here as well, since ideological differences between sectors are limited compared to Canada, yet it arguably has had more of a history of ideologically based political debate. However, we should acknowledge that the timing of the surveys (1980 for the United States and 1983 for Canada) coincided with a period when size of the state issues were important in both.

The results confirm the impression that, so far as political attitudes are concerned, sectoral differences may be confined to those in higher status occupations. That certainly seems to be true for Canada and Norway—and perhaps for Sweden. The lack of a similar pattern in the United States is not easy to understand. Following Brint (1984) one might look to younger cohorts in social science and arts-related public sector occupations for signs of greater left-wing attitudes, but that could not be done with these data.[18] Perhaps the relatively small size of the U.S. public sector, which means there are proportionately fewer professionals as well as managerial and technical personnel employed in the provision of services such as health, gives these categories a different character than in countries with larger state sectors. Rose (1985, table 1.5) reports that 48.7 percent of public employees in the United States are engaged in the provision of health, education, and welfare services, compared to 53.8 percent in Sweden. However, the U.S. public sector has proportionately more teachers than any European country (ibid., 17). Another possible compositional effect could have been produced by the presence of proportionately more military personnel in the U.S. public sector, but the data did not permit this to be checked.

Finally, we might consider these results in a somewhat different light. Predictions regarding the attitudes and behavior of bureaucrats were developed mainly by analyzing the utility functions of those in senior bureaucratic positions with budgetary responsibilities. By extending coverage to the entire public sector, I have tapped into an area with more complex interactions and incentives, such as those linked to differences in the functions performed by organizations within the public sector. Given this complexity, we perhaps should be more impressed with the evidence of the sectoral divisions we do find. Wherever sectoral differences exist, with the exception of the attitudes of Norwegian blue-collar workers, they always find public sector employees to the left of private sector employees, not the other way around. Moreover, they are more apparent among members of occupations most likely to be involved in policy making.

APPENDIX
Question Wording and Control Variables
for Great Britain, the Netherlands, and the United States

Left/Right Self-Placement

Great Britain: In 1964 and 1966, respondents were asked to locate themselves on a left/center/right scale and were scored 1, 2, or 3, depending on the choice made. In 1983 they were asked to locate themselves on a scale running from −10 on the extreme Left to 10 on the extreme Right.

Netherlands: In 1971 and 1972, respondents were scored from 1 to 7 from left to right. In 1981 and 1982, the range was from 1 to 10.

United States: Respondents were asked to place themselves on a scale running from 1 (extremely liberal) to 7 (extremely conservative).

Cutting Services Versus Improving Services

Great Britain: In 1979, respondents were asked to choose among seven responses from "very strongly in favour of cutting taxes" to "very strongly in favour of keeping up services." In 1983, respondents were asked to place themselves on a scale running from −10, indicating support for increased spending on social services, to 10, indicating a preference for lower taxes.

The Netherlands: In 1971, respondents were dichotomized according to whether they supported raising taxes for general services or supported lowering taxes. In 1982, they were scored from 1 to 5 on the basis of degree of agreement or disagreement with the proposition that income taxes should be raised to keep social services.

United States: In 1980, respondents were scored on a 7-point scale running from "government should provide fewer services, even in areas such as health and education, in order to reduce spending" to "government should continue the services it now provides even if it means no reduction in spending." In 1984, the ends of the scale were "the government should provide fewer services, even in areas such as health and education in order to reduce spending" and "it is important for the government to provide many more services, even if it means an increase in spending."

Cutting Versus Increasing Social Spending

Great Britain: In 1974 and 1979, respondents were asked whether social services and benefits should be cut back a lot, cut back a bit, stay as they are, or whether more social services and benefits were needed. To facilitate comparison with U.S. data, in 1983 a social-spending scale was created by combining responses to questions dealing with cuts or increases to spending on poverty, pensions, and education.

United States: Scales were constructed in 1982 and 1986 by combining responses on questions about government spending on social security, food stamps, and student loans.

Nationalization Versus Privatization

Great Britain: From 1964 to 1983 respondents chose from among four options—a lot more industries should be nationalized; only a few more industries should be nationalized; no more industries should be nationalized, but industries that are now nationalized should stay nationalized; and some of the industries that are now nationalized should become private companies. In 1983, they were also asked to choose a position from −10 (nationalize) to 10 (privatize).

Control Variables

Great Britain: In addition to public versus private sector, the control variables used were gender, home ownership, union membership, subjective class, and position in the occupational hierarchy (Whiteley 1986).

Netherlands: In addition to public versus private sector, the control variables used were frequency of church attendance, union membership, subjective class, gender, and age (Irwin 1982).

United States: In addition to public versus private sector, the control variables used were race, subjective class, religion, gender, and an interaction term distinguishing white southerners (Stanley, Bianco, and Niemi 1986).

Scale Construction in Canada, Norway, Sweden, and the United States

The questions used to construct the left/right index for Canada, Norway, Sweden, and the United States and the preamble to them were worded as follows (in translation):

> We should like to ask you a few questions about possible changes in the way the economy and business are run. For each of the following statements

tell me if you strongly agree, somewhat agree, somewhat disagree, or strongly disagree with it.

• Corporations benefit owners at the expense of workers and consumers.

• During a strike, management should be prohibited by law from hiring workers to take the place of strikers.

• It is possible for a modern society to run effectively without the profit motive.

• If given the chance, nonmanagement employees at the place where you work could run things effectively without bosses.

• The energy crisis will not be fully solved until the government controls the major energy companies.

NOTES

1. The data are all from national election studies made available by the Inter-University Consortium for Political and Social Research to the University of British Columbia Data Library. Neither the archives nor the principal investigators are responsible for the analyses or interpretations presented here.

2. The only exceptions are for the Netherlands. Left versus right self-placement in 1971 and 1972 and the trade-off question in 1971 were coded as dichotomies.

Specific questions about industrial sectors were used to classify respondents as public or private sector in Great Britain and the Netherlands for all years, and for the United States in 1984 and 1986. For earlier years, a method based on census industrial classifications was used (Blais, Blake, and Dion 1990).

3. Where possible, interaction terms were used to test for within-sector differences associated with occupation or type of bureaucracy (central administration versus state enterprise). The only significant differences of this type appeared for Britain in 1983. State enterprise employees were more hostile to privatization than the public sector in general, while both were more hostile than private sector workers. Public sector workers in teaching and health fields were significantly more left wing than other public sector workers.

4. This generalization should be treated cautiously, since attitudes toward social spending in Great Britain were measured in a different fashion in 1983 (see appendix).

5. The U.S. data also contained questions on spending for defense, foreign aid, environmental protection, crime fighting, the space program, cities, blacks, and programs to curb drug abuse. There was no sectoral effect for any of them.

6. The data were made available by the Inter-University Consortium for Political and Social Research to the University of British Columbia Data Library. Neither the archives nor the principal investigator, Erik Olin Wright, are responsible for the analyses or interpretations presented here. The U.S. and Swedish surveys were conducted in 1980, that for Norway in 1982, and for Canada in 1983.

7. The reasoning in this paragraph is the same whether we consider attitudes to be the product of self-interest associated with occupational sector or an artifact of self-selection into public employment. In a political context, with more ideological debate, recognition of self-interest and consciousness of personal ideological commitments should both be more apparent. For an interesting discussion of the self-interest/self-selection question for Britain, see Alt and Turner (1982).

8. Calculations using data in Budge and Fairlie (1983, tables 2.2, 2.3) show that the issues in these categories constituted 10.8 percent of the total number of salient election issues in Canada, 28 percent in Norway, 46.7 percent in Sweden, and 21.6 percent in the United States.

9. The responses to each question were scored 1 for strongly agree, 2 for somewhat agree, 4 for somewhat disagree, and 5 for strongly disagree. Each item had a score of at least 0.45 on the first principal component in each country. The scale was constructed so that higher scores were given for right-wing answers. For exact question wording, see the appendix.

10. These conclusions were reached after including the left/right index score as one of the independent variables in regressions on measures of partisanship in each country. The other independent variables were chosen on the basis of work by Borre (1984), LeDuc (1984), Stanley, Bianco, and Williams (1986), and Sarlvik and Holmberg (1985). These variables were also used in a subsequent analysis that treats the left/right score as the dependent variable.

The variables male, working class, Catholic, Jewish, noncharter language, black, union member, and public sector are all dummy variables; age is actual age in years, and education and income are ordinal variables based on rankings provided in the data set. The working-class classification is based on a subjective measure of class position. Noncharter language identifies respondents in Canada whose mother tongue is neither English nor French. Analysis of the Canadian data also included controls for region. However, their presence in the regression made no difference to the public sector effect, and they were omitted in the analyses reported here. In Sweden and Norway, degree of sympathy scores for the programs of social democratic and labor parties were used as dependent variables. The dependent variables in the United States regression were a simple Democratic versus other (including independent) dichotomy and an ordinal measure from strong Democrat through independent to strong Republican. The choice of dependent variable makes little difference in the results.

The presence of three significant parties in Canada dictated the use of three dependent variables—Progressive Conservative versus other identification, NDP versus other, and Liberal versus other. A left/right score was statistically significant in regressions involving the first two, but not for the Liberals.

11. When each item in the index is considered separately, significant sectoral differences appear for Canada on corporate greed and corporate power; for Norway on the profit motive and controlling oil companies; for Sweden on corporate greed and prohibiting hiring strikebreakers; and for the United States only on corporate greed.

12. Except for the U.S. private sector, the sample figures for Sweden and the United States are similar to those reported by Rose (1985, table 1.6) using official sources for 1980—89 percent and 82 percent, respectively, for public and private sectors in Sweden, and 22 percent and 23 percent in the United States.

13. The white-collar service category is numerically significant only in Sweden, where all but one member was classified as public sector. In Canada and Norway, the group is much smaller and is divided evenly between public and private sectors, hence the relevant public sector interaction term appears only in the equations for these two countries. The residual category not represented in the regressions by a separate dummy variable consists of a mixture of private sector occupations containing relatively few members each: clergy, creative and entertainment, and crafts.

14. This conclusion is also supported for Norway by simply adding a working-class/public sector interaction term to the models reported in table 9.2. The possibility of functional differences within the public sector has been examined by the addition of separate terms for teachers and medical workers. In both Norway and Canada, teachers prove to be significantly more left wing than other public sector workers, but the latter are still more left wing than the private sector as whole. In Canada and the United States, it is possible to divide public sector employees by level (federal or provincial). The only difference appears for Canada, where federal employees are significantly more right wing than provincial employees. However, the effect is probably due to the fact that teachers are overwhelmingly found in the provincial public sector.

13. With union membership included, the public blue-collar variable just misses statistical significance ($t = 1.78$).

16. The t-ratios are 1.64 and -1.80 for the professional coefficient and public sector interaction term, respectively, in the model without union membership; and rather less, 1.48 and -1.46, if union membership is included.

17. The t-ratio for the public managerial and technical term is -1.34 with union membership included and -1.38 with union membership excluded.

18. A plausible alternative, estimation of a model incorporating a variable to isolate those in the teaching profession, showed no significant difference in the attitudes of teachers compared to others in the public sector.

REFERENCES

Aberbach, Joel D., Robert D. Putnam, and Bert A. Rockman. 1981. *Bureaucrats and politicians in western democracies.* Cambridge, Mass.: Harvard Univ. Press.

Alt, James, and Janet Turner. 1982. The case of the silk-stocking socialists and the calculating children of the middle class. *British Journal of Political Science* 12:239–48.

Blais, André, Donald E. Blake, and Stéphane Dion. 1990. The public/private sector cleavage in North America: The political behavior and attitudes of public sector employees. *Comparative Political Studies* 23:381–403.

Blais, André, and Stéphane Dion. 1987. Les employés du secteur public, sont-ils différents? *Revue française de science politique* 37:76–97.

Borre, Ole. 1984. Critical electoral change in Scandinavia. In Dalton, Flanagan, and Beck 1984, 330–64.

Breton, Albert. 1974. *The economic theory of representative government.* New York: Macmillan.

Brint, Steven. 1984. "New class" and cumulative trend explanations of the liberal political attitudes of professionals. *American Journal of Sociology* 90:30–71.

Buchanan, James M. 1977. Why does government grow? In *Budgets and bureaucrats: The sources of government growth,* ed. Thomas E. Borcherding, 3–18. Durham, N.C.: Duke Univ. Press.

Budge, Ian, and Dennis J. Fairlie. 1983. *Explaining and predicting elections: Issue effects and party strategies in twenty-three democracies.* London: Allen and Unwin.

Cameron, David. 1986. The growth of government spending: The Canadian experience in comparative perspective. In *State and society: Canada in comparative perspective,* ed. Keith Banting. Toronto: Univ. of Toronto Press.

Dalton, Russell J., Scott C. Flanagan, and Paul Allen Beck, eds. 1984. *Electoral change in advanced industrial democracies.* Princeton, N.J.: Princeton Univ. Press.

Dunleavy, Patrick, 1980. The political implications of sectoral cleavages and the growth of state employment, 2, Cleavage structure and political alignment. *Political Studies* 28:527–49.

Granberg, Donald. 1987. A contextual effect in political perception and self-placement on an ideology scale: Comparative analyses of Sweden and the U.S. *Scandinavian Political Studies* 10:39–60.

Hibbs, Douglas A., Jr., and Henrik Jess Madsen. 1981. Public reactions to the growth of taxation and government expenditure. *World Politics* 33:413–35.

Irwin, G. A. 1982. Patterns of voting behavior in the Netherlands. In *The economy and politics of the Netherlands since 1945,* ed. R. T. Griffiths, 199–222. The Hague: Martinus Nijhoff.

Ladd, Everett Carll, Jr. 1979. Pursuing the new class: Social theory and survey data. In *The New Class?* ed. B. Bruce-Briggs, 101–22. New York: McGraw-Hill.

Lafferty, William M., and Oddbjorn Knutsen. 1984. Leftist and rightist ideology in social democratic states: An analysis of Norway in the midst of the conservative resurgence. *British Journal of Political Science* 14:345–67.

LeDuc, Lawrence. 1984. Canada: The politics of stable dealignment. In Dalton, Flanagan, and Beck 1984, 402–24.

Lewis, Alan, and Diane Jackson. 1985. Voting preferences and attitudes on public expenditures. *Political Studies* 33:457–66.

Lewis, Gregory B. 1990. In search of the Machiavellian milquetoasts: Comparing attitudes of bureaucrats and ordinary people. *Public Administration Review* 50:220–27.

Meier, Kenneth John. 1975. Representative bureaucracy: An empirical analysis. *American Political Science Review* 69:526–46.

Niskanen, William A. 1971. *Bureaucracy and representative government.* Chicago: Aldine Atherton.

OECD. 1985. *Historical Statistics: 1960–1985.* Paris: Organization for Economic Cooperation and Development.

Ornstein, Michael. 1986. The political ideology of the Canadian capitalist class. *Canadian Review of Sociology and Anthropology* 23:182–209.

Ornstein, Michael, and H. M. Stevenson. 1984. Ideology and public policy in Canada. *British Journal of Political Science* 14:313–44.

Rose, Richard. 1985. The significance of public employment. In *Public employment in western nations,* ed. Richard Rose, 1–53. Cambridge: Cambridge Univ. Press.

Sarlvik, Bo, and Soren Holmberg. 1985. Social Determinants of party choice in Swedish elections, 1956–1982. Paper presented to Congrés de l'Association internationale de science politique, Paris.

Stanley, Harold W., William T. Bianco, and Richard G. Niemi. 1986. Partisanship and group support over time: A multivariate analysis. *American Political Science Review* 80:969–76.

Whiteley, Paul. 1986. Predicting the labour vote in 1983: Social backgrounds versus subjective evaluations. *Political Studies* 34:82–98.

Wuthnow, Robert, and Wesley Shrum. 1983. Knowledge workers as a "new class." *Work and Occupations* 10:471–87.

10

JEAN-MICHEL COUSINEAU AND
ANNE-MARIE GIRARD

Public Sector Unions, Government Expenditures, and the Bureaucratic Model

The Niskanen work, *Bureaucracies and Representative Government* (1971), makes explicit references to labor market, bureaus, and their relations with their factor suppliers. "For several reasons," it argues, "the bureaucracy is the last stronghold of wage and factor price discrimination" (31). The work continues by explaining the source of such discrimination:

> The first basis for wage and factor price discrimination is that bureaus are often monopoly suppliers of some services. These bureaus are thus also monopoly buyers of those labor skills and material factors that are specialized in the production of these monopolized services. Infantry officers are paid less than pilots in the same staff or management position, for example, because infantry officers have few alternative employments where they can market their specialized skills. . . . Hospitals discriminate in their recruitment of nurses, and local governments discriminate in hiring several types of personnel. (31)

In short, the Niskanen model predicts, in the absence of a union, a lower wage in the public sector than in the private sector. However, contrary to the standard monopsonistic model in the private sector, it predicts higher employment than otherwise would be in a competitive profit-seeking firm: "Such opportunities for monopsonistic discrimination are exploited by bureaus, because, as I shall demonstrate later, this increases both the bureau's budget and output" (31). In the presence of a union, however, wage discrimina-

257

tion may well disappear as far as "unions have destroyed most wage discrimination (among those employees with comparable skills in a given firm) in the private labor market." Thus, the Niskanen model predicts lower wages, but higher employment in the public sector with the absence of a union. Unions, on their part, might eliminate part or all of the wage discrimination effect. Finally, as an extension to the Niskanen model, we might predict that unions in a bureaucracy, as representatives of a part of the bureaucracy, will increase the pressure on the bureau's budget and output. In this chapter, we first review the evidence on the incidence of unions on compensation, employment, and output in the public sector in order to determine whether these predictions receive empirical support. Our first four sections cover the literature on wages, fringe benefits, employment, and government expenditures. The last section discusses the consistency of these results with alternative models. Finally, our conclusion analyzes the consistency between those same empirical results and the Niskanen model.[1]

Union Wages Effects

The impact of public sector unionism on wages is not unambiguous. First, it is true that public sector unionism faces a particularly inelastic demand for its services. However, its bargaining power will largely depend upon the legal framework in which it is inserted. Unions without the legal right to strike, and that face large penalties for pursuing a strike, cannot be that powerful. However, public sector unionism, as well as unions in the private sector, must bring to their members some return for their dues. Higher wages than otherwise is a form of return for an asset that is not free. Thus, from a strict monetary perspective, unions must bring up a wage differential in order to subsist. Studies about the impact of public sector unionism on wages clearly show that, in most circumstances, it has a positive and significant impact on public sector wages. Most of these studies proceed by estimating a wage equation model controlling for different independent variables, which include a union status variable. The estimated impact of public sector unions on wages is further derived from the regression coefficient of this union status variable.[2]

As shown in table 10.1, except for municipal workers, public sector unionism brings about a 5 percent to 7 percent wage differential for public sector employees (fire fighters, police officers, hospital workers, and teachers). For municipal workers, however, the impact appears to be somewhat larger. It falls in the range of 9 percent and even gets to the 15 percent level or so that is currently estimated in the private sector (Lewis 1988). All in all, the estimated impact of public sector unions on wages appears to be, at most, equal to the estimated impact of private sector unions. In most cases, with the exception of a few municipal employees, it is significantly lower.[3] For fire fighters, two studies found quite low estimates—below 2 percent (Ichniowski 1980); Ashenfelter 1971) for very large cities. Mehay and Gonzalez (1986) and Ashenfelter (1971) found close to a 10 percent differential (for medium-sized cities). In the pioneer work of Ashenfelter, one must note, however, that only one control variable was introduced in the model—cost of living.

In the case of police officers, we also find two relatively low estimates, but one is larger than 10 percent. Hospital workers received an average of 6.8 percent wage differential, covering non-professional workers, registered nurses, and other categories of hospital worker. Teachers also received a 6 percent wage differential that varied between 0.6 percent and 21 percent. This former estimate (Baugh and Stone 1982) diverges from the whole set of results, but such an estimate was to be expected, given the inflationary period in which wage settlements were negotiated. Cousineau and Lacroix (1977) showed that wage elasticities, with regard to inflationary expectations, were quite large in the Canadian public sector. Wilton (1986) also attributes this unusual elasticity to catch-up adjustments. All in all, every study concluded in equal wage adjustments of public and private sectors over a long-range period (e.g., full cycle). Freund (1974) also found an insignificant impact of public sector union variables on the differential rate of change of money wage growth.[4]

In summary, our conclusions stand for a lower wage effect of unions in the public sector. Further evidence for Canada is given

TABLE 10.1
Effect of Public Unions on Public Sector Wages
(percent)

Study	Effect of Unions on Wages
FIRE FIGHTERS	
Ashenfelter (1971, tables 2 and 3)	
Cities over 50,000	1.0
Cities 25,000–50,000	9.5
Ehrenberg (1973, table 4)	7.5
Ichniowski (1980, table 1)	1.8
Mehay and Gonzalez (1986, table 3)	9.4
Mean	5.8
POLICE	
Bartel and Lewin (1981, table 1)	6.4
Ehrenberg and Goldstein (1975, table 1)	6.9
Feuille and Delaney (1986, table 1)	1.4
Hall and Vanderporten (1977, table 1)	3.1
Kearney and Morgan (1980, table 2)	1.0
Mehay and Gonzalez (1986, table 2)	10.9
Mean	5.0
HOSPITAL WORKERS	
Becker (1979, table 2)	
Nonprofessional workers	7.0
Cain et al. (1981, table 8)	
Registered nurses	1.0
Licensed practical nurses	13.0
Nonprofessional workers	4.0
Feldman and Scheffler (1982, table 3)	
Secretaries	11.0
Housekeepers	8.0
Registered nurses	6.2
Licensed practical nurses	6.8
Fottler (1977, table 3)	
Nonprofessional workers	4.5
Mean	6.8
TEACHERS	
Baird and Landon (1972, p. 415)	4.9
Baugh and Stone (1982, table 1)	
1974	7.0
1977	21.0

Study	Effect of Unions on Wages
Chambers (1977, table 1)	
Unified districts	7.7
Elementary districts	12.5
Frey (1975, table 9)	0.6
Hall and Carroll (1973, p. 836)	1.8
Holmes (1976, p. 330)	7.0
Kasper[a]	2.0
Lipsky and Drotning (1973, p. 30)	2.4
Schmenner (1973, table 1)	11.7
Thornton (1971, table 2)	3.7
Mean	6.9
OTHER MUNICIPAL WORKERS	
Edwards and Edwards (1982a, table A-3)	
Sanitation workers	9.1
Edwards and Edwards (1982b, table 2)	
Sanitation workers	7.7
Ehrenberg and Goldstein (1975, table 1)	
Financial administration	8.5
General control	6.8
Streets and highways	16.0
Sewerage and sanitation	16.0
Parks and Recreation	13.6
Water supply	5.1
Schmenner (1973, table 3)	0.0
Valetta (1989, p. 436)[b]	5.0
Zax and Ichniowski (1988, table 12.8)[c]	4.8
Zax (1989, table 2)	8.5
Mean	8.4

a. Estimate from Freeman (1986).

b. Includes police, fire, sanitation (other than sewerage), streets and highways, finance, and general control personnel.

c. Includes police, fire, streets and highways, sanitation, and refuse collection departments.

by the study of Simpson (1985), which finds a substantive and quite significant negative impact of a public sector dichotomic variable in its estimated equations for both public and private unionized workers. The magnitude of this impact is in the order of −5.3 percent (ibid., table 2). Thus public sector unionism cannot, on the whole, be blamed for having a higher wage differential than what private sector unionism can bring.[5]

A few other auxiliary results are also worth attention. First, as shown in table 10.2, the significant effect of a monopsony variable in eight out of nine studies. This is evidence of the presence of monopsony power of governments in the labor market for public employees.[6] Such results do have important implications. They show that, while there is a comparison being made between union and nonunion wages in the private sector, there is also a comparison being made between union monopoly wages and (more or less) competitive wages. In the public sector, the same estimates rather suggest that the comparison is between union wages and monopsony wages.[7]

Another important empirical result reported in numerous studies is that public sector unionism brings wage differentials for women especially (Becker 1979; Freeman 1985; Smith 1977). Given the overwhelming evidence on wage discrimination for female workers in the private sector, this also confirms that a slight wage differential for public female workers is evidence of a more efficient wage policy in that sector, and that public sector unions significantly contribute to such a policy.

Finally, table 10.3 provides additional information on the impact of city managers on wages and fringe benefits. In both cases it shows that the presence of a city manager has a positive impact on wage differentials. It must also be noted that the size of this impact is comparable to, if not greater than, the public sector union impact on wages. Unions do not appear to be the sole agents of wage differentials between the public and private employees. On the whole, the overall results of the impact of public sector unionism on wages do not appear to be as great as many might expect at first.

Fringe Benefits

Research in the field of fringe benefits is not as extensive as in the case of wage differentials. However, as shown in table 10.4, if public sector unionism has anything to do with labor costs, it

TABLE 10.2
Existence of a Monopsony Variable

Study	Government Function Studied	Affects Wages
Becker (1979, table 2)	Hospital nonprofessional workers	No[a]
Delaney (1988, table 7)	Teachers	Yes
Feldman and Scheffler (1982, table 3)	Hospital workers	Yes
Fottler (1977, table 2)	Hospital workers	Yes
Hall and Vanderporten (1977, table 1)	Police	Yes
Landon and Baird (1971, table 1)	Teachers	Yes
Lipsky and Drotning (1973, table 2)	Teachers	Yes
Mehay and Gonzalez (1986, tables 2,3)	Police and fire fighters	Yes
Baird and Landon (1972, table 1)	Teachers	Yes

a. Statistically insignificant.

TABLE 10.3
Effect of City Managers on Public Sector Wages and Fringe Benefits
(percent)

Study	Government Function Studied	Effects of City Managers
Edwards and Edwards (1982b, table 2)	Sanitation workers	
	Wages	+1.8[a]
	Fringe benefits	+9.3[a]
Ehrenberg (1973, table 4)	Fire fighters, wages	+7.4
Ehrenberg and Goldstein (1975, table 1)	General municipal workers, wages	
	Financial administration	+5.1
	General control	+17.4
	Streets and highways	+3.7
	Sewerage and sanitation	+1.9[a]
	Parks and recreation	+4.6
	Water supply	+1.3[a]
Feuille and Delaney (1986, p. 239)	Police, wages	+7.5
Feuille, Delaney and Hendricks (1985, p. 19)	Police, fringe benefits	+19.5
Ichniowski (1980, p. 210)	Fire fighters	
	Wages	+3.9
	Fringe benefits	+7.4

a. Statistically insignificant.

seems to be in the area of fringe benefits. Feuille, Delaney, and Hendricks (1985) and Edwards and Edwards (1982b) find at least a 25 percent effect of public sector unions on fringe benefits. Becker (1979), Ichniowski (1980), and Bartel and Lewin (1981) find a lower estimate for the fringe benefits effects, but it is found larger than their wage effects. The respective comparative numbers are 8.8 percent versus 7.0 percent, 8.2 percent versus 1.8 percent, and 8.9 percent versus 6.4 percent. Finally, Cain et al. (1981) and Hunter and Rankin (1988) mention a much larger impact of public sector unions on fringe benefits than on wages (not quantified in percentage by the authors).

Following the work of Bartel and Lewin (1981) and Ichniowski

TABLE 10.4
Effect of Public Unions on Public Sector Benefits
(percent)

Study	Government Function Studied	Effects of Unions
Bartel and Lewin (1981, table 3)	Police	+8.9
Becker (1979, table 3)	Hospital workers	+8.8
Edwards and Edwards (1982b, table 2)	Sanitation workers	+26.0
Feuille, Delaney, and Hendricks (1985, p. 19)	Police	+31.3
Ichniowski (1980, table 3)	Fire fighters	+8.2

(1980), public sector unions influence each of the three main components of fringe benefits; that is to say, time paid but not worked (sick leave, vacation, holidays, etc.), insurance premiums, and pension funds. Fringe benefits have a long history as a major part of a public sector employee compensation package. Union effects may well exacerbate politicians' interest in differing costs (hidden costs) or reflect the preference of long-tenure workers.

Employment Effects

The public sector union effect on employment is also ambiguous, at least in theory. Given the negative elasticity of employment to wages, an indirect effect of public sector union on employment is negative. Ceteris paribus, increases in labor costs are expected to reduce employment. But given the potential for union workers and their union representative to influence labor demand for their product, it is also expected that public sector unionism will contribute to produce a net positive effect on public employment.

At least five studies report a positive net effect of public sector unions on public employment: Zax (1985; 1989), Masters and Robertson (1988), Eberts (1984), and Benecki (1978). However, one study finds a large negative and significant impact (−30 percent, Benecki) for very large cities (over 100,000). In fact, in that study,

the net positive effect of public sector unions is found to be significant only in the case of small size cities (between 10,000 and
24,000). Eberts (1984) also finds a positive and significant effect
but does not provide the full information on his specification and
on other estimated coefficients. The Masters and Robertson study
applies to international data but uses a union power index rather
than the standard degree of unionization or union status variables
that would allow a precise percentage estimate of public sector
unionization impact on public employment. Finally, Zax and Zax
and Ichniowski provide the 4.3 percent, 3.1 percent, and 11 percent estimates, respectively, that are shown in table 10.5. This
same table also reports unnoticed and possibly unexpected effects
of public sector unionism; that is, work overload. For teachers,

TABLE 10.5
Effect of Public Unions on
Public Sector Employment and Work Load
(percent)

Study	Government Function Studied	Effects of Unions
Employment		
Valetta (1989, p. 436)	Police, fire, sanitation (other than sewerage), streets and highways, finance and general control personnel	+19.0
Zax (1985, table 3)	General municipal workers	+4.3
Zax and Ichniowski (1988, table 12.1)	Four functions in the municipalities	+11.0
Zax (1989, table 2)	General municipal workers	+3.1
Workload		
Chambers (1977, table 1)	Teachers	+1.5
Hall and Carroll (1973, pp. 840–41)	Teachers	+4.9
Register (1988, table 3)	Hospital workers[a]	+16.5

a. Public and private hospitals.

direct and indirect employment effects combine in such a way that the ratio of teachers to pupils falls in the presence of a public sector bargaining unit. Chambers (1977) also finds a similar but smaller effect.

Finally, in a study of hospital costs, Register (1988) found that day patients per hospital workers raised quite dramatically with the level of unionization. Thus, for those two well-defined sectors, unionization does not contribute to overemployment per se but to the overloading of organized workers.

Public Expenditures

Given the previous results on different aspects of public sector expenditures, one is led to conclude that public sector unions might well increase total budget expenditures. In fact, unions do have an effect on wages and fringe benefits as well as public employment, even if in certain special circumstances the employment effect is compensated by workload effects. But three studies directly examined the total effect of public sector unionism on public expenditures. As shown in table 10.6, all but one study (Benecki 1978), for very large cities) conclude a net positive and significant effect of public sector unionism on public expenditures. Thus, in most cases, the hypothesis that public sector unions contribute to higher government expenditures is supported. The total impact of public sector unionism on government expenditures could well be on the order of 6 percent on average. It does not exceed 13 percent but could be nonsignificant or even negative in certain circumstances.

Discussion

The objective of the previous sections was to assess the impact of public sector unions on wages, fringe benefits, employment, and public expenditures. Our review of the literature shows that such an impact is present: public sector unions do increase wages,

TABLE 10.6

Effect of Public Unions on Total Public Sector Expenditures

Study	Government Function Studied	Effects of Unions
Benecki (1978, table 2)	General municipal workers	
	Cities over 100,000	−28.5
	Cities 50,000–99,999	+1.3
	Cities 25,000–49,999	+12.4
	Cities 10,000–24,000	+9.6
Chambers (1977, table 1)	Teachers	
	Unified districts	+3.7
	Elementary districts	+11.7
Gallagher (1978, table 2)	Teachers	+9.0
Gallagher (1979, tables 3, 4)	Teachers	
	Low-wealth districts (equalized assessed valuation per ADA below $19,000)	+4.17[a]
	Medium-wealth districts (equalized assessed valuation per ADA between $19,000 and $25,000)	+8.0
	High-wealth districts (equalized assessed valuation per ADA above $26,000)	+12.6

a. Statistically insignificant.

fringe benefits, employment, and public expenditures. Is this evidence consistent with the Niskanen model? In fact, the results are consistent with three classes of theoretical models that bear quite different public policy implications.

The first of these models is the double-power model. Public sector unions would bring both monopoly wages and higher demand for public sector employment. As shown in figure 10.1, the double-power model implies that public sector unions shift the wage-employment combination from *a* to *b* (monopoly power effect) along the same demand curve and then from *b* to *c* (the special interest group effect) from one (lower) labor demand curve to the other (higher). The empirical evidence previously discussed provides support for a total displacement effect from point *a* to point *c* in figure 10.1 (higher wages and higher employment). Such evidence is reenforced by the presence of an indirect effect of total expenditures on employment. Zax and Ichniowski (1988) recently developed and presented impressive evidence on such an indirect effect for the U.S. municipal sector.

One may be tempted to argue that such a model is consistent with the Niskanen (1971) theory. However, strictly speaking, bureaucrats do not shift both the levels of wages and employment in

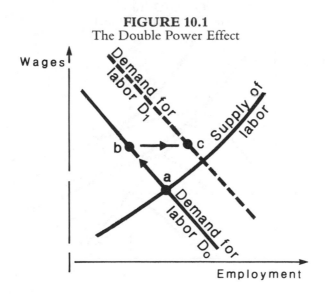

FIGURE 10.1
The Double Power Effect

this latter theory. In fact, in the initial Niskanen approach, they (the bureaucrats) fix higher levels of the employment for a given wage. Thus, as far as empirical evidence on the impact of unions on government expenditures is concerned, it does not provide much insight into this initial version of the Niskanen model.

The second of these models, however, is clearly consistent with the revised Niskanen (1975) approach (but also see Migué and Bélanger 1974). It is the cooperative model.[8] In the presence of bureaucrats who attempt to maximize the difference between the budget allowed and the normal costs of production (an equivalent of profit maximizers for discretionary expenditures), contracts can be reached at both higher wages and employment levels. Figure 10.2 shows a circumstance where first, at the going wage rate, bureaucrats fix the employment level at the corresponding level of maximum discretionary budget (*EB*). But second, the presence of a union forces the bureaucrats to reduce this excess budget at a level *EB'* or *EB''*. At *EB'*, a better contract is reached at point *e,* where the excess budget is the same as for point *c* (pure monopoly effect), but the utility of the union leaders (or members) is greater (U functions represent the level of utility for union leaders or members: the further they are from the origin, the greater is the utility).

FIGURE 10.2
The Cooperative Model

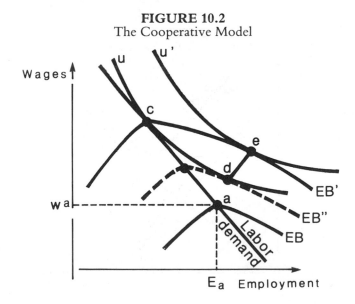

At EB'', the level of utility or satisfaction of the union leaders or members is kept the same; but then, at point d, the excess budget of the bureaucrats is superior (the lower the EB curve, the greater is the level of excess budget available to the bureaucrat).

The line that joins d to e describes the contract curve between unions and bureaucrats. Employment and wage levels are both shown to be higher than the alternative wage-employment combination without a union (point a), but the union wage effect also appears to be smaller than the pure monopoly (cf. private sector) effect of unions. The empirical evidence discussed earlier also supports a positive effect of public sector unions on wages and employment (such as point d or e) that is lower than the pure private sector monopoly effect (point c), but also suggests lower wages effects of public sector unions, which is consistent with the cooperative model.

There is also a third possible model that leads to similar predictions: the monopsony power model. In this model, the employer (government or public) is large enough to be the exclusive or the main employer of a group of workers (teachers, nurses, library technicians, etc.) and it is expected that, in the absence of a union, such an employer will pay lower wages and hire fewer employees. The well-known predicted effect of a union in this model is that both employment and wages will raise in the presence of a union. As illustrated in figure 10.3, the union wage (w^u) as well as the union employment level (E^u) are greater than the alternative monopsony wage and employment levels (w^m and E^m, respectively).

Given the presence of monopsonistic effects in the public sector labor market, the evidence on the public sector union impact on both wages and employment is also consistent with such a model of a positive countervailing power.

Conclusion

Our search for the evaluation of the public sector unions on public expenditures lead us to the following observations:

1. Public sector employees tend to have lower wages when there is no union in the bureaucracy.

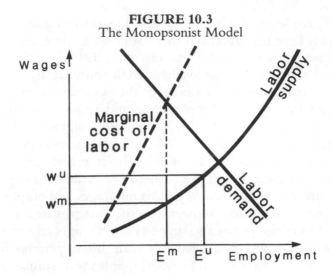

FIGURE 10.3
The Monopsonist Model

2. Public sector unions do raise wages, but significantly less than the private sector unions.

3. Fringe benefit effects of public sector unions appear to be quite substantial and significant.

4. Employment effects tend to be positively correlated with the presence of a public sector union.[9]

5. Total expenditures generally tend to rise in the presence of a public sector union.

In summary, if we recall the predictions of the Niskanen model, we first see support of a monopsony power of the bureaucracy in the absence of a union. Also, as expected, unions tend to bring wage differentials, but not as important differentials as private sector unions bring. However, since wages are only a part of total compensation, public sector employees may well receive an equivalent total compensation in the form of a different combination between wages and fringe benefits. Finally, as an extension to the Niskanen model, we observed that unions in a bureaucracy, as representatives of a part of the bureaucracy, increase the pressure on total budget and employment expenditures. In this way, the Niskanen model can be said to fit the data. However, as shown earlier, these same results or part of them could also be consistent with alternative models.

APPENDIX
Summary of Studies of Government Functions

Study	Government Function Studied	*N,* Year and Method of Collection	Dependent Variable	Independent Variable
Ashenfelter (1971)	Fire fighters	201 cities of 25,000–100,000, 1961–1966; cross-section/time-series pooled data	Average hourly wage, average annual salary, average hours per week	Cost-of-living, presence of a union
Baird and Landon (1972)	Teachers	44 school districts of 25,000 to 50,000 enrollment, 1967–1968; cross section	Average starting salary	Logarithm of the number of districts in the same country, per capita income, percentage of the revenue from local sources, effective property tax rate, dummy variable equals 1 if negotiations are held, percentage of teachers in the district who are members of the NEA, percentage of teachers in the district who are members of the AFT

Study	Government Function Studied	N, Year and Method of Collection	Dependent Variable	Independent Variable
Baugh and Stone (1982)	Teachers	Wage level regression, cross section: 617 teachers, 1974 (kindergarten through secondary); 1,037 teachers, 1977 (kindergarten through secondary). Wage change regression, cross section: 318 teachers, 1974–1975; 233 teachers, 1977–1978 (kindergarten through secondary)	Natural logarithm of the hourly wage	Race, experience, sex education, dummy variable equals 1 if SMSA is one of 44 largest, dummy variable equals 1 if member of a union
Bartel and Lewin (1981)	Police	215 cities of at least 25,000, 1973; cross section	Wage equation of minimum salary for police privates, hourly	Median family income, city size, population density, median value of housing in the community, geographic re-

Study	Sample	Dependent variables	Independent variables
		minimum wage for police privates, maximum salary for police privates, average salary for all police officers; fringe benefits equation of expenditures for all fringe benefits, expenditures for retirement benefits	gion dummies, mayor-council form of government, commission form of government, opportunity wage, presence of collective bargaining; dummy variable equals 1 if the city has a written labor agreement covering wages, hours, and conditions of employment for police personnel
Becker (1979)	Hospital nonprofessional workers	Natural logarithm of average hourly money wage rate, fringe benefits total compensation for the ith occupation	Percentage of turnover, percentage of females, median county income, beds, teaching hospital, population of county, monopsony, government reimbursement, union dummy variable equals 1 if occupation is covered by a collective bargaining agreement, number of bargaining units in the hospital, dummy variable equals 1 if the occupation is nonunion but located in a union hospital
	506 to 619 nonprofessional occupations, including kitchen helpers, maids, nurse's aides, ward clerks, and switchboard operators; cross section		

Study	Government Function Studied	N, Year and Method of Collection	Dependent Variable	Independent Variable
Benecki (1978)	General municipal employees	66 cities over 100,000; 94 cities 50,000–100,000; 207 cities 25,000–50,000; 347 cities 10,000–25,000; 1972; cross section	Expenditures (general and personnel), revenue (intergovernmental and tax), debt (total, long term, short term)	Population, population density, percentage of population nonwhite, percentage of foreign extraction, median age, median family income, value added by manufacturing in the municipality (whether or not municipality is satellite city and has municipal government), institutional bargaining variables, percentage of employees organized for negotiating purposes
Cain et al. (1981)	Hospital workers	5,000 employees in hospital industry, 1973–1976; cross-section/time-series pooled data	Average hourly earnings	Race, sex, marital status, age, education, part-time work, region, size of place of residence, union status

| Chambers (1977) | Teachers | Salaries, ratio of teachers/pupils, school spending/pupil | 39 elementary districts and sample of 50 unified districts within 6 largest SMSAs in California; 1970–1971; cross section | Control variables not reported in the study, dichotomous dummy variable equals 1 if formal negotiations occurred, fraction of teachers covered by formal bargaining contracts |
| Edwards and Edwards (1982a) | Municipal sanitation workers | Hourly wage rate | 175 cities, 95 with public collection systems and 80 with private systems, 1974; cross section | Hourly wage of production workers in manufacturing, 1 minus the unemployment rate of all workers, race, education, number of households served in the city, density of population, total population, median family income, dichotomous variable equals 1 when some or all sanitation workers are union members |

Study	Government Function Studied	N, Year and Method of Collection	Dependent Variable	Independent Variable
Edwards and Edwards (1982b)	Municipal sanitation workers	102 cities of 5,000 to over 700,000, 1977; cross section	Hourly wage rate, fringe benefits, and total compensation	Hourly wage of production workers in manufacturing, minus the unemployment rate, race, education, number of households served, density of population, tons of refuse per household, total population, number of collections per week, percentage of households in cities receiving backyard pickup, median family income, dummy variable equals 1 if city has a council-manager form of government, dummy variable equals 1 when some or all sanitation workers are union members
Ehrenberg (1973)	Fire fighters	270 cities 25,000–250,000, 1969; cross section	Entrance and maximum annual salary for fire fighters, average annual salary for	City manager form of government, commission form of government, population density, median value of housing, median family income, aver–

			all department employees, entrance and maximum hourly salary for fire fighters, average annual salary for all department employees	age hourly earnings of manufacturing production workers, median education level, race, presence of a union, presence of a written contract
Ehrenberg and Goldstein (1975)	All	478 cities over 25,000, 1967; cross section	Average monthly earnings (log)	Form of government, per capita grants from higher levels of government, median education, percentage of population that is black, population density, median income level, median value of single-family housing, average monthly earnings of manufacturing production workers, proportion of category employees represented by unions or employee associations

279

Study	Government Function Studied	N, Year and Method of Collection	Dependent Variable	Independent Variable
Feldman and Scheffler (1982)	Hospital workers: registered nurses, practical nurses, secretaries, housekeepers	942 hospitals, 1977; cross section	Natural log of average annual salaries for full-time registered staff nurses with 3-year diploma, natural log of average annual salaries for full-time licensed practical nurses with 2-years' experience in a hospital, natural log of average hourly wages for full-time general secretaries, natural log of hourly wages for full-time housekeeping employees	State of local government hospital ownership, nonprofit hospital, proprietary hospital, fraction of county hospital beds located in four largest hospitals, county per capita income, county urbanization index, county cost of living, average annual wages of employees in offices of physicians and surgeons, average annual wages of employees in wholesale and retail trade, average annual wages of employees in service industries, average monthly state aid for dependent children per recipient family, dummy variable equals 1 if occupation was unionized in 1975 or later, dummy variable equals 1 if occupation is unionized, 1968–1974, dummy variable equals

				1 if occupation is unionized before 1968, dummy variable equals 1 if there was a strike or slowdown in 1976–1977, percentage of hospitals in state with a collective bargaining agreement in 1975, occupation not unionized but has collective bargaining agreement covering other occupations
Feuille and Delaney (1986)	Police	900 cities, 1971–1981; cross-section/time-series pooled data	Patrol officer's maximum annual salary, patrol officer's minimum annual salary	Population, crime rate, city density, per capita-income, median value of residential housing, percentage of residents who are black, form of government, dummy variable equals 1 for city manager, dummy variable equals 1 for being outside SMSA, average manufacturing wage, regional dummy variables, written police collective bargaining agreement, arbitration availability, current arbitration use, postarbitration use

281

Study	Government Function Studied	*N*, Year and Method of Collection	Dependent Variable	Independent Variable
Feuille, Delaney, and Hendricks (1985)	Police	500 to 600 cities over 25,000, 1971–1980; cross-section/time-series pooled data	Log of the dollar amount spent on fringe benefits (retirement and insurance contributions) per police officer	Population, crime rate, city density, per capita income, median value of residential housing, percentage of city residents who are black, form of government dummy variable equals 1 for city manager, dummy variable equals 1 for being outside SMSA, average manufacturing wage, regional dummy variables, written police collective bargaining agreement, arbitration availability, current arbitration use, past arbitration use
Fottler (1977)	Hospital nonprofessional workers	21 SMSAs, 1966, 1969, 1972; cross section	Average weekly wage	Cost of living, concentration ratio, federal ratio, proportion of women, source of control (0 = private, 1 = public), proportion of nonprofessional employees covered by collective bargaining contract

Freund (1974)	All	Percentage change in average weekly earnings	40–80 cities over 50,000, 1965–1971; cross-section/time-series pooled data	Change in work force composition, average percentage of high-wage-change occupations, average SMSA unemployment rate, percentage of change in nongovernment wages, percentage of change in government expenditures, relative municipal wages, percentage of change in cost of living in SMSA, percentage of unionization of city work force, public sector strike activity, compulsory arbitration, legal prohibition against collective bargaining and political activities
Frey (1975)	Teachers	Logarithm of base pay	298 school districts with more than 750 pupils average daily attendance, New Jersey, 1964–1970; cross-section/time-series pooled data	Wages for nurses, district size, median family income of the community, property tax base per pupil, state aid per pupil, collective bargaining

Study	Government Function Studied	N, Year and Method of Collection	Dependent Variable	Independent Variable
Gallagher (1978; 1970)	Teachers	133 Illinois public school districts with enrollment 500–4,000 average daily attendance (ADA), 1974; cross section	Total school district operating budget per ADA, total teacher salary expenditures per ADA, nonteacher expenditures per ADA	School district wealth (measured by equalized assessed property valuation per ADA), percentage of district's students enrolled in grades 9–12, log of ADA, percentage of the certified staff with advanced degrees beyond the bachelor's level, percentage of the district population with a college degree, formal collective bargaining agreement
Hall and Carroll (1973)	Teachers	118 elementary school districts, Illinois 1968–1969; cross section	Mean salary, student–teacher ratio	Median family income, percentage of white-collar workers, ADA, percentage of teachers who are male, mean years teaching experience, state aid per pupil, operating expenditures per pupil, student–teacher ratio, population, collective bargaining agreement

Hall and Vanderporten (1977)	Police	141 cities over 50,000, 1973; cross section	Minimum annual salary for police private, maximum annual salary for police private, average annual salary for all police department personnel	Crime rate, median family income, number of retail, service, and wholesale establishments per 1,000 population, median income of male craftsmen, monopsony power, parity of police and fire fighter salaries, population, written labor contract, formal collective negotiations
Holmes (1976)	Teacher	24,915 full-time class room teachers employed by 456 independent Oklahoma school districts, 1974–1975; cross section	Gross contract salary	Sex, race, total years experience, years experience in district, education, total revenue per ADA, union activity and extent of organizational activity

Study	Government Function Studied	N, Year and Method of Collection	Dependent Variable	Independent Variable
Hunter and Rankin (1988)	Police and fire fighters	24 large urban areas, 1976; cross section	Total compensation: total payments per employee, including pay for time not working, pensions and direct salaries; paid compensation: payment per employee for salary and direct labor costs; hidden compensation: payments per employee not directly observable, such as pension benefits and leave time, vacation and holiday pay, and fringe benefits	Population, percentage change in population, per capita income, felonies per 1,000 population, Herfindahl index, municipal government workers per 1,000 adult population, dummy variable equals 1 if municipal workers have right to organize and bargain collectively under state law

Ichniowski (1980)	Fire fighters	1,015 cities, 1976; 597 cities, 1966–1976; 307 cities that exclude those with "not reported or not applicable" union status; cross section and cross-section/time-series pooled data	Total compensation, wage and salary expenditures, total salary, hours per week on duty, maximum salary, entrance salary, fringe benefits, retirement benefits, insurance benefits	Population, opportunity wage, fire insurance rating, alarms per 1,000 people, per capita income, median value of single-family housing, per capita general revenue from own sources, percentage of population nonwhite, geographic region dummy variable, government type, land area, contract, international association of local fire fighters
Kearney and Morgan (1980)	Police	147 south central cities of 10,000 and over, 1976; cross section	Entrance salary and maximum salary of police patrolman, benefits, mean salary of police employees, mean salary plus benefits	Average earnings service employees, percentage of nonwhite, median years education, population size, per capita personal income, per capita general revenue from own sources, crime rate, percentage police officers belonging to employee organizations that bargain over compensation

Study	Government Function Studied	N, Year and Method of Collection	Dependent Variable	Independent Variable
Landon and Baird (1971)	Teachers	136 school districts; 69 districts with enrollments of 25,000 to 50,000, 43 districts with enrollments of 50,000 to 100,000, 24 districts with greater than 100,000, 1966–1967; cross section	District's contractual salary for teacher with no prior experience	Monopsony power, per capita income in county, percentage total school revenues from local sources, effective property tax rates by district
Lipsky and Drotning (1973)	Teachers	696 school districts in New York state (except New York city), 1967–1968; cross section	Base salary, salary of teacher with 7 years experience and 30 hours earned credit beyond bachelor degree, salary of teacher with 11 years experience and 60 hours	Pupil-teacher ratio, total enrollment percentage of teachers in a district with advanced degrees, percentage of teachers in a district with 3 years of seniority or less, dummy variable equals 1 if district in downstate New York, true value per pupil, instructional costs per pupil, debt service

			earned credit beyond bachelor degree, mean salary	per pupil, union dummy variable equals 1 if district has contract
Masters and Robertson (1988)	All	20 OECD nations, 1965–83; cross-section/time-series pooled data	Average annual proportion of the total civilian labor force employed in the public sector, or average annual rate of growth in public employment	Union power index, gross domestic product, unemployment, earnings, leftist cabinet
Mehay and Gonzalez (1986)	Police, fire fighters, and general municipal employees	445 cities of 25,000 to 350,000 located in 24 states in the southern and western regions, 1982; cross section	Monthly wage rate	State legal barriers to incorporation, rate of annexation by city, number of municipalities in county, opportunity wage, per capita income, population, median age, population density, rate of growth of community, per capita intergovernmental aid, regional dummy variable

Study	Government Function Studied	N, Year and Method of Collection	Dependent Variable	Independent Variable
Register (1988)	Hospital workers	275 hospitals from 13 urban areas and 114 hospitals in Ohio, 1984; cross section	Average annual wage paid to nonsupervisory personnel, average product of labor function, ratio of total expenditures to in-patient days	Percentage of hospital employment made up by the medical staff, registered nurses, licensed practical nurses, cost of living, region dummies, dummy variable equals 1 for union hospitals; ratio of beds to total personnel, total full-time equivalent personnel, natural log of predicted wage, ratio of out-patient visits to in-patient days, facilities and services index, ratio of surgeries per admission, intensive care days per in-patient day, regional dummy variables, union dummy variables equal 1 for union hospitals; natural log of predicted wage, intensive care days per in-patient day, ratio of out-patient visits

				to in-patient days, ratios of surgeries per admission, facilities and services index, regional dummy variables, general medical and surgical acute care days, subacute care days, out-patient visits, ratio energy costs to beds, interest payments to beds, union dummy variables equals 1 for union hospitals
Schmenner (1973)	Police, fire fighters, teachers, general municipal employees	11 large cities, 1962–1970; cross-section/time-series pooled data	Minimum police and fire fighter salaries, average monthly earnings for common function employees, minimum salary for teacher with no experience	Opportunity wage, assessment per capita, percentage change in tax rate, city population, work stoppages by employees per area, school district dummy, fraction of unionized employees, existence of formal collective bargaining agreement

Study	Government Function Studied	N, Year and Method of Collection	Dependent Variable	Independent Variable
Shapiro (1978)	All	99–1,136 males 45–59 years old, 1971; cross section	Natural logarithm of hourly wage rate for blue-collar and white-collar workers	Years of schooling, work experience, dummy variables equal 1 if respondent "not married," spouse present," dummy variables equal 1 if respondent has health problem, regional dummy variable, population size dummy variables, dummy variables equal 1 if wages set by collective bargaining
Thornton (1971)	Teachers	83 school districts in cities of at least 100,000, 1969–1970; cross section	Salary levels	Opportunity-cost variable, district size, pupil-teacher ratio, percentage full-time classroom teachers with less than standard teaching certificates, dummy variables equal 1 if the district negotiated collective salary agreement in previous year with formally recognized teacher organization

Valetta (1989)	Police, fire, sanitation, streets and highways, finance and general control, personnel	681 cities, 1980: cross section	Expenditures per capita, total revenue per capita, property taxes per capita	Population, income per capita, median housing value, median household income, population percentage with income below 75 percent of the poverty line, city unemployment rate, percentage of renter-occupied housing units, educational attainment, median age, percentage of blacks, region dummies, department dummies, dummy variable indicating the presence of a collective bargaining contract for the department, legal index variable used to control different laws regulating public sector collective bargaining across states and departments
Zax (1985)	General municipal employees	839 cities, 1975, 1977, 1979; cross-section/time-series pooled data	Man hours per capita is 10,000, employees per capita is 10,000, annual work hours per employee	Union strength (other variables not reported)

293

Study	Government Function Studied	N, Year and Method of Collection	Dependent Variable	Independent Variable
Zax (1989)	Streets and highways, public welfare, police, fire, sanitation	5,144 cities, 1977–82; cross-section/time-series pooled data	Employment per capita, monthly payrolls per employee	Occupation, percentage of adults with college education, median age, unemployment rate, population, percentages of population that are black, Hispanic, aged less than 16, aged greater than 64, living in the same dwelling as in 1975, percentage of families with incomes below poverty level, median family income, interquartile range of family income, median owner-occupied housing value, percentage owner-occupied housing value, percentage owner-occupied, percentage of structures 5 years old or less, dummies for department, geographic division, counties and jurisdictions in SMSAs, 9 dummy variables describing state laws governing local pub-

| Zax and Ichniowski (1988) | Police, fire, streets and high-ways, sanitation and refuse collection | 463 municipali-ties, four func-tions, 1977–1930, 1982; cross-section/time-series pooled data | Pay per full-time employee, em-ployment per 10,000 | lic sector unionization, dummy variable for bargain-ing unit represents depart-ments in which any employ-ees are covered by bargaining unit; dummy variable for asso-ciations representing depart-ments in which any employ-ees belong to labor organiza-tion, none covered by bargain-ing unit |
| | | | | Function dummy variables, year dummy variables, 1970 population, population changes 1960–1970, 1970–1980, the percentage of popu-lation that is Hispanic, black, of foreign stock, has high school education, is below the poverty level, median family income, median value of hous-ing, percentage of housing that is 1-unit structure, me-dian education, median earn-ings of male operatives, ratio |

Study	Government Function Studied	N, Year and Method of Collection	Dependent Variable	Independent Variable
				of nonworking to working individuals; percentage of white-collar workers, central city dummy variable; 8 variables describing characteristics of the municipal government, 6 bargaining laws, a right-to-work dummy variable, union (bargaining unit) and association (dealing unit) dummy variables; other more complex equations are also developed and estimated.

NOTES

1. This project was funded by the SSHRC. We wish to thank professors André Blais and Claude Montmarquette of Université de Montreál and William Niskanen of Cato University for their comments on a draft of this chapter. Our main bibliographical source was the *Journal of Economic Literature*. It covers most of the U.S. and Canadian journals, but also a good sample of the European economic literature. However, in our review of the literature, it was found that almost all references were based on U.S. data, with the exception of one international study and a few Canadian studies that are noted in the text.

2. The appendix covers the studies examined from which we retained what we thought to be representative estimates. Most of the studies are cross sectioned, but a few are based on a pooling of cross sections and time series. Only two studies are based on an after/before methodology. The conclusion does not substantially differ, however, whatever the methodology.

3. Freeman (1986) and Lewis (1988) also arrived at similar conclusions. Many reasons can explain the variability in the results. We would like to note further that the rules of the game (right to strike, presence of a collective agreement, union affiliation, arbitration rights or use) frequently affected the estimates, as expected. But because other factors also affect these same estimates, we were unable to isolate one from the others. The direction and magnitude of the bias in the average estimates cannot therefore be ascertained on this a priori basis.

4. For a study on the dynamic effects of the degree of unionization on short-term employment and wage adjustments in the U.S. municipal sector, see Lewis and Stein (1989).

5. To our knowledge, no econometric evidence is available on the comparison of total workers compensation, that is, wages plus fringe benefits between private and public employees on the basis of such a union/nonunion cross classification.

6. Even if this piece of evidence provides clear support to the Niskanen model, we reserve our discussion on the consistency between our empirical results and the Niskanen model until the end of the chapter.

7. A monopsony wage is a wage settled below the efficient and competitive wages.

8. Zax (1985) explicitly suggests the use of such an approach.

9. Productivity effects are not considered in this review of the literature because of a lack of such studies at a significant aggregate level and

also because of the difficulty of constructing largely admitted measures of productivity in the public sector.

REFERENCES

Ashenfelter, Orley. 1971. The effect of unionization on wages in the public sector: The case of fire fighters. *Industrial and Labor Relations Review* 24(2): 191–202.

Baird, Robert, and John H. Landon. 1972. The effect of collective bargaining on public school teachers' salaries: Comment. *Industrial and Labour Relations Review* 25(3): 410–17.

Bartel, A. and David Lewin. 1981. Wages and unionism in the public sector: The case of police. *Review of Economics and Statistics* 63:53–59.

Baugh, William H., and Joe A. Stone. 1982. Teachers, unions, and wages in the 1970s: Unionism now pays. *Industrial and Labor Relations Review* 35(3): 368–76.

Becker, Brian E. 1979. Union impact on wages and fringe benefits of hospital nonprofessionals. *Quarterly Review of Economics and Business* 19(4): 27–44.

Benecki, Stanley. 1978. Municipal expenditure levels and collective bargaining. *Industrial Relations* 17(2): 216–30.

Cain, Glen C., Brian D. Backer, Cathy G. McLaughlin, and Albert E. Schwenk. 1981. The effect of unions on wages in hospitals. In *Research in labor economics 4*, ed. Ronald G. Ehrenberg, 191–320. Greenwich, Conn.: JAI Press.

Chambers, Jay G. 1977. The impact of collective bargaining for teachers on resource allocation in public school districts. *Journal of Urban Economics* 4(3): 324–39.

Cousineau, J.-M., and R. Lacroix. 1977. *Wage determination in major collective agreements in the private and public sectors.* Ottawa: Economic Council of Canada.

Delaney, John T. 1988. Teachers' collective bargaining outcomes and trade offs. *Journal of Labor Research* 4(4): 363–75.

———. 1984. Union effects on teacher productivity. *Industrial and Labor Relations Review* 37(3): 346–58.

Edwards, Linda N., and Franklin R. Edwards. 1982a. Wellington-winter revisited: The case of municipal sanitation collection. *Industrial and Labor Relations Review* 35(3): 307–18.

———. 1982b. Public unions, local government structure and the compensation of municipal sanitation workers. *Economic Inquiry* 20:405–25.

Ehrenberg, Ronald G. 1973. Municipal government structure, unionization, and the wages of fire fighters. *Industrial and Labor Relations Review* 27(1): 36–48.

Ehrenberg, Ronald G., and Gerald S. Goldstein. 1975. A model of public sector wage determination. *Journal of Urban Economics* 2(3): 223–45.

Feldman, Roger, and Richard Sheffler. 1982. The union impact on hospital wages and fringe benefits. *Industrial and Labor Relations Review* 35(2): 196–206.

Feuille, Peter, and John T. Delaney. 1986. Collective bargaining interest arbitration, and police salaries. *Industrial and Labor Relations Review* 39(2): 228–40.

Feuille, Peter, John T. Delaney, and W. Hendricks. 1985. Police bargaining, arbitration, and fringe benefits. *Journal of Labor Research* 6(1): 7–20.

Fottler, Myron D. 1977. The union impact on hospital wages. *Industrial and Labor Relations Review* 30(3): 342–55.

Freeman, Richard B. 1985. How do public sector wages and employment respond to economic conditions? NBER Working Paper 1653. Cambridge, Mass.: National Bureau of Economic Research.

———. 1986. Unionism comes to the public sector. *Journal of Economic Literature* 14:41–86.

Freeman, R. B., and C. Ichniowski, eds. 1988. *Public sector workers unionize.* Chicago: Univ. of Chicago Press for National Bureau of Economic Research.

Freund, James. 1974. Market and union influences on municipal employee wages. *Industrial and Labor Relations Review* 27(3):391–404.

Frey, Donald E. 1975. Wage determination in public schools and the effects on unionization. In *Labor in the public and nonprofit sectors,* ed. Daniel S. Hamermesh, 183–219. Princeton, N.J.: Princeton Univ. Press.

Gallagher, Daniel G. 1978. Teacher bargaining and school district expenditures. *Industrial Relations* 17(2):231–37.

———. 1979. Teacher negotiations, school district expenditures, and taxation levels. *Educational Administration Quarterly* 15(1):67–82.

Gunderson, Morly, and W. Craig Riddell. 1988. Labour market economics, theory, evidence and policy in Canada. 2d. ed. Toronto: McGraw-Hill Ryerson.

Hall, Clayton W., and Norman Carroll. 1973. The effect of teachers' organizations on salaries and class size. *Industrial and Labor Relations Review* 26(2): 834–41.

Hall, Clayton W., and Bruce Vanderporten. 1977. Unionization, monopsony power, and police salaries. *Industrial Relations* 16(1): 94–100.

Holmes, Alexander B. 1976. Effects of union activity on teachers' earnings. *Industrial Relations* 15(3): 328–32.

Hunter, William J., and Carol H. Rankin. 1988. The composition of public sector compensation: The effects of unionization and bureaucratic size. *Journal of Labor Research* 9(1): 29–42.

Ichniowski, Casey. 1980. Economic effects of the fire fighters' union. *Industrial and Labor Relations Review* 33(2): 198–211.

Kasper, Hirschel. 1972. The effects of collective bargaining on public school teachers' salaries: Reply. *Industrial and Labor Relations Review* 25(3): 417–23.

Kearney, Richard, and David R. Morgan. 1980. The effect of employee organizations on the compensation of police officers. *Journal of Collective Negotiations* 9(1): 17–31.

Landon, John H., and Robert N. Baird. 1971. Monopsony in the market for public school teachers. *American Economic Review* 61(5): 966–71.

Lewis, Gregg H. 1988. Union/nonunion wage gaps in the public sector. In Freeman and Ichniowski 1988, 323–61. See also Comment by Harry Holzer in the same volume, 361–63.

Lewis, Gregg H., and L. Stein. 1989. Unions and municipal decline. *American Politics Quarterly* 17(2): 208–22.

Lipsky, David B., and John E. Drotning. 1973. The influence of collective bargaining on teachers' salaries in New York State. *Industrial and Labor Relations Review* 27(1): 18–35.

Masters, Marick F., and John D. Robertson. 1988. The impact of organized labor on public employment: A comparative analysis. *Journal of Labor Research* 4(4): 347–61.

Mehay, Stephen, and Rodolfo A. Gonzalez. 1986. The relative effect of unionization and interjurisdictional competition on municipal wages. *Journal of Labor Research* 7(1): 79–93.

Migué, Jean-Luc, and Gérard Bélanger. 1974. Towards a general theory of managerial discretion. *Public Choice* 17(1): 24–43.

Niskanen, William A. 1971. *Bureaucracy and representative government.* Chicago: Aldine Atherton.

———. 1975. Bureaucrats and politicians. *Journal of Law and Economics* 18(3): 617–44.

Register, Charles A. 1988. Wages, productivity, and costs in union and nonunion hospitals. *Journal of Labor Research* 9(4): 325–45.

Schmenner, Roger W. 1973. The determination of municipal employee wages. *Review of Economics and Statistics* 55(1): 83–90.

Shapiro, David. 1978. Relative wage effects of unions in the public and private sectors. *Industrial and Labor Relations Review* 31(2): 193–204.

Simpson, Wayne. 1985. The impact of unions on the structure of Canadian wages: An empirical analysis with microdata. *Canadian Journal of Economics* 17(1): 164–81.

Smith, Sharon P. 1977. Government wage differentials. *Journal of Urban Economics* 4(3): 248–71.

Spizman, Laurence M. 1980. Public employee unions: A study in the economics of power. *Journal of Labor Research* 1(2): 265–73.

Thornton, Robert J. 1971. The effects of collective negotiations on teachers' salaries. *Quarterly Review of Economics* 11(4): 37–46.

Valetta, Robert G. 1989. The impact of unionism on municipal expenditures and revenues. *Industrial and Labor Relations Review* 42(3): 430–42.

Wilton, D. 1986. *Public sector wage compensation, in Canadian labour relations,* ed. W. C. Riddell. Toronto: Univ. of Toronto Press.

Zax, Jeffrey S. 1985. Municipal employment, municipal unions, and demand for principal services. NBER Working Paper 1728. Cambridge, Mass.: National Bureau of Economic Research.

———. 1989. Employment and local public sector unions. *Industrial Relations* 28(1): 21–31.

Zax, Jeffrey S., and Casey Ichniowski. 1988. The effects of public sector unionism on pay, employment, department budgets and municipal expenditures. In Freeman and Ichniowski 1988, 323–61. See also comment by Harry Holzer in the same volume, 361–63.

11

B. GUY PETERS

The European Bureaucrat:
The Applicability of
Bureaucracy and Representative Government
to Non-American Settings

William Niskanen's (1971)*Bureaucracy and Representative Government* has staked out an important position in the study of public bureaucracies. His book has been much praised and much damned, but such controversy is often the mark of an important contribution to scholarship. In this chapter I devote very little time to praising or damning the book on the basis of its own internal logic or its arguments as presented in the somewhat sparse and abstract language of economics. That task has already been undertaken successfully by a number of scholars (Kogan 1973; Jackson 1982; Coneybeare 1984; Smith 1988; Blair and Dion 1988). Rather, I am interested in the applicability of the model presented in *Bureaucracy and Representative Government* to policy-making systems outside the United States. Any critique of the work, and any discussion of possible means of reconciliation between the empirical evidence presented in this chapter and the argument of the book, are reserved for the conclusion.

That being said, however, I will make one fundamental point about explicating and testing the Niskanen model: we do not have access to information that would allow us to know the preferences and the objective functions of civil servants and politicians in a number of European countries (or indeed in the United States). Any empirical examination of the model, therefore, must be done using only surrogate measures. Further, because the values of these surrogate measures depend largely on the outcomes of the policy-making process, we will in most instances be measuring the *success*

303

of bureaucratic entrepreneurs in achieving their (presumed) goals and not the existence of those goals. For example, if employment in the public bureaucracy does not increase over time, this does not necessarily mean that bureaucrats did not want larger budgets and personnel allocations but only that they were unsuccessful. We could examine public records, biographies, and the like to attempt to understand motivations behind budget requests, but that evidence is likely to be spotty and would provide limited evidence about underlying demands. However, given that the ability of the bureaucracy to mislead sponsors and to achieve their goals is also an important component of the model (Niskanen 1971, 138–54), finding little evidence of success is still important.

One additional point that should also be made about the problem of testing this model is that many outcomes compatible with it could also be compatible with other utility-maximizing models of organizational behavior (for a review see Orzechowski 1977). For example, Downs's (1967) discussion of bureaucratic behavior posits much of the same aggressiveness on the part of bureau managers to increase budgets and personnel allocations, although the posited motivations are different. The assumed motivation in Downs's model is more organizational—ensuring especially the survival of the organization even in the face of possible future budget cuts—than it is for the personal benefit of bureau chiefs.

Although both models predict many of the same behaviors and have some of the same cynicism about the behavior of bureaucratic agencies (e.g., that service to clients and public policy as a whole are means to an end rather than ends in themselves), the two models could also produce different predictions if individual and collective goals diverged. A consideration of a divergence of goals would also arise in the context of the new institutionalism within political science, which attempts to explain behavior in government by institutional rather than individual variables (March and Olsen 1984). From the institutionalist perspective, maximizing behavior on the part of a bureau could be seen as meeting the perceived needs of that bureau, rather than the more personal motivations of its leadership.

At a further level of removal from the Niskanen model, it could also be argued that bureaucrats behave rationally but have very different objective functions than the ones posited by *Bureaucracy and Representative Government*. For example, Alan Peacock (1983)— no great friend of bureaucracy or big government—has argued that rather than being highly ambitious and self-seeking, bureaucrats are better understood as being extremely lazy and as attempting to maximize on-the-job leisure rather than budgets. This model, while functioning within the same utility-maximizing framework, would have different predictions about the behavior of bureau chiefs based on different assumptions about their underlying demand functions. Similarly, although Tullock (1965) does discuss imperialism in bureaucracies, much of his analysis is concerned with evasion of accountability rather than bureaucratic expansionism.[1] Thus, we could accept utility maximization in a bureaucracy without accepting all the assumptions presented by Niskanen.

The European Bureaucrat

My intention is to examine the European bureaucrat in light of Niskanen's (1971) description of the motivations and actions of bureaucrats derived primarily from the U.S. perspective. It can be argued that the Niskanen book is peculiarly American in its description and analysis of public bureaucracies. The book's argument depends to a large extent upon the existence of relatively autonomous agencies having direct relationships with their legislative sponsors, and to some extent on that sponsor being structured in an equally decentralized manner. That decentralization also allows substantial latitude to specialist committees and subcommittees of the sponsoring institution to support their favorite agencies. Further, from reading *Bureaucracy and Representative Government,* it is not at all clear whether the central protagonist in the model, the bureau chief, is a career civil servant or short-term political appointee (Heclo 1977; Mackenzie 1987). The latter official may have a great deal to gain by demonstrating his or her prowess in manipulating the political system for higher budgets, although it is less clear that the former would, and political appointees are much more likely to be in leadership roles in Washington than in other national capitols. There are a number of other points that could demonstrate the close connection of the arguments contained in the book to the executive system of the United States. It is useful, therefore, to attempt to extend the geographical domain of the analysis and to determine how well the model as presented can explain behavior in the executive branch in other industrialized, democratic political systems.

The difficulty is, however, that there appears to be as much variance among European countries as there is between Western European countries and the United States. Rather than there being a single European bureaucrat and a single European policy-making system, there are as many of these as there are countries, and each has characteristics that should affect the applicability of the Niskanen model. Therefore, it is desirable to develop some analytical statements about the structure of administrative systems in Western Europe, the characteristics of civil servants, the characteristics of sponsoring organizations, and the nature of the public expenditure mix being implemented. Each of the above factors has some influence on the capacity of an agency to evade control, to produce excessive amounts of its goods and services, and to expand its budget. The particular variables will be selected on the basis of their potential utility for explicating the Niskanen model within Western Europe and for explaining variance in the applicability of the model. This will be an attempt to "move away from the simple equation of budgetary expansion with bureaucratic utility and specify *under what circumstances* bureaucrats will successfully be able to extract 'bureaucratic surplus' from budgetary increases, in what form . . . and to what degree" (Hood, Huby, and Dunsire 1984, 177). We may not be able to meet all the demands presented in that one sentence, but we should be able to determine some of the conditions under which the model operates.

Structural Characteristics

We first examine characteristics of European administrative systems that should affect the capacity of the bureaucracy to seek its own goals, such as expanded budgets or increased personnel allocations, through the policy-making process. There are several features of the structure of public bureaucracies that should have an influence on the success of bureaucrats. Not only can we hypothe-

size that these structural features influence the relative success of
bureaucratic entrepreneurs, but they may in fact help to create
those entrepreneurs. For example, a highly decentralized administrative system may create conditions very similar to those existing
in the private market, and relatively small organizations may believe themselves to be isolated and devoid of any meaningful institutional support. In such a decentralized setting, survival very
quickly becomes equated with growth, as organizations believe
they must protect their heartlands through the generation of budgetary and personnel fat (Downs 1967). Viewed from Niskanen's
rather than Downs's perspective, decentralization within the bureaucracy may mean that an agency can escape the detailed scrutiny of the sponsor and therefore have the opportunity to maximize its budget.[2]

Decentralization. The most obvious characteristic of bureaucratic systems affecting the capacity of bureau chiefs to pursue
their own goals is the level of centralization or decentralization.
Everything else being equal, we would hypothesize that more
decentralized bureaucratic systems would provide a greater capacity to pursue individual goals than would more centralized ones.[3]
The Niskanen model was developed for the United States, with a
decentralized administrative system permitting agencies substantial autonomy from their cabinet departments and an ability to
pursue goals that, if not antithetical to the department or the president, may at times be only tangentially connected (Seidman and
Gilmour 1986). Thus, the underlying conception of bureaucratic
expansionism arises in the context of a decentralized bureaucratic
system engaged in something approaching a *bellum omnia contre
omnes*.

Most European political systems are not as decentralized as that
of the United States, but some do come quite close. The Swedish
government, for example, administers most programs through a
number of quasi-autonomous agencies and boards (*styrelsen* and
centrala ambetsverk), which have real but limited ties to the ministry
responsible for their policies (Hadenius 1979). The government of
Finland has a rather similar pattern of agency autonomy (Stahlberg
1988), and the other two Scandinavian countries also allow substantial autonomy, although less than Sweden. The boards (at least in

Sweden) are able to pursue their own budget requests (Tarschys and Eduards 1975), although there are requirements for coordination with the sponsoring ministry. In short, these organizations should have the latitude to pursue any goals with minimal interference from above and to make their own arrangements over personnel and budgets.[4]

At the other end of the centralization spectrum is the United Kingdom, with ministries as the principal form of organization in central government, and limited autonomy or even organizational differentiation beneath that level (Pollitt 1983; Peters 1988; Hogwood 1988). In this organizational format, components of the ministry would have little or no capacity to influence their own budget but, rather, must accept the allocations made to them through the ministry budget. Some organizations (nonministerial bodies) are granted a quasi-autonomous status and have been more successful than most in extracting resources (Ashford 1989) from the central agencies. Most components of British ministries are, however, at the mercy of the Treasury and their own minister. We would therefore expect, as some empirical analysis has already substantiated (Hood, Huby, and Dunsire 1984; Hood, Dunsire, and Thomson 1988), that British government organizations would experience little success in pursuing their own goals through the policy-making and budgetary processes.

Between the two extremes lie countries such as France and Italy, which, although relying on ministries as the principal building blocks of government, have well-articulated organizational structures within each ministry (Darbel and Schnapper 1972; Rigaud and Delcros 1986; Cassesse 1988). Although the numerous bureaus that exist within a French or Italian ministry do have an identity and often a legally defined mission, they still exist within a hierarchical ministerial structure. West Germany represents a special case. In some ways extremely decentralized, with most administrative functions being performed at the *Land* level, within each of the *Länder* the administrative structures are hierarchical and legally controlled and, consequently, allow relatively little opportunity for pursuing individualized agency goals.

Competitiveness. Closely related to the degree of decentralization is the degree of competition for resources permitted within it.

However, administrative systems may be decentralized without there being manifest competition for resources. The means of suppressing competition are largely in the hands of the sponsors, who may force collective decision making in cabinet on expenditures and reinforce the power of central financial ministries. They may also strengthen legislative organizations for dealing with spending issues. In addition, the ethos of the civil services themselves may restrict competition. This ethos is especially important when the service considers itself an elite body within government that is dedicated to public service rather than to self-seeking (Goodin 1982). While such a self-portrait may be somewhat disingenuous, it may be widely accepted enough to reduce the amount of budgetary aggrandizement actually experienced.

Some mechanisms for the control of competition, however, do remain within the administrative structure itself. In particular, the degree to which organizations are enmeshed within coordinative mechanisms may substantially influence their capacity to go it alone and to attempt to achieve greater budgetary success. For example, the French government has developed an elaborate set of coordinative committees operating at three levels within the executive branch—civil service, *Matignon,* and *Élysée*—which greatly reduces the capacity of an administrative agency to operate unilaterally (Fournier 1987). The institutionalization of the office of *secrétariat général du gouvernement* has further reduced the autonomy of ministries and agencies (Py 1985). I have already pointed out that the structure of ministries in France is highly articulated, with a large number of seemingly independent levels and offices (Darbel and Schnapper 1972), but any autonomy of those organizations is greatly reduced by the coordinative structures.

To some extent, the same reduction and control of autonomy might be found being exercised over the decentralized Scandinavian boards and agencies. Although nominally rather independent, they are coordinated through membership on each other's advisory boards and committees (in addition to formal controls in the budgetary process). These advisory bodies are very important in policy making in Scandinavia, and civil servants from other ministries or boards account for a significant proportion of the membership on these committees (Johansen and Kristensen 1982; Kvavik

1980; Olsen 1985). In these cases, the coordination, rather than coming from above in the form of the political executive, comes laterally through cooperation with other bureaucratic organizations. This approach to coordination may be very effective given the cooperative policy styles of the Scandinavian countries (Anton 1980; Meijer 1969), but it would be difficult to transplant to other political cultures.

In addition to these structural arrangements for coordination, the nature of civil service systems themselves may make for greater coordination than has been found in the United States. In part, this is a result of the higher level of integration of European bureaucracies when compared to their counterparts in the United States (Self 1972). In addition, the corps system found most notably in France (Baecque and Quermonne 1981; Kessler 1986), but also in other systems derivative of the French, permits coordination across agencies. This is especially true for corps such as the Inspection des Finances and the Cours des Comptes, which monitor public expenditure and have representatives in most agencies and in most ministerial cabinets. This makes any individualistic or imperialistic actions on the part of a single agency substantially more difficult.

At this point, we should perhaps take a short excursion into the theory of bureaucratic behavior as developed by Niskanen. He identified monopoly supply (both of services and of information) as being at the root of the problems identified in public bureaucracy. Therefore, the creation of competitive bureaus was considered a central means of addressing the problem and of reducing the capacity of bureaus to extract excessive budgets from a sponsor. The above argument concerning the virtues of coordination and centralization may appear to run directly contrary to that logic. We must distinguish, however, between bureaucratic organizations that are competitive within the same policy area from those that are competitive simply by seeking funds from the same budgetary process. Decentralized competition through the budgetary process may simply reinforce the monoply of each agency within its own area of expertise, while coordination and centralization may, in fact, minimize that monopoly. There are, of course, arguments on behalf of the "musk ox phenomenon" (Hogwood and Peters 1983; Goodin

1975), in which nominally competitive bureaus compete against their mutual enemy, the sponsor. In most instances, however, coordination will minimize rather than exacerbate the negative effects of decentralization.[5] Therefore, we must be very careful in specifying the nature and extent of competitive bureau development if this is to be a remedy for the problems that have been identified in bureaucratic politics.

Although there are some basic patterns of centralization and decentralization in administrative structures, attempts at administrative reform have produced, and continue to produce, some interesting opportunities to ascertain the impact of structure on the behavior of bureaucrats. On the one hand, there have been attempts to decentralize government substantially. In France and Belgium, a number of *administrations de mission* have been created to meet specific program needs (Timsit 1987; Rigaud and Delcros 1986). These bodies are organized outside the structures of the ministries, are headed by a single individual (perhaps the ultimate bureau chief), and are given broad grants of power to pursue their goals. *Projektgruppen* in Germany are similar organizations, although perhaps not quite so independent (Lepper 1983). Finally, the most radical change of all is the British proposal to devolve most government functions onto a series of agencies largely independent of ministerial control (Jenkins, Cairnes, and Jackson 1988). This reform, which has already begun to be implemented, if successful, would transform a highly centralized system of administration into a highly decentralized system, and would constitute a natural laboratory for studying the impact of changing structures on bureaucratic goals and performance. Issues of parliamentary accountability (among other problems) may yet prevent the full implementation of these proposals, but we would anticipate the creation of a whole new cadre of bureaucratic entrepreneurs if they were implemented fully.

At the other end of the dimension, there have been proposals to reduce the decentralization of Swedish administration and to curtail some of the powers of the boards (Ruin 1989). For a variety of reasons (interestingly, some of them budgetary), the idea that there is a need for additional political control over administration has become more popular (Mellbourn 1986; see also SOU 1985). By reducing the power of the decentralized boards, it is hoped that politicians will be able to produce more of what they promise during electoral campaigns, rather than being so much at the mercy of the permanent bureaucracy. In this case, however, the desired results appear very much an attack of Downs's idea of being able to pursue different policies through the bureaucracy, rather than Niskanen's notion of supplanting public policy goals with the private goals of the bureaucratic leaders.

Interest Group Connections. In addition to decentralization, administrative systems also differ in the extent to which the agencies (or bureaus, or whatever they may be called) have close ties to interest groups. Further, the extent to which such ties are recognized as an integral part of the governing process will also have an impact on the capacity of the interest groups to shape the policy of the public organization (Peters 1989). In this case, we hypothesize that, everything else being equal, the greater the legitimate role accorded interest groups in the policy making of a public organization, the less is the capacity of the leaders of that organization to pursue their own goals through the policy-making process. We expect this for several reasons. First, the more interest groups are associated with a public organization, the less autonomy that organization is able to exercise. If, as in many European countries, the agency must consult an advisory board composed of interest group members and circulate a petition (*remiss*) seeking advice about policy, it will have little capacity to do what they as bureaucrats want to do to feather their own nests. Certainly consultation need not equal control, but it may come very close to being that when the decisions, and the grounds on which they are made, are widely circulated. Further, in societies that value consultation and consensus in policy making, like Scandinavia, Austria, and Switzerland, a ministry would find it difficult to make policy decisions that stray too far from the advice that it had been given.

Following from the discussion of corporatism, close links of an administrative agency to an interest group would imply that the organization would be under pressure to pursue *purposive* goals, rather than the *reflexive* goals implied by the Niskanen model (Mohr 1973). In other words, a close link with an interest group would tend to generate goals within the organization that would satisfy the needs of clients, even if they did not necessarily satisfy the original wishes of the legislature. Further, the goals derived from an association with an interest group would be less likely to meet the more personal needs of the organization leadership. Of course, in the by now famous iron triangles in U.S. politics, the two goals appear to have become closely intertwined. However, we have to question the extent to which that is a peculiarly U.S. phenomenon, which also reflects to some extent the decentralized nature of the sponsor. Other political systems may have phrases that capture some of the same meaning—*Ressorts* in Germany (Scharpf, Reissert, and Schnabel 1976) and *familles d'espirit* in France (Gremion 1979)—but even there the symbiotic linkages characteristic of the United States are absent. Again, activities in the European systems appear closer to Downs's ideas about the manner in which public goals might be deflected than they do to those expressed in the Niskanen book.

The above discussion implies a one-on-one, symbiotic relationship between an interest group and an agency, which is certainly the model that has been applicable to the United States. That relationship has been changing significantly through the development of issue networks and policy communities (Heclo 1978; Walker 1989; Campbell 1988). A wider array of interest groups are now involved in policy decisions, which may in turn actually strengthen the agency's capacity to do what it (and its leadership) wants to do. In Western Europe, corporate (Schmitter 1974) and corporate pluralist (Rokkan 1966; Heisler 1979) arrangements have weakened the capacity of any one interest group to dominate the policy making of an agency. This is especially true in the broadly consultative corporate pluralist arrangements common in Scandinavia (Kvavik 1980). Again, however, the breadth of the consultative arrangements may be sufficiently great to permit substantial agency autonomy, especially given the autonomy already granted to boards and agencies in those countries.

Instruments of Accountability. To some extent, the predictions of the Niskanen model represent a failure to enforce that old bureaucratic virtue—accountability. If agencies are, in fact, being allowed to expand almost at will, they are not being held accountable fiscally (or in policy terms) for their actions. We could argue that the structuring of public bureaus in many industrialized democracies permits government organizations to function with little direct accountability and hence with greater opportunity to pursue their own, reflexive goals. To understand the possibility of avoiding accountability requires some idea of the changing nature of that virtue (Day and Klein 1987). At one end of a spectrum is strict legal accountability (see Gruber 1987), in which the agency's actions are closely reviewed by the legislature, the courts, or perhaps superior executive organizations. The increasing volume and complexity of public policy makes this type of accountability virtually impossible to enforce in the late twentieth century. At the other end of the spectrum is market accountability, in which the actions of a government bureau are subjected to the indirect, but nonetheless real, discipline of the market, and the organization is forced to break even, or at least to justify its subsidy (Pierce 1981). Many government programs are not suitable for this type of accountability, although quasi markets can be created for many activities. One of the justifications for the creation of the new agency structure in the United Kingdom, for example, is to be able to enforce something approaching market accountability on services that would, at least in principle, be marketable.

It appears that many contemporary public organizations fall between these two ideal types of accountability. These organizations are neither subjected to strict legal accountability nor to the rigors of the marketplace. As a consequence, they are able to behave relatively autonomously and to pursue their own goals. One of the characteristics of modern public organizations is that they have been able to carve out a sphere of relative autonomy in the midst of large, complex governments. The very size and complexity of government enhances the capacity of organizations to create those areas of autonomy, because it becomes difficult for any sponsor to monitor all that happens in government. Therefore, we will need to examine the nature of the sponsoring organizations to determine to what extent these institutions have attempted to equip themselves for the challenges posed by diffuse responsibility and hybrid accountability.

Individual Characteristics

In addition to the characteristics of the administrative institutions in Western Europe, we also must pay some attention to the nature of the individuals who occupy positions in the public bureaucracy. There are some important factors in common across European governments, with perhaps the most important being the elite status and widespread public respect of European civil servants in comparison to their U.S. counterparts. This respect does, as should be expected, provide those European civil servants substantial latitude in policy making. There are also, however, important differences among European public personnel systems that affect the capacity of civil servants to exercise the autonomous power seemingly required by the Niskanen model. While some of the characteristics (discussed below) do refer to the attributes of specific individuals who may occupy roles in the public bureaucracy, most refer to the nature of personnel systems taken as wholes.

Career Structures. Several factors in the career structures of the public bureaucracy could be hypothesized to affect the ability and desire of civil servants to maximize their budgets. One is the extent to which careers are within a single agency or department. In the United States, the majority of civil servants remain within the same department, or even the same bureau, for their entire career. The same is true for a number of European countries, with some countries allowing the agencies themselves to do the recruiting rather than using a centralized personnel organization.[6] On the other hand, in some European countries, for example, the United Kingdom, civil servants tend to be moved around among departments during the early portion of their careers, in order to cultivate a broader view of government and its work than can be gained from any particular organization. Such a career structure develops the trust, the institutional commitment, and the extended time perspective that may restrain any tendency to "shoot the moon" in the budgetary process (Heclo and Wildavsky 1974). Everything else being equal, we expect careers within a single organization or only a few organizations to be associated more with the budget-maximizing behavior than diverse career patterns would be. It would be difficult with a single organization career, however, to distinguish between budget-maximizing behavior designed to protect and defend services being provided to clients (Downs) from the same behavior being motivated by personal ambitions (Niskanen).

Somewhat similar questions arise about movement between the public and private sectors and its impact on budget-maximizing behavior in government. The arguments here, however, could go either way. On the one hand, individuals who anticipate that their entire career will be in government, whether within a single organization or not, can be hypothesized to be more likely to engage in budget-maximizing behavior than those with more varied careers. In the first place, for those who remain within government, their only chance for improving their economic positions may be through the expansion of the agency budget. The evidence on whether such expansion indeed benefits those at the top of the organization, with the greatest opportunity to influence the budget, is very spotty (Dunleavy 1985) but, if nothing else, such behavior may be *perceived* as a means to that end. Conversely, if individuals plan to spend only a portion of their careers in government, and especially if they intend to finish their career in the private sector, they may have less interest in pushing for larger budgets than in building a reputation as an effective manager; such a reputation would be enhanced by producing lower rather than higher budgets. Actually, much the same may be true for someone with a career entirely in the civil service, if the desired destination is the treasury or a similar central agency with a reputation for financial probity and careful budgeting.

On the other hand, individuals who are in government for a short period of time have a very short time horizon. They may believe that they have to accomplish something fast, and the quickest way to prove their effectiveness may be to get more money. Numerous studies of ministers and political executives point to the ability to "fight one's corner," to protect and expand the organization as a central feature in the success of a public manager. Therefore, a more open career structure in government may be associated with greater budget maximization, rather than less. In addition, the short-term manager need not worry about long-term effects or the efficiency of programs. Their job may be simply to do *something* fast.

Another feature of the career systems of Western European public bureaucracies that has potential importance for the applicability of the Niskanen model is the politicization of the bureaucracy. Unlike the United States and the United Kingdom, where attempts are made to separate political from career appointments, the two types of appointments may be fused in European bureaucracies (Meyers 1985; Mayntz, 1984). For example, civil servants in Germany may declare their party allegiance (Derlien 1988), which in turn will improve their chances of receiving a top government position—assuming that the proper party is in power. Partisan commitment by bureaucrats may reduce the willingness of bureau chiefs to pursue different goals from those of their sponsor. With a partisan commitment, the bureau chief will be under more pressure to pursue the goals of the government, rather than to pursue individual goals. Of course, partisanship is no talisman against self-seeking, as close observation of any legislature would quickly reveal, but it may serve as a check on more overt utilization of the public budget for personal rewards.

Roles and Values. Finally, individual values and role conceptions that a civil servant brings to the job may influence the extent to which he or she engages in budget-maximizing behavior. Most Western European countries have well-institutionalized, career, civil servants, with long histories of public service. Further, the role of the civil servant is often expressed in legalistic rather than political or entrepreneurial terms. To assume that all European civil servants are interested only in the law and in public service would be naive (see Page 1985), but it is important to understand the significant differences that do exist between European and U.S. civil servants (Aberbach, Putnam, and Rockman 1981). Although we as scholars can readily understand that German or Scandinavian civil servants play a political role, they may think of their legal obligations first. This can be a significant restraint on their latitude of action.

An alternative way to consider the question of roles and values in civil service is to consider the position of the state in these countries. Particularly in contrast to the United States (Skowronek 1982), most European countries are state-centric (Dyson 1980). In addition, the civil service is regarded as the dutiful servant of the state. With this prestigeous and powerful position, we might expect the civil service—especially the senior civil service as a general social elite for these societies—extract what it wants from the remaining components of government. This estimate is in contrast with the structural arguments, as well as with the legalitistic description of the role of civil servants, discussed above. Further, the prestige and the concept of service may further restrain self-seeking through the budgetary process.

The Sponsor

The third set of variables affecting the ability of bureaucratic agencies to achieve any success at budget maximization are those associated with the sponsor of the agency. In the Niskanen model, it appears to be assumed that this sponsor is singular (but see Tullock 1965, 82–106) and, given its derivation from the U.S. experience, that the sponsor is a legislative committee or subcommittee. Given the (then) well-established norms of behavior in the U.S. Congress, if an agency was successful in extracting the desired budget level from the relevant subcommittee, it would be almost certain to get that amount from the full house (Fenno 1966). That model for the United States is overly simplistic, but the situation facing agencies in Western Europe is even more complex. As a consequence, it appears more difficult for those agencies to really win in the budgetary game. (Of course, most agencies in the United States have found the outcomes of the real budgetary game much more problematic than the easy victories portrayed in the Niskanen book.)

A variety of factors inhibit the capacity of agencies, or even entire ministries, in Western European countries from adopting anything like a budget-maximizing strategy that could produce for them the fiscal latitude being sought. Perhaps the most important limiting factor is the expertise and the status of the sponsors. In addition to some concerns about the legislature and its committees, the average administrator in Western Europe must first worry about the ministry of finance or its equivalent central agency (Campbell and Szablowski 1979). These organizations tend to be much more expert and better informed than legislative committees—even legislative committees with substantial experience and staff, such as those in the United States. The minister of finance will have a staff of experts monitoring expenditure requests, making it more difficult for an agency to slip any excess fat through the process.

Several other factors in addition to expertise reinforce the budgeting capacity of a European ministry of finance. First, unlike a legislative committee, the ministry of finance is rarely connected with any spending interests or serving any electoral constituency. The major constituency of a ministry of finance is one that respects financial probity. As Kristensen (1980) points out, budgetary expansion is usually a private good, but controlling expenditures may be a public good. In addition, the minister of finance tends to be in a strong political position. In almost all cases, this is the second most important position in the cabinet (second only to the prime minister), and tends to have the strong support of the prime minister. In addition, the minister of finance may be granted special powers in cabinet meetings. For example, in Germany, a vote of one-half of the cabinet (which must include the chancellor) is necessary to overturn a decision by the minister of finance (Johnson 1983, 113). Further, organizations such as the Treasury in Britain tend to be the pinnacle of a civil service career. Hence, anyone who wants to climb the career ladder may adopt a "Treasury view," with its ruthless skepticism about public expenditure, early in his or her career. Finally, the respect with which ministries of finance are treated within the civil service (especially one with a unified career structure) tends to produce little resistance to their decisions. When there is resistance, the rules and procedures for resolution tend to favor the sponsor, not the spender.

Although we argue that in general the sponsor is a more formidable opponent for a spending agency in Europe than in the United States, there are still important differences in the capability of these controlling institutions. Some of the differences are readily apparent and identifiable. For example, in some countries (Italy and Belgium for example) there is a separate ministry of the budget responsible for overseeing expenditure requests. The division of responsibilities for oversight between such a ministry and the ministry of finance may weaken the sponsor. Likewise, the powers of the sponsor are reduced if revenue decisions are separated from expenditure decisions and if they are dealt with by government at different times. The constraints imposed by revenue demands are important for keeping expenditures (and hence the success of budget maximizers) lower, even if the budget is not formally balanced. Likewise, if, as in the British Treasury prior to 1968 and after 1981, personnel powers are combined with financial powers, the capacity of the sponsor to curtail budget maximizers is enhanced. Finally, the presence of special cabinet powers for the finance minister (as in the example of Germany) also limits the likely success of budget maximizers. These factors are combined in table 11.1 to provide some idea of the relative powers of financial control in ministries in Western European democracies.

In addition to the powers of central agencies in controlling public expenditure, the ministers in line ministries may be able to exercise a good deal of control over their own organizations. It is sometimes very easy to critique the capacity of ministers to counteract the desires of their own civil servants (Rose 1974; Katz 1986; Peters 1981), and this can be done humorously as well as seriously.[7] However, different political systems appoint ministers with differing capacities (Blondel 1988), and some ministers, even in the most difficult systems to control (Headey 1974), have proven perfectly capable of managing their own departments and, if necessary, imposing budgetary restraint. It may be the case, however, that the minister does not want to impose restraint on agencies but would very much like to maximize his own budget— for service to clients or for personal aggrandizement. Further, he or she may want to do this to prove prowess, as mentioned earlier (Kaufman 1980). Here again we encounter the defintional problem of just who the bureau chief really is. Is it the minister responsible for the entire ministry, or is it the senior permanent civil servant, for example, the permanent secretary or the Staatssekretar? Or is the bureau chief farther down in the hierarchy, the head of an office or a bureau or a section? Given the huge differences in the organizational structure of governments, it may be difficult to determine who has the incentive and the capability to engage in budget-maximizing behavior (Peters 1988). In addition, as Dunleavy (1985) points out, those who have the incentive rarely have the power, and vice versa.

In addition to the formidable powers possessed by ministries of

TABLE 11.1
Powers of the Executive as Sponsor, Fifteen Countries

Country	Ministerial Decentralization	Coalition	Finance Minister	Special Procedures	Summary
Austria	Low	Moderate[a]	Moderate	No	Moderate
Belgium	Moderate	Broad	Weak	No	Weak
Denmark	Moderate	Broad	Moderate	Yes	Moderate
Finland	High	Moderate	Moderate	No	Moderate
France	Low	Narrow	Moderate	No	Moderate
Germany	High	Narrow	Moderate	No	Moderate
Ireland	Low	Narrow	Moderate	No	Strong
Italy	Low	Broad	Weak	No	Weak
Netherlands	Low	Broad	Moderate	Yes	Moderate
Norway	High	Moderate	Moderate	No	Weak
Portugal	Low	Moderate	Moderate	No	Moderate
Spain	Low	Narrow	Moderate	No	Moderate
Sweden	High	Moderate	Moderate	Yes	Moderate/weak
Switzerland	Moderate	Moderate	Moderate	No	Moderate
United Kingdom	Low	One party	Strong	Yes	Strong

[a] Recently a "grand coalition."

finance and their counterparts, and those possessed by ministers in the line agencies, parliaments (as yet another manifestation of the sponsor) in Western Europe are not without their own powers. It has become conventional to downplay the capacity of legislatures to make effective decisions in contemporary presidential democracies, but some legislatures have made rather effective counterattacks against executive dominance (Suleiman 1986). These counterattacks have been especially important in budgeting, where parliaments have sought to regain their control of the purse strings—one of the original sources of their power. The powers of legislatures in many Western European governments are, however, severely constrained by the need to build coalition governments. The bargaining that precedes the forming of coalition governments often involves side payments to constituencies, and thus taking tough stances against certain categories of expenditure may be difficult. Thus, countries with single-party governments (the United Kingdom), or with limited coalitions (Germany, Sweden), may be able to exercise greater control than those with broader coalitions (Belgium).

The assertion, or reassertion, of legislative power can come through a number of devices. One is strengthening legislative committees for both making legislation and overseeing the bureaucracy. Another means is to develop staffs and an analytic capacity to scrutinize public expenditures. This includes performing such scrutinies before appropriations and after expenditure (the traditional postaudit function of legislatures). The final change is in the development of specialized procedures to ensure closer inspection of budgets and to place the burden of proof on those who want to increase an appropriation. In the most extreme case, as in Sweden (Ericksson 1983), the government may assume an automatic budget cut rather than an increase. No legislature in Western Europe has undertaken all these reforms, but most have undertaken some (Schick 1986). In so doing, they have greatly strengthened their position as sponsors for the bureaucracy. Some judgments about the probable comparative strengths of legislatures in controlling the bureaucracy are presented in table 11.2.

Finally, some political systems have developed specialized organizations for advising the government on programs and public expenditures, and these have served as yet another barrier to the

TABLE 11.2

Strength of Parliament as Sponsor, Seventeen Countries

Country	Right to Amend	Separate Budget Committee	Referral to Functional Committee	Staffing	Summary
Austria	Yes	Yes	No	Low	Medium
Belgium	Yes	Yes	Yes	Medium	High
Denmark	Yes	Yes	No	Medium	Medium
Finland	Yes	Yes	Yes	Medium	High
France	No	Yes	No	Low	Low
Germany	Yes	Yes	Yes	High	High
Greece	No	Yes	Yes	Low	Low
Ireland	No	Yes (several)	No	Medium	Medium
Italy	No	Yes	Yes	Medium	Medium
Luxembourg	Yes	Yes	No	Medium	Medium
Netherlands	Limited	No	Yes	Low	Low
Norway	Yes	Yes	Yes	Medium	High
Portugal	Yes	Yes	Yes	Low	Medium
Spain	Yes	Yes	No	High	High
Sweden	Yes	Yes	Yes	High	High
Switzerland	No	Yes	No	High	Medium
United Kingdom	No	No[a]	No[a]	Low	Low

Source: Inter–Parliamentary Union, 1986.

a. Referred to various select committees rather than to standing committees.

success of budget-maximizing bureaucrats. For example, the Stats-
kontoret in Sweden is designed as a body to give management
advice to (and to some extent to scrutinize) organizations in government. Very early in the era of retrenchment, the Danish government established an office to routinely review existing expenditure
programs (Wurtzen 1977). The Netherlands Scientific Council on
Government Policy serves as an analytic enterprise, offering high-
quality advice on policy proposals. Even the Central Policy Review Staff in Britain functioned for a time as a source of policy
advice for the entire cabinet, with some real impact on specific
policy choices (Blackstone and Plowden 1988). While at times they
do not have a specific client—and lose influence because of that—
these bodies still provide another source of analysis and additional
ammunition that a sponsor can use for control.

In short, the description of the resources available to governments in Western Europe should indicate that sponsors are not
lonely, ignorant funders of public programs, as appears to be implied by the Niskanen argument. Rather, government institutions
have ample sources of advice, which should enable them to distinguish the budget-padding program from the service-enhancing
program. This does not mean that the sponsor would always select
the latter type of program over the former, only that there is no
monopoly of information that would require the sponsor to trade
public money for information about a program. Perhaps especially
important is the fact that there is by now a multiplicity of advisory
bodies in most European governments, some responsible to the
executive (collectively, or to individual ministers), some responsible to the legislature (collectively, or to committees), and some
operating independently. Further, outside of government, consult-
ing firms have begun to market their services much as they do in
the United States. To be able to deceive its sponsor readily, as is
implied by the Niskanen argument, the bureau has to be extremely
lucky, extremely devious, or perhaps both.

Public Programs

The final factors affecting the ability of a bureau chief to maximize his or her budget, and probably also affecting the desire to do

so, are the nature of the programs being managed and the types of expenditures (defined in economic terms) associated with the program. The impact of programs can be considered in at least two ways. First, certain policy areas tend to experience greater success than others, everything else being equal. Therefore, a bureau chief who wants to budget maximize for his or her personal gain (as is often assumed) would do well to select a program of this type to manage. Second, the composition of budgets in some agencies makes it easier to appropriate any increases for personal benefits of the bureau chief than is possible in other agencies. Again, anyone who wants to be a budget maximizer should carefully select a program in advance if he or she expects to be successful.

As noted earlier, some policy areas tend to experience greater budgetary success than do others (Davis, Dempster, and Wildavsky 1974). This success may come about for several reasons. In some cases, the successful program is one popular with legislators and political executives, as to some extent defense has been in the United States. In other instances, the program may be an entitlement program, so that most spending increases can be justified as fulfilling the existing commitments of government, rather than an exercise of discretion. Other programs are associated with interest groups that have gained political power, even if they do not represent a large segment of the population; agriculture in most industrialized countries is an obvious example. Finally, a program may be complex and technical, and the managers of the program may be able to appeal to their own expertise to overcome opposition. For whatever reasons, however, we expect bureaus whose programs fall into any of these categories to have greater budgetary success than organizations that cannot use any of these arguments.

Although aggregate budgetary success may be influenced by the nature of the policy area, the ability of the bureau chief to appropriate any of the budget surplus (fat) that might be created will be influenced by the composition of his or her budget. For example, Dunleavy (1985) has developed useful distinctions among three components of the existing budget for any agency. (1) The core budget (those portions of the budget spent for maintaining the agency's own operations, e.g., salaries and equipment) is the component of the budget of greatest utility to the budget-maximizing bureau chiefs. (2) The bureau budget contains the core budget as well as those parts of the agency's program spending that are directly spent, and for which the agency is directly responsible to the sponsor. This may include contracts let to the private sector. (3) The program budget contains the bureau budget (and thereby the core budget) plus funds to implement the agency's programs, even if the ultimate spending authority resides in the public sector outside the bureau. Thus, the category includes money passed on to local governments.

Clearly the money in the core budget is more available for personal utilization by the bureau chief than is money in either of the other two categories, and programs that have more of this type of budget money will be most valuable to a budget-maximizing bureau chief—at least one in the Niskanen mold. A bureau chief in the Downs's mold, on the other hand, tends to be indifferent toward these types of expenditures or might actually favor the bureau or program budgets. This is true, because the latter two categories of funds facilitate direct services to clients and therefore might be more difficult for a sponsor to reduce; or it might be because the bureau chief is committed to the agency's program of service (Dich 1973). As Hood, Huby, and Dunsire (1984) point out, the budget-maximizing bureaucrat model needs to be specified more precisely in order to determine just when and where maximization is most possible, and most desirable, for the bureau chief.

Another point to be made about program type is that some programs are more readily monitored than others. That is, output from some programs can be identified more readily, and related to inputs more readily, than is true for other programs. Almost by definition, the output of programs creating almost pure public goods, for example, defense, are not readily subject to close monitoring of outputs. In addition, there are severe difficulties in measuring the output of more private goods, for example, education, when the true beneficiaries and the timing of the benefit are not clear (Byatt, 1977). Of course, given that the strategy of the budget-maximizing bureau chief appears to be to avoid control through avoiding accountability, programs that cannot be readily scrutinized are preferred to other types of programs. When the difficulty of scrutiny can be combined with political popularity, or with technical complexity (as with national defense in most countries), this type of program becomes a natural locus for a manager to adopt a maximization strategy.

Type of program and type of expenditure do intersect, but not always in ways favorable to the budget-maximizing bureau chief. For example, if entitlement programs are indeed among the most successful organizations in extracting money from government (which they appear to be), this may be particularly beneficial to the bureau chief. This is because most of the money generated by entitlement programs comes in the form of bureau or program expenditures, which is passed on to clients. In general, programs that devote a larger proportion of their total budget to exhaustive expenditures—especially personnel—are the most likely candidates for the budget-maximizing bureaucrat. If the goal of the bureaucrat is to devote as much as possible of the agency's budget to his or her own personal goals, then he or she should attempt to maximize the core budget. Again, however, a bureaucrat following Downs's logic might be more interested in program or bureau budgets because of the direct link to clients and the greater protection from cuts.

This discussion emphasizes the comparative advantages of certain spending programs for a budget-maximizing bureau chief. The same argument, however, can be used to address cross-national comparisons. For example, defense programs, a natural policy area for the budget maximizer, have been the source of much greater expenditure in the United States than in most Western European countries. Likewise, transfer expenditures, for example, social service programs, have relatively little capacity to generate exploitable benefits for a bureau chief, even if he or she is successful in increasing the budget. Social programs constitute a substantially larger proportion of public expenditure in Western Europe than in the United States. Again, the United States is particularly well suited to the budget-maximizing model, while most of Western Europe is not. Even in Europe, however, there are still important differences in the levels of expenditure for different purposes (see table 11.3), which may be related to some differential levels of budgetary success for bureaucrats.

TABLE 11.3
Expenditures by Function, Sixteen Countries, 1985
(percent)

Country	Defense	Social Services	Economic Services	Debt Interest
Austria	3.1	54.4	14.6	6.0
Belgium	5.3	41.4	12.2	9.4
Denmark	5.4	39.1	7.5	16.8
Finland	5.2	44.5	21.4	10.2
France	7.3	58.5	7.2	5.8
Germany	9.3	68.4	7.4	6.5
Greece	10.8	41.2	4.9	11.1
Ireland	3.1	38.6	15.0	17.3
Italy	3.2	38.9	13.2	12.8
Netherlands	5.1	46.4	10.7	13.2
Norway	7.9	45.6	19.5	7.4
Portugal	n.a.	n.a.	n.a.	n.a.
Spain	4.4	60.9	11.6	8.4
Sweden	6.6	49.6	6.8	5.9
Switzerland	10.3	63.0	12.2	6.3
United Kingdom	13.3	41.1	8.9	8.3

Source: International Monetary Fund, annual.

Testing the Model

We have, to this point, been discussing conditions hypothesized to predict the capacity of a bureau chief to engage in budget-maximizing behavior. In general, these conditions are almost all less favorable for the bureau chief in Europe than they are in the United States.[8] However, among Western European nations, there are also substantial differences among these variables, so should expect different outcomes in different European countries. Some *very rough* ratings that sum the observed differences along these dimensions for a number of European countries are provided in table 11.4.

At least two alternative research strategies are available. The first is to attempt some measurement (even if only subjective rating scales) of each dimension and then relate those measures to some measures of the dependent variables—indicators of budget

TABLE 11.4
Likelihood of Budget Maximization, Fourteen Countries

Country	Executive Strength	Legislature Strength	Program Mix	Summary
Austria	Moderate	Moderate	Unfavorable	Mixed
Belgium	Low	High	Unfavorable	Mixed
Denmark	Moderate	Moderate	Unfavorable	Mixed
Finland	Moderate	High	Mixed	Mixed
France	Moderate	Low	Unfavorable	Mixed
Germany	Moderate	High	Unfavorable	Mixed
Ireland	High	Moderate	Favorable	Mixed
Italy	Low	Moderate	Favorable	Mixed
Netherlands	Moderate	Low	Mixed	Mixed
Norway	Low	High	Mixed	Mixed
Spain	Moderate	High	Unfavorable	Mixed
Sweden	Weak	Moderate	Favorable	High
Switzerland	Moderate	Moderate	Unfavorable	Low
United Kingdom	High	Low	Unfavorable	Low

maximization—to ascertain which of the independent variables is most closely associated with the budgetary success of agencies. The alternative approach is to select several extreme cases to determine if there are indeed important differences among these countries in the apparent success of bureaus in the budgetary process. If there are such differences, then it is likely that the dimensions we have identified do have some relationship to agency success and, therefore, that the general model merits additional research. In part, for reasons of time and available research materials, we adopted the second strategy and focus on four countries: the United Kingdom, France, Germany, and Sweden. The United Kingdom and Sweden appear to fall at the opposite ends of a spectrum of European countries to which the Niskanen model is applicable: it is apparently least applicable to the United Kingdom and most applicable to Sweden. In the United Kingdom, the hierarchical arrangement of ministries, the strength of the Treasury, numerous procedural devices (cash limits, etc.), and a single-party government make such maximizing behavior unlikely. In Sweden, on the other hand, the decentralization of the administrative and personnel systems make such behavior more likely. Both France and Germany fall in the middle of the spectrum of applicability, but for somewhat different reasons.

In the empirical research that has already been conducted to test the Niskanen model, a number of dependent variables have been utilized. All of these variables were surrogate measures for the unmeasured attributes of motivations and demand curves of bureau chiefs (Lane 1987; Sorenson 1987). With that caveat, research can still determine if the model has any plausibility in the real world of government: if there is sufficient evidence that the outcomes of the model appear as predicted, then we may be able to infer the underlying motivations of the bureau chiefs. The first step is to identify the dependent variables that capture the meaning of the model's predictions.

One of the most comprehensive analyses of the Niskanen model was performed by Hood, Huby, and Dunsire (1984). Their analysis of British central government used four types of dependent variables. One was the overall level of public expenditure compared to the expenditures that might have been expected if the costs of government had only increased in line with inflation. This was assumed to measure the ability of the bureaucracy to keep their gravy train running. Beneath that broad measure, the authors examined level of civil service pay relative to total public expenditure. With reference to public sector personnel, Hood, Huby, and Dunsire examined the ratio of top civil servants to total civil service employment, and a rough measure (the number of private secretaries in government) of the perquisites available to top civil servants. These measures were examined in the aggregate and, in some cases, were disaggregated to the department level. In each case, there was little evidence to support a budget-maximizing model of bureaucratic behavior in Britain. Given my previous analysis of the structural characteristics of British government, I would not have expected great agency success—and that expectation was certainly confirmed.

The analysis of the United Kingdom appears to touch on most of the relevant surrogate measures of budget-maximizing behavior, and therefore I will attempt to replicate (and to some extent, extend) that analysis in this chapter. In particular, I am interested in the following six measures.

1. *Overall expansion of public expenditure.* Although I am reasonably confident of what will be discovered here, this variable will still serve as a useful backdrop against which to examine more nuanced changes within the public sector.

2. *Total public employment as a percentage of the work force.* This is a reasonably direct test of the model, because increasing the personnel allocation of a bureau is assumed to enhance the power, prestige, pay, and perquisites of the bureau chief. Further, even in the restatements of the basic model, for example, Dunleavy's theory on growth in total public employment, could be valuable in creating new positions for managers. This would not directly benefit the bureau chief, but it might improve his or her position with other members of the bureau.

3. *Total wages and salaries as a percentage of public expenditure.* This is another reasonably direct test of the importance of personnel and salaries to the budget-maximizing bureaucrat. I assume that if the basic Niskanen model is correct, salaries will be an increasing component of public expenditure.

4. *Salary scale expansion or compression.* If budget-maximizing bureau chiefs are actually able to use their budget increases to improve their own lot in life, then I would expect them to enhance their own pay and perquisites. The test of this is the extent to which salaries at the top of the scale have increased relative to all public sector salaries. I would also want to know if the senior bureaucracy has been able to keep its own purchasing power in line with inflation and with general wage movements in the economy.

5. *Senior civil servants as a percentage of total civil service employment.* One reason for expanding the size of public employment is to create more senior positions, which will be able to command high salaries and enhanced perquisites. In fact, some analysts argue that budgetary expansion benefits not so much the bureau chief as those in the lower echelons of management, who are able to move into newly created senior positions. The evidence on this point is limited but is still important for understanding the dynamics of the public sector.

6. *Qualitative analysis of where government growth occurs.* Dunleavy (1985) argues that the Niskanen model is most applicable to the growth and development of already existing line agencies. Is this

where the action is in the growth of contemporary governments in Western Europe?

The combination of all these factors should provide a reasonably fair and comprehensive test of the Niskanen model, remembering all the while that we are depending on surrograte measures.

Findings and Analysis

I have been able to marshall evidence for all Western European countries for some of the variables mentioned above and for the selected sample of four countries for all the dependent variables. Thus, the analysis will provide a reasonably nuanced picture of what has been happening with Western European bureaucracies and the extent to which they conform to the Niskanen model. I will present the information in the order of the dependent variables mentioned above. In most instances, the data will be presented from 1950 to the present, but that may be impossible for some variables. Covering such a long time period is desirable (see Rose and Peters 1978) to ascertain the effects of the postwar economic (and public sector) boom and the effects of contraction forced by economic and ideological change. In particular, it is important to see if bureaucracies maintain gains in the face of widescale retrenchment.

Total Public Expenditure

Total public expenditure has increased substantially in all Western European countries in the time period we are considering (see table 11.5). This is certainly true in absolute terms and is also true in reference to economic aggregates, such as gross domestic product. This growth was most pronounced in 1955–1975, but in some countries has continued, albeit at a slower rate. In itself, expansion of public expenditure proves nothing about the success of bureaucratic agencies in expanding their own core budgets; that can be ascertained in the separate analysis of the composition of public expenditure. What total expenditures do demonstrate, however, is that government is able to extract resources from the economy

TABLE 11.5
Growth of Public Expenditure as percentage of
Gross Domestic Product, Seventeen Countries, 1950–1987

Country	1950	1960	1970	1980	1987	Change 1950–1986	Change 1980–1987
Austria	24.0	32.1	39.2	48.9	52.5	118.8	7.4
Belgium	22.6	30.3	36.5	50.8	52.5	131.4	3.0
Denmark	23.4	26.1	40.2	56.2	58.3	149.1	3.7
Finland	25.5	26.7	30.5	36.5	42.0	64.7	15.1
France	32.0	34.6	38.9	46.4	51.8	61.9	13.6
Germany	30.8	32.0	38.6	48.3	46.8	51.9	−3.1
Greece	15.1	17.4	22.4	30.5	43.0	184.8	41.0
Ireland	34.1	32.6	39.6	50.9	54.7	60.4	7.5
Italy	22.9	30.1	34.2	46.1	50.7	121.4	10.0
Luxembourg	27.6	30.5	33.1	54.8	51.7	87.3	−5.7
Netherlands	26.5	33.7	43.9	57.5	60.1	126.8	4.5
Norway	27.6	29.9	41.0	50.7	49.9	80.8	−1.6
Portugal	14.4	17.0	21.6	35.9	43.9	204.9	22.3
Spain	11.6	13.7	22.2	32.9	41.7	259.5	26.7
Sweden	23.0	31.1	43.3	61.6	63.6	176.5	3.3
Switzerland	19.8	17.2	21.3	29.3	30.5	54.0	4.1
United Kingdom	31.9	32.6	39.8	46.0	43.2	35.4	−6.1

Source: OECD monthly; OECD annual.

that can serve as the raw material for bureaucratic expansion. Bureaucratic expansion of the type described by Niskanen may occur without overall expenditure growth, if sufficient resources can be shifted out of program and bureau budgets to core budgets, but an expanding total expenditure pie makes expansion of bureau personnel budgets that much easier.

Although there has been some expansion of public expenditure in all Western European countries, that expansion has not been uniform. The largest percentage increases of public expenditure (as a percentage of gross domestic product) have occurred in the later-developing countries such as Portugal, Spain, Greece, and in Sweden and Denmark. The slowest rates of expansion (although having among the highest levels of public expenditure relative to the gross domestic product) have come in the larger European countries such as France, Germany, the United Kingdom, as well as in Switzerland and Ireland. Thus, if we harken back to our hypotheses about the applicability of the Niskanen model to different European countries, it appears that there is one strike against the model here. The expansion of the public sector appears to have been associated more with developmental factors and with ideological change than with the nature of the bureaucracy.

The major piece of consoling news for the budget-maximizing model is that the Thatcher government was not able to fully constrain the expansion of public expenditure in Britain, even though it was ideologically inclined to do so and should have used the available levers in the Treasury and in its own commitment to do so. Some governments have reduced total public expenditure relative to gross domestic product in the 1980s, but in most, public expenditure appears to have a life of its own. In most countries, the continued growth of public expenditure has been more a function of entitlement programs and transfer expenditures than growth in public sector salaries and consumption expenditures. If anyone has been the beneficiary of the expansion of the public sector in European countries, it is not the civil service (Gretton and Harrison 1982; Hennessy 1988; Hood, Huby, and Dunsire 1984).

Public Employment

It is conceivable that a government could reduce public expenditure while still increasing its own levels of employment. This could be done by shifting resources out of transfer programs and into programs involving large numbers of direct public employees, by hiring more low-paid and part-time workers, by reducing public sector salaries, or by some combination of these. The evidence for most of Western Europe is that, although public employment increased during the 1950s, 1960s, and into the 1970s, that growth has slowed or reversed (OECD, 1982; Martin, 1982; Rose et al., 1985), and the public sector now absorbs a smaller proportion of total employment. In some instances, the shift out of public sector employment has been very dramatic (Cusack, Notermans, and Rein 1989). Further, several of the managerial changes mentioned earlier—for example, using more part-time employees—

have been adopted, so that government consumed quite a bit less personnel time in the late 1980s than it once did.

Determining total public employment is an increasingly difficult task, as governments disguise their true size from taxpayers (Peters and Heisler 1983; Salamon 1981). Therefore, I am not concerned with peripheral employment but with employment in central government. In addition to greater ease in data collection, this is also the segment of government toward which the Niskanen model is most clearly directed. Central government is not itself a homogenous category and contains not only spending ministries but organizations dedicated to reducing, or at least minimizing, expenditures. It is, however, a category that is generally comparable across countries. As shown in table 11.6, after increasing during the 1950s and 1960s and into the 1970s, central government employment constitutes a declining share of total employment in the economy in each of the four countries under investigation. Again, this may represent the hiving off, or decentralizing, of some policy areas, but even that appears to be an admission of defeat for a bureaucracy intent on increasing its own size and power.

Employment in Senior Grades

An additional change in employment that should occur in the bureaucratic aggrandizement hypothesized by Niskanen is an increase in employment in the top grades of the civil service. If the goal of the strategy is to produce private benefits, one of the more important of those benefits would be an increase in the number of openings in the senior grades of the civil service. These positions not only have higher salaries but greater perquisites, and some may even provide the occupants the quiet life that Peacock (1983) argues they are seeking. Further, in terms of organizational politics, the creation of additional senior positions would provide the bureau chief a means of rewarding his or her loyal supporters.

Everything else being equal, we should expect some upward movement of civil service grades. First, as the work of government becomes more complex and technical, more professionals have to be hired. Second, privatization and decentralization of policies will be associated with declining total employment, especially at lower

TABLE 11.6
Central Government Employment as a
Percentage of the Civilian Labor Force, 1950–1985

Year	United Kingdom	France	Germany	Sweden
1950	4.7	5.0	0.4	5.9
1960	4.1	7.1	0.5	6.1
1970	4.6	8.5	3.0	5.9
1975	4.7	10.1	3.2	6.6
1980	4.3	9.8	3.2	7.1
1985	3.9	9.1	3.0	6.9

Source: Rose et al. 1985; national sources.

Note: National definitions of central government employment vary; the figures are comparable within countries across time but not necessarily across countries.

ranks. Senior jobs will be retained to oversee the implementation of privatized policies, if nothing else. Therefore, even without the exercise of power on the part of the bureaucracy, we might expect some shifting of the composition of public employment.

The evidence on this point is somewhat disparate (table 11.7). In Germany and Sweden, the number of chiefs relative to total public employment (central government only) has declined slightly, although there is sufficient movement up and down from year to year to indicate that this is not any strong trend. In Britain, as Hood, Huby, and Dunsire (1984) note, there has been virtually no change in the composition of the civil service. In France there has been a slight increase in the number of senior positions, although sufficiently slight to cause one to wonder if this is really the manifestation of an omnipotent public bureaucracy. As noted earlier, the changing demands on government may be the cause of some upward movement of the grade structure within public administration, and the wide swings in government in France (Stevens 1985) may have generated some new positions.

Expenditures on Personnel

Even if there has been a declining number of civil servants, the Niskanen model of the expansion of the public bureaucracy could

TABLE 11.7
Senior Central Government Civil Servants as a
Percentage of Total Civil Service, 1960–1985

Year	France	Germany	Sweden	United Kingdom
1960	0.51	0.86	1.31	0.18
1970	0.44	0.54	1.10	0.10
1975	0.43	0.50	1.08	0.10
1980	0.37	0.46	0.73	0.11
1982	0.40	0.44	0.70	0.10
1985	0.52	0.42	0.61	0.11

Sources: Ministère de la Fonction Publique et du Plan, annual; *Statistisches Jahrbuch für die Bundesrepublik Deutschland,* annual; Statistiska Centralbyrån, annual; Hood, Huby, and Dunsire 1984; Central Statistical Office, annual.

Note: Definitions of civil servants vary. Data is comparable within countries but not necessarily across countries. German and Swedish figures were calculated from salary levels rather than from job titles.

be supported through this aggregated analysis if it could be shown that the wage bill for government, including perquisites such as pensions and other fringe benefits, increase over time. The total personnel costs of government are an especially important consideration, given the central position of benefits such as index-linked pensions in the demonology of critics of the civil service (Levine 1988; Cmnd. 8147). If indeed the upper echelons of government are to feather their own nests and those of their associates in the civil service through expansion, then the resources of government should logically be increasingly devoted to wages, salaries, and benefits. This does not, however, appear to have been the case at all; personnel costs actually appear to be a declining portion of total public expenditure.

The information contained in table 11.8 demonstrates that, for all Western European democracies, the personnel costs of central government tend to be a declining rather than increasing component of public expenditure. A similar decrease appears to have occurred for the personnel costs of subnational government, although there the change is less pronounced. There are some definite differences among the countries in the rate at which personnel

TABLE 11.8
Central Government Wages and Salaries as a Percentage of Total Public Expenditure, Sixteen Countries, 1975 and 1987

Country	1975	1987	Percentage Change, 1975–1987
Austria	10.5	9.7	−7.6
Belgium	17.3	13.4	−22.6
Denmark	17.4	12.3	−29.3
Finland	13.2	9.9	−25.0
France	17.3	17.3	0.0
Germany	9.8	8.4	−14.3
Greece	39.6	26.9	−32.0
Ireland	13.7	14.1	3.9
Italy	15.0	10.7	−28.6
Luxembourg	23.2	19.2	−17.2
Netherlands	11.2	9.0	−19.6
Norway	11.1	7.9	−28.8
Spain	45.9	16.8	−63.4
Sweden	9.2	5.9	−35.9
Switzerland	6.6	6.2	−6.1
United Kingdom	14.9	13.9	−6.7

Source: International Monetary Fund, annual.

costs have decreased in these governments (as well as in the absolute levels of personnel expenditures), and these data cover a relatively short period. Still, there is a very clear pattern of declining personnel costs. In many cases of large decreases in personnel costs, the government has privatized some functions it had previously implemented with its own personnel. This, in turn, may mean that the remaining agencies have been able to expand their own personnel expenditures and improve the economic conditions of those who remain in government. The loss of personnel through privatization, however, may mean that the bureaucracy (including, in this case, organizations such as nationalized industries) is not nearly as effective in protecting itself against the other political branches of government as has been assumed. When real political demands were placed on it, the bureaucracy has had to accede.

If we look in somewhat greater detail at the four cases on which we are concentrating the analysis, we see a very similar pattern. During the 1950s and early 1960s, the personnel cost component of total public expenditure increased. This growth appears to be in part because government as a whole was expanding, and more people were required to perform the jobs government had acquired. The growth of spending for personnel also appeared to be a function of the importance attached to the public sector at that time and the consequent need to adequately reward public employees. After about 1970, the share of total public expenditure devoted to personnel costs leveled off and then began to decrease slowly. Again, this was a function of shifting priorities, the relative growth of transfer programs, the privatization of programs, and a declining emphasis on the civil service as the bulwark of the nation. For whatever reason, however, this decline in personnel expenditures did occur, and the civil service does not appear to be very successful in defending its economic position in any of the countries.

Salary Compression or Expansion

If the purpose of holding a senior position in the civil service is to improve the occupant's own lot in life, then one of the clearest ways to do so is to improve the salary being received. Further, if the senior civil service has the power they are alleged to possess, then they should be able to force such salary improvements through the political process. Salary increases can be justified on the basis of comparability to similar jobs in the private sector, on the basis of need to recruit and retain individuals, or on the basis of keeping up with other economic aggregates, especially prices (Lauxmann 1974). For whatever reasons, if the civil service is at once self-interested and capable of manipulating its sponsor, it should be able to generate such gains. In some cases, because of the unified salary scales within a civil service system, differential benefits for senior civil service may not be possible, but if there is sufficient power, then the entire service should at least be able to keep up with other salaries in the economy—and perhaps surpass them.

Again, the evidence in support of a model of bureaucratic self-aggrandizement and bureaucratic power is far from compelling. First, taken as a whole, average salaries and wages for the civil service in Western European democracies for which there is adequate data are very little different from overall salaries and wages in the economy (Heller and Tait 1983). This lack of difference is especially surprising given that government tends to employ a larger proportion of technical and professional employees than do most industries, and given that professionalism in government has been increasing (Levine 1988; Rose et al. 1985). In short, the civil service does not appear to have been able to elevate its salaries or to extract special treatment; it appears to be treated very little different (except perhaps for fringe benefits) than other groups of employees.

If we look more closely at the four countries we have selected for analysis, additional findings of the same sort emerge. First, rather than widening salary differentials, with the senior civil service improving its own salaries differentials have been tightening in most countries (see table 11.9). For example, while in 1951 the top civil service positions in Germany received 650 percent higher salaries than did the lowest echelons of the *Beamten,* in 1987 that top official received only a 310 percent higher salary. Some salary compression occurred in Britain during the 1970s, but since that time there has been a significant widening of differentials. The termination of the Priestley scheme for relating pay for most civil servants, the hostility of the Thatcher government toward the civil service, and the work of the top salaries review body in protecting the salaries of the top of the service, combined to disadvantage lower echelons of the civil service. The degree of salary compression in Sweden was, however, even more dramatic than that in Germany. The available evidence for France is inconclusive, in part because of the complexity of the machinations of the *grille.* In addition, the final salary for a senior civil servant in France may depend a great deal on allowances and discretionary bonuses (Pougnard 1980). Some limited evidence on the salaries of members of the *grand corps* (Kessler 1986; Duvilliers and Pauti 1975) does indicate that at least in that powerful component of the civil service there has been some salary compression.

It appears once again that the numerous constraints built into civil service systems—and increasingly into employment in West-

TABLE 11.9
Salary Compression:
Highest Civil Service Salary as Multiple of Lowest, 1950–1987

Year	Sweden	Germany	United Kingdom
1950	13.4	7.5	7.1
1960	11.8	6.4	6.2
1965	11.1	5.9	
1970	10.6	5.6	5.9
1975	6.8	4.4	
1980	6.0	4.3	5.5
1984	5.6	4.3	10.2
1985	5.6	4.3	12.6
1986	5.5	4.2	16.1
1987	5.2	4.1	16.2

Sources: Statistiska Centralbyrån, annual; Statistisches Bundesamt, annual; Central Statistical Office, annual.

ern economies in general—have tended to minimize or nullify any impact of bureaucratic power on their own financial rewards. In particular, strong civil service unions in Sweden and Germany have pressed for lower differentials and better pay for those at the bottom of the hierarchies. In the context of Social Democratic politics and solidaristic wage policies in Sweden, such demands were virtually impossible to oppose. This was true even with a bourgeois government in office. In terms of our hypotheses about the relative power of bureaucracy in different countries, the observed findings are the inverse of what was expected. Top British civil servants appear to have had the greatest success, while those in Sweden have enjoyed the least.

Public sector wages and salaries have been able to keep up with—and in some cases to surpass—inflation, but this has been true for wages in almost all sectors of industrialized economies. The data in table 11.10 indicate that real salaries for the top civil service positions in these countries have been close to inflation but well below wage movements in the economy as a whole. In short, although sufficiently powerful to maintain their position relative to inflation, the public service has not been able to pull away from other segments of the economy. This is true despite the conven-

TABLE 11.10
Public Sector Wage Movements
Compared to Economy, 1950–1985
(index values)

Country and Year	Public Sector Salary[a]	Consumer Prices	Nonagricultural Wages
France			
1950	100	100	100
1960	187	185	196
1965	220	228	228
1970	250	281	364
1975	416	427	716
1980	675	702	1,370
1985	909	1,110	2,378
Germany			
1950	100	100	100
1960	147	135	164
1965	185	161	266
1970	237	220	381
1975	334	262	611
1980	425	410	838
1985	489	509	1,024
Sweden			
1950	100	100	100
1960	127	161	145
1965	181	195	271
1970	206	242	417
1975	289	352	602
1980	566	580	1,223
1985	828	892	1,808
United Kingdom			
1950	100	100	100
1960	134	147	139
1965	178	174	243
1970	201	218	358
1975	378	408	733
1980	745	798	1,480
1985	1,089	1,129	2,206

Sources: International Labour Office, annual; Ministère de la Fonction Publique et du Plan, annual; Statistisches Bundesamt, annual; Statistiska Centralbyrån, annual; Central Statistical Office, annual.

a. Highest paid category.

tional wisdom in many circles that the absence of a market restraint on salaries means that the senior civil service is able to extract substantial wages for itself. If anything, the lower echelons of the civil service—because of unions and their real ability to disrupt the life of citizens—have done better than the top. Gustafsson's (1976) characterization of the public sector in Sweden appears to hold true for public sectors in most other industrialized countries: it is a good place to start but not a good place to finish a career.

The compression of public sector salaries, and the apparent inability of the senior civil service to improve its own conditions—relative to other segments of the economy and even relative to other segments of the public sector—must be understood in the context of the contemporary politics of the public sector. A combination of a shift to the right of the political consensus in many European countries, the importation of private sector methods of pay determination (performance pay, job weighting, etc.) in the public sector (Chiver 1988), and union demands to improve the conditions of the low-paid worker in the public sector have combined to place a cap on top salaries while allowing wages and salaries at the bottom to creep upward. Further, the United Kingdom the concept of strict comparability of public and private sector salaries has been abrogated by the government (Cmnd. 8590), so that the government pays what the market will bear rather than attempting to compensate the civil service fairly relative to the remainder of the economy. At best, methods of indexing public sector salaries and wages have remained in place. The political conditions of the late 1970s and early 1980s were not conducive to improving the salaries of the top civil service workers, although compression in most countries had begun long before that time.

Qualitative Changes

Finally, is has been argued that the Niskanen model is particularly applicable to line departments in the mainstream of government (Dunleavy 1985) and that, to the extent that alternative organizational arrangements for delivering public services are developed, the model is less likely to be successful. In some ways this argument appears to run counter to the logic of the Niskanen model, that decentralized administrative systems permit greater budget-maximizing behavior than more centralized systems. That, however, assumes that all this activity is occurring within the context of a single central government. When public functions are moved out of that central government into autonomous or quasi-autonomous organizations with limited connections to government, the logic becomes somewhat different. When public functions are hived off, they are more likely to become subject to a variety of methods for enforcing accountability, including the market. Further, off-line organizations are less likely to be protected against claims of accountability simply because they are a public organization now that they are at least in part in the private sector. Finally, the actions of autonomous organizations may become more visible to clients and the public when they are forced to stand alone in the economy and society, rather than being components of larger government entities. All of these changes in their conditions may make success at budget maximization less probable.

The available evidence about changes in delivery systems among the European countries is mixed. On the one hand, there has been substantial interest in the development of off-line organizations for service delivery (Hood and Schuppert 1988; Barker 1982; Sharkansky 1978) and some evidence of their continuing development. Even for organizations that remain entirely within the public sector, there is some evidence of greater autonomy and less direct control by the ministries. On the other hand, an earlier investigation found that, in France, the principal area of organization activity is within the ministries themselves, while in Sweden, the principal locus of organizational activity is on the periphery (Peters 1988). Locus of organization does not appear to affect public expenditure or personnal changes. The real impact of such organizational differences may appear at a much finer level of control over policy. In the United Kingdom, however, it does appear that organizational format is important for control: the Thatcher government invested a good deal of effort in "quango bashing" (Holland and Fallon 1978); subsequently, it created its own quangos. In summary, the evidence on this point is inconclusive. There is a wide range of organizational arrangements in

European governments, but they have had little apparent impact on the success of public bureaucracies in budgeting.

Conclusions

This chapter has covered a good deal of territory, I hope conceptually as well as geographically. It attempted to explicate how the Niskanen model of bureaucratic budget maximization and expansion can be understood and tested within the context of Western European countries. Their bureaucratic systems are at once very different from one another and from that of the United States. I attempted to order and organize this diversity by discussing several dimensions along which these systems vary, identifying the feature that might influence the applicability of the budget-maximizing model.

The evidence obtained provides rather little empirical support for the Niskanen model. In general, European bureaucracies have not manipulated their systems of government in ways that maximize their own budgets and improve the economic positions of their members—especially of their top-level members. There are several qualifications to a sweeping statement that the model was not supported. One is that the time period being investigated does appear to make a difference. Bureaucracies did somewhat better during the 1950s and 1960s, and even into the 1970s, than they have since. This changing fortune is almost certainly a function of changing economic circumstances and changing political fashions. Some of the apparent loss of political power by the bureaucracy—for example, salary compression and attacks on perquisites—began however, prior to the 1980s.

Another qualification is that the conditions of the lower echelons of the European public bureaucracies did improve during the postwar era. During a period of perceived affluence, it was easy to increase wages with some assurance, since economic growth would pay for those increases. Further, the public sector was increasingly unionized during the postwar period, and these unions have been strong advocates for improved compensation for the lower echelons. Finally, the skills required for many jobs have now

raded, for example, the computerization of clerical and
secretarial work, and with greater skills has come increased pay.
This is not what the budget-maximizing model of the bureaucracy
would have predicted, but these have been important changes in
the public sector.

It is impossible to deny that there has been substantial growth
and development in the public sector during the postwar period.
What is possible to deny, however, is that this growth has benefited the senior civil service more than other government workers.
The most obvious beneficiaries appear to have been the clients of
public programs, rather than the workers administering those programs. To the extent that workers have been beneficiaries, it has
been the lower echelons who have been advantaged the most.

This discussion does not mean, however, that the public bureaucracy is not an important political actor in Western European
politics. There is simply too much systematic and anecdotal evidence to think otherwise. What it does indicate is that the power
of the bureaucracy apparently is exercised differently, and perhaps
for different purposes, than is assumed in many of the rational
choice approaches to bureaucracy. That power may be used to
maximize service to clients rather than to maximize personal benefits. Or it may be used to change (or defend) policies that have
nothing to do with direct benefits to the civil service. Finally, it
may be used to defend the status quo and the powerful position
of the civil service, which may require self-effacement rather than
self-aggrandizement. The public bureaucracy may by now have
become too central a policy maker in contemporary governments
to allow it to engage in the type of self-seeking implied in the
Niskanen model. This is probably true in the United States; it is
certainly true in Europe.

NOTES

1. Budgetary expansion may, however, be used rationally to evade
accountability. For example, it can be argued that ministries in Belgium
have pushed for higher appropriations in order to make the issue "how
much," rather than "for what," when budget time comes.

2. An additional insight into organizational strategies for developing

and utilizing budgetary fat or slack can be gained from the literature on the population ecology of organizations. See Britain and Freeman (1980) and Zammuto (1988).

3. By decentralization here I am referring primarily to placing operations and power outside ministries or to differentiating the organizational structure of a ministry and then allocating power to the lower echelons of those structures. I am referring only incidentally to giving additional policy-making powers to subnational governments.

4. Although seemingly extremely autonomous, the boards are coordinated and controlled by legal requirements. Some requirements apply to the conduct of all boards, while others are specific to individual boards.

5. To Niskanen's point about competitive organizations could be added the more general considerations raised by Martin Landau (1969) as "the rationality of redundancy."

6. Again, any personnel recruiting by individual agencies is conducted in the context of well-articulated legal criteria for appointment as a civil servant.

7. Every paper on this general subject requires a reference to *Yes, Minister* (Lynn and Jay 1981). This is mine.

8. The major exception to this generalization is the power of Congress as a sponsor in the United States. Despite the common characterization as a weak controller, Congress does have a sizable staff, substantial expertise in most public programs, and the Congressional Budget Office to enhance its capacity to scrutinize public expenditure issues.

REFERENCES

Aberbach, J. D., R. D. Putnam, and B. A. Rockman. 1981. *Politicians and bureaucrats in western democracies.* Cambridge, Mass.: Harvard Univ. Press.

Anton, T. J. 1980. *Administered democracy.* Boston: Martinus Nijhoff.

Baecque, F. de, and J.-L. Quermonne. 1981. *Administration et politique sous la Cinquieme République.* Paris: Presses de la Fondation nationale des sciences politiques.

Barker, A. 1981. *Quangos in British goverment.* London: Macmillan.

Blackstone, T., and W. Plowden. 1988. *Inside the think tank.* London: Heinemann.

Blais, A., and S. Dion. 1988. Are bureaucrats budget maximizers? The Niskanen model and its critics. Department of Political Science, Univ. of Montreal.

Blondel, J. 1988. Ministerial careers and the nature of parliamentary government: The cases of Austria and Belgium. *European Journal of Political Research* 16:51–71.

Brittain, J. W., and J. H. Freeman. 1980. Organizational proliferation and density dependent selection. In *The organizational life cycle,* ed. J. R. Kimberly and R. H. Miles. San Francisco: Jossey-Bass.

Byatt, I. G. R. 1977. Theoretical issues in expenditure decisions. In *Public expenditure: Allocation among competing ends,* ed. M. V. Posner. Cambridge: Cambridge Univ. Press.

Campbell, C., and G. Szablowski. 1979. *The superbureaucrats: Structure and behaviour in central agencies.* Toronto: Macmillan.

Campbell, J. C. 1988. Afterword on policy communities: A framework for comparative research. *Governance* 2:86–94.

Cassesse, S. 1988. Italy. *Public administration in developed democracies,* ed. D. C. Rowat. New York: Marcel Dekker.

Central Statistical Office. Annual. *Civil Service Statistics.* London: HMSO.

Chiver, K. 1988. Flexible pay in the civil service. *Public Money* 8:51–54.

Cmnd. 8147. 1981. *Inquiry into the value of pensions* (Scott Report). London: HMSO.

Cmnd. 8590. 1982. *Inquiry into civil service pay* (Megaw Report). London: HMSO.

Coneybeare, J. 1984. Bureaucracy, monopoly and competition: A critical analysis of the budget maximizing model of bureaucracy. *American Journal of Political Science* 28:479–502.

Cusack, T. R., T. Notermans, and M. Rein. 1989. Political-economic aspects of public employment. *European Journal of Political Research* 17:441–500.

Darbel, A., and D. Schnapper. 1972. *Le système administratif.* Paris: Mouton.

Davis, O. A., M. A. H. Dempster, and A. Wildavsky. 1974. Toward a predictive theory of the federal budgetary process. *British Journal of Political Science* 4:419–52.

Day, P., and R. Klein. 1987. *Accountabilities: Five public services.* London: Tavistock.

Derlien, H.-U. 1988. Reprecussions of government change on the career civil service in West Germany: The case of 1969 and 1982. *Governance* 1:50–78.

Dich, J. S. 1973. *Den herskende klasse.* Copenhagen: Borgen.

Downs, A. 1967. *Inside bureaucracy.* Boston: Little, Brown.

Dunleavy, P. 1985. Bureaucrats, budgets and the growth of the state: Reconstructing an incremental model. *British Journal of Political Science* 15:299–320.

Duvilliers, P., and J.-M. Pauti. 1975. *Rémunération et avantages sociaux dans la fonction publique*. Paris: Berger-Levrault.

Dyson, K. H. F. 1980. *The state tradition in Western Europe*. Oxford: Martin Robertson.

Ericksson, B. 1983. Sweden's budget system in a changing world. *Public Budgeting and Finance* 3:64–80.

Fenno, R. F. 1966. *The power of the purse: Appropriation politics in Congress*. Boston: Little, Brown.

Fournier, J. 1987. *Le travail gouvernmental*. Paris: Dalloz.

Goodin, R. E. 1975. The logic of bureaucratic back-scratching. *Public Choice* 21:53–67.

———. 1982. Rational politicians and rational bureaucrats in Washington and Whitehall. *Public Administration* 60:23–41.

Gremion, C. 1979. *Profession: Décideurs*. Paris: Gauthier Villars.

Gretton, J., and A. Harrison. 1982. *How much are public servants worth?* Oxford: Basil Blackwell.

Gruber, J. E. 1987. *Controlling bureaucracies: Dilemmas of democratic governance*. Berkeley, Calif.: Univ. of California Press.

Gustafsson, S. 1976. *Lönebildning och lönestruktur inom den statliga sektorn*. Stockholm: Industriens Utredningsinstitut.

Hadenius, A. 1979. Ämbetsverk, Styrelsen. *Statsvetenskapliga tidskrift* 81:19–32.

Headey, B. 1974. *British cabinet ministers*. London: Macmillan.

Heclo, H. 1977. *A government of strangers*. Washington, D.C.: Brookings.

———. 1978. Issue networks and the executive establishment. In *The new American political system*, ed. A. King. Washington, D.C.: American Enterprise Institute.

Heclo, H., and A. Wildavsky. 1974. *The private government of public money*. Berkeley: Univ. of California Press.

Heisler, M. O. 1979. Corporate pluralism: Where is the theory? *Scandinavian Political Studies* 2:277–98.

Heller, P. S., and A. A. Tait. 1983. *Government employment and pay: Some international comparisons*. Washington, D.C.: Internatioal Monetary Fund.

Hogwood, B. W. 1988. The rise and fall and rise of the department of trade and industry. In *Organizing governance, governing organizations*, ed. C. Campbell and B. G. Peters. Pittsburgh, Pa.: Univ. of Pittsburgh Press.

Hogwood, B. W., and B. G. Peters. 1983. *Policy dynamics*. Brighton: Wheatsheaf.

Holland, P., and M. Fallon. 1978. *The quango explosion*. London: Conservative Political Centre.

Hood, C., A. Dunsire, and S. Thomson. 1988. Rolling back the state: Thatcherism, Fraserism and bureaucracy. *Governance* 1:243–70.

Hood, C., M. Huby, and A. Dunsire. 1984. Bureaucrats and budgeting benefits: How do British central government departments measure up? *Journal of Public Policy* 4:163–79.

Hood, C., and G. F. Schuppert. 1988. *Delivering Public Services in Western Europe.* London: Sage.

International Labour Office. Annual. *Year Book of Labour Statistics.* Geneva: ILO.

International Monetary Fund. Annual. *Government Finance Statistics Yearbook.* Washington, D.C.: IMF.

Inter-Parliamentary Union. 1986. *Legislatures of the World.* New York: Facts on File.

Jackson, P. 1982. *The political economy of bureaucracy.* Oxford: Phillip Allen.

Jenkins, K., K. Cairnes, and A. Jackson. 1988. *Improving management in government: The next steps.* Ibbs Report. London: HMSO.

Johansen, L. N., and O. P. Kristensen. 1982. Corporatist traits in Denmark, 1946–1976. In *Patterns of corporatist policymaking,* ed. G. Lehmbruch and P. C. Schmitter. London: Sage.

Johnson, N. 1983. *State and government in the Federal Republic of Germany.* 2nd. ed. Oxford: Pergamon.

Jordan, A. G., and J. J. Richardson. 1987. *Government and pressure groups in Britain.* Oxford: Clarendon Press.

Katz, R. S. 1986. Party government: A rationalistic concept. In *Visions and Realities of Party Government,* ed. F. G. Castles and Rudolf Wildenmann. Berlin: deGruyter.

Kaufman, G. 1980. *How to be a cabinet minister.* London: Sidgwick and Jackson.

Kessler, M.-C. 1986. *Les grands corps de l'état.* Paris: Presse de la Fondation Nationale des Sciences Politiques.

Kogan, M. 1973. *Comments on Niskanen's* bureaucracy: Servant or master? London: Institute of Economic Affairs.

Kristensen, O. P. 1980. The logic of bureaucratic decision-making as a cause of government growth: Or why the expansion of public programmes is a private good and their restriction is a 'public good.' *European Journal of Political Research* 8:249–64.

Kvavik, R. 1980. *Interest groups in Norwegian politics.* Oslo: Universitetsforlaget.

Landau, M. 1969. The rationality of redundancy. *Public Administration Review* 29:346–58.

Lane, J.-E. 1987. The concept of bureaucracy. In *Bureaucracy and political choice*. London: Sage.

Lauxmann, F. 1974. *Was sind uns die beamten wert?* Stuttgart: Deustsche Verlag.

Lepper, M. 1983. Internal structure of public office. In *Public administration in the Federal Republic of Germany,* ed. K. König, H. J. von Oertzen, and F. Wagener. Boston: Kluwer.

Levine, C. H. 1988. Human resource erosion and the uncertain future of the US civil service: From policy gridlock to structural fragmentation. *Governance* 1:115–43.

Lynn, J., and A. Jay. 1981. *Yes, minister: The diaries of a cabinet minister.* Vol. 1. London: British Broadcasting Corp.

Mackenzie, G. C., ed. 1987. *The in-and-outers*. Baltimore, Md.: Johns Hopkins Univ. Press.

March, J. G., and J. P. Olsen. 1984. The new institutionalism: Organizational factors in political life. *American Political Science Review* 78: 734–49.

Martin, J. 1982. Public sector employment trends in western industrialized economies. In *Public finance and public employment,* ed. R. H. Haveman. Detroit, Mich.: Wayne State Univ. Press.

Mayntz, R. 1984. German federal bureaucrats and administration: A functional elite between policy and administration. In *Bureaucrats and policymaking,* ed. E. N. Suleiman. New York: Holmes and Meier.

Meijer, H. 1969. Bureaucracy and policy formation in Sweden. *Scandinavian Political Studies* 4:103–16.

Mellbourn, A. 1986. *Bortom det starka samhellet.* Stockholm: Carlssons.

Meyer, M., W. Stevenson, and S. Webster. 1985. *Limits to bureaucratic growth.* Berlin: de Gruyter.

Meyers, F. 1985. *La politisation de l'administration.* Brussels: Institut International des Sciences Administratives.

Ministère de la Fonction et du Plan. Annual. *La fonction publique de l'état.* Paris: La Documentation Française.

Mohr, L. B. 1973. The concept of the organizational goal. *American Political Science Review* 67:470–81.

Niskanen, W. A. 1971. *Bureaucracy and representative government.* Chicago: Aldine Atherton.

OECD. 1982. *Employment in the public sector.* Paris: Organization for Economic Cooperation and Development.

———. Monthly. *National accounts of OECD member countries.* Paris: OECD.

———. Annual. *OECD economic outlook.* Paris: OECD.

Olsen, J. P. 1985. *Organized democracy.* Bergen: Universitetsforlaget.

Orzechowski, W. 1977. Economic models of bureaucracy: Survey, extensions, evidence. In *Budgets and bureaucrats,* ed. T. E. Borcherding. Durham, N.C.: Duke Univ. Press.

Page, E. C. 1985. *Political authority and bureaucratic power.* Knoxville: Univ. of Tennessee Press.

Peacock, A. T. 1983. Public x-inefficiency: Informational and institutional constraints. In *Anatomy of government deficiencies,* ed. H. Hanusch. Berlin: Springer.

Peters, B. G. 1981. The problem of bureaucratic government. *Journal of Politics* 43:56–82.

———. 1988. *Comparing public bureaucracies.* Tuscaloosa: Univ. of Alabama Press.

———. 1989. *The politics of bureaucracy.* 3d. ed. New York: Longman.

Peters, B. G., and M. O. Heisler. 1983. Thinking about public sector growth. In *Why government grows,* ed. C. L. Taylor. Beverly Hills, Calif.: Sage.

Pierce, W. S. 1981. *Bureaucratic failure and public expenditure.* New York: Humanities Press.

Pollitt, C. 1983. *Manipulating the machine.* London: Allen and Unwin.

Pougnard, P. 1980. Les traitements. *La Fonction Publique* 2. Paris: Les Cahiers Français.

Py, R. 1985. *Le secrétariat général du gouvernement.* Paris: La Documentation Française.

Rigaud, J., and X. Delcros. 1986. *Les institutions administratives Françaises, le fonctionnement.* Paris: Dalloz.

Rokkan. S. 1966. Norway: Numerical democracy and corporate pluralism. In *Political oppositions in western democracies,* ed. R. A. Dahl. New Haven, Conn.: Yale Univ. Press.

Rose, R. 1974. *The problem of party government.* London: Macmillan.

Rose, R., and B. G. Peters. 1978. *Can government go bankrupt?* New York: Basic Books.

Rose, R., et al. 1985. *Public employment in western nations.* Cambridge: Cambridge Univ. Press.

Ruin, O. 1989. The duality of Swedish central administration: Ministries and central agencies. In *Comparative public administration,* ed. A. Frazamand. New York: Marcel Dekker.

Salamon, L. B. 1981. Rethinking public management. *Public Policy* 29:255–75.

Scharpf, F. W., B. Reissert, and F. Schnabel. 1976. *Politikverflechtung: Theorie und emperie des kooperativen foederalismus.* Kronberg: Scriptor.

Schick, A. 1986. Macro-budgetary adaptations to fiscal stress. *Public Administration Review* 46:124–34.

Schmitter, P. C. 1974. Still the century of corporatism? *Review of Politics* 36:85–131.

Seidman, H., and R. Gilmour. 1986. *Politics, power and position*. 4th. ed. New York: Oxford Univ. Press.

Self, P. 1972. *Administrative theories and politics*. London: Allen and Unwin.

Sharkansky, I. 1978. *Whither the state?* Chatham, N.J.: Chatham House.

Skowronek, S. 1982. *Building a new American state*. Cambridge: Cambridge University Press.

Smith, B. C. 1988. *Bureaucracy and political power*. Brighton, Sussex: Wheatsheaf.

Sorenson, R. 1987. Bureaucratic decision-making and the growth of public expenditures. In *Bureaucracy and public choice*, ed. J. E. Lane. London: Sage.

SOU. 1985. *Regeringen, myndigheterna och myndigheternas ledning*. Stockholm: Sveriges Offentliga Utredningar.

Ståhlberg, K. 1988. Finland. In *Public administration in developed democracies*, ed. D. C. Rowat. New York: Marcel Dekker.

Statistiches Bundesamt. Annual. *Statistiches Jahrbuch für die Bundesrepublik Deutschland*. Wiesbaden: Statistiches Bundesamt.

Statistika Centralbyrån. Annual. *Statsanställda*. Stockholm: Statistika Centralbyrån.

Stevens, A. 1985. "L'alternance" and the higher civil service. In *Socialism, the state and public policy in France*, ed. P. G. Cerny and M. A. Schain. London: Frances Pinter.

Suleiman, E. N. 1986. *Parliaments and parliamentarians in democratic politics*. New York: Holmes and Meier.

Tarschys, D., and M. Eduards. 1975. *Petita: Hur svenska myndigheter argumenter för högre anslag*. Stockholm: Publica.

Timsit, G. 1987. *Administrations et êtats: Etude comparée*. Paris: Presses Univ. de France.

Tullock, G. 1965. *The politics of bureaucracy*. Washington, D.C.: Public Affairs Press.

Walker, J. 1989. Introduction: Policy communities as global phenomena. *Governance* 2:1–4.

Wurtzen, H. 1977. Strukturrationalisering af det offentliges virksomhed: Et dansk forsog. *Nordisk Administrativt Tidskrift* 58:5–17.

Zammuto, R. F. 1988. Organizational adaptation: Some implications of organizational ecology for strategic choice. *Journal of Management Studies* 25:105–20.

ANDRÉ BLAIS AND
STÉPHANE DION

Conclusion:
Are Bureaucrats Budget Maximizers?

The empirical findings reviewed in the eleven chapters of this book are extremely varied; some findings tend to support the budget-maximizing bureaucrat model, but others are inconsistent with it or suggest that the model should be substantially amended. In this conclusion, we highlight what we believe to be the major findings and discuss their implications.

First, there is ample evidence that *bureaucrats systematically request larger budgets*. This simple but basic fact has been known for a long time. In his classic *The Politics of the Budgetary Process,* Wildavsky asserts that "it is usually correct to assume that department officials are devoted to increasing their appropriations" (1964, 19). Indeed, Niskanen was aware of Wildavsky's work and quotes him in his book. His characterization of the bureaucrat's maximand was quite consistent with political scientists' common knowledge in the late sixties.

Unfortunately, the evidence on this commonsense proposition is rather thin. The many studies that examined budget requests and appropriations (see, for instance, Kamlet and Mowery 1983) fail to report average increases. We suppose they do not care to discuss a pattern (requests for large increases) that is part of the conventional wisdom. The fact that the proposition has not been challenged leads us to believe that it is likely to be true. And at least one study strongly confirms it. Leloup and Moreland (1978) analyzed 500 cases of requests and appropriations in thirty-six agencies of the

U.S. Department of Agriculture between 1941 and 1971; they report that the mean request is a 41 percent increase. The case studies reviewed by Lynn (chapter 3) lead to the same conclusion: the great majority of bureaucrats want and ask for more money. Our own study (chapter 8) also shows that they are more likely to vote for parties more favorable to state intervention.

The assumption that bureaucrats seek larger budgets is shared by the other players in the game; Aucoin (chapter 5) notes that budget control procedures have been put in place by politicians of all persuasions who are convinced that bureaucrats do indeed seek to maximize their budgets. Finally, studies of budget proposals by school superintendents in the United States convey the same message. Taxes are assessed as high as they can be without having to go to the voters. When the proposal has to be approved by referendum, it is often turned down, and the subsequent proposed budget has to be reduced. The whole pattern is in accord with the budget-maximizing hypothesis (Kiewiet, chapter 6).

There remains the question of whether requesting a budget increase entails a maximizing strategy. Case studies indicate that few bureaucrats seek extremely large increases in their budgets (Lynn, chapter 3). This could correspond to a long-term maximizing strategy; bureaucrats know, to quote Wildavsky "there is a reasonable range within which a decision can fall and they just follow ordinary prudence in coming out with an estimate near the top" (22). They request moderate annual increases in order to maximize their total budget over the long haul. It could also be that bureaucrats' prime value is security (Peters 1978, 175) and that, while they certainly welcome a somewhat larger budget, they do not aim for very large increases. To the extent that he or she is risk aversive (Kahneman and Tversky 1984), the bureaucrat will also be more concerned with preventing or resisting budgetary cuts than with obtaining the largest possible increase. The evidence, therefore, supports a budget-boosting strategy as much as (or perhaps even more than) a budget-maximizing one (Blais and Dion 1990).

Second, it is clear that *bureaucrats do not benefit much financially from budget increases.* Peters (chapter 11) reports that personnel costs are a declining share of public expenditure and the gross domestic product in most countries. Furthermore, there has been a narrowing of salary differentials within the public sector. As a consequence, salaries for top civil servants have lagged behind wage movements in the whole economy. Cousineau and Girard (chapter 10) note that the impact of unions on wages is lower in the public sector.

Current research (Young, chapter 2) also indicates little relationship between the growth of bureaus and bureaucrats' salaries. This is so in great part because seniority is a crucial ingredient of the bureaucratic labor market; Johnson and Libecap (1989) observe that in the United States, automatic grade step increases account for two-thirds of a typical bureaucrat's salary gain over the first eighteen years of employment. The evidence, it should be stressed, is not as devastating for the model as it might first appear. The Grandjean study, reviewed by Young, concludes that the hypothesis that bureau growth contributes to better career opportunities is incomplete but useful. Likewise, the Johnson-Libecap study produced at least one positive result (Young, chapter 2). Furthermore, each study presents certain lacunae; we lack a panel analysis of individual careers over a long period of time. Still, it is hard to dispute Young's conclusion that "any benefits likely to accrue to bureaucrats who succeed in obtaining larger staffs and budgets for their agency seem . . . small" (ibid.).

This raises an interesting enigma. Why is it that bureaucrats systematically request larger budgets if it is not in their best interest to do so? Three possible answers can be offered. First, bureaucrats may seek increased budgets because of their values, regardless of their self-interests. The case studies reviewed by Lynn (chapter 3), as well as the interviews analyzed by Campbell and Naulls (chapter 4), indicate that many civil servants are mission-minded: they are committed to improve the quality of service to the public. To the extent that their mission entails an increased budget, they will press for it. Likewise, the propensity to request larger budgets could reflect a more general leftist orientation in the public sector (Blake, chapter 9). A second interpretation is that senior bureaucrats seek larger budgets because they define their interest not in financial terms, as it is measured in the empirical literature, but rather in terms of power, prestige, and promotions, all of which are facilitated by a larger budget. Unfortunately, we do not have any direct evidence on this particular hypothesis. A third possibility is that the majority of bureaucrats mistakenly believe that it is in their interest to get increased budgets.

There is scant evidence to assess the validitiy of these three interpretations. However, we find it difficult to believe that bureaucrats systematically misread their interests or behave without considering them at all. Perhaps the most plausible view is that they seek larger budgets because they believe these budgets are warranted (the value interpretation) *and* improve their lot (the utility hypothesis).

Third, *bureaucrats have a substantial impact on budgetary outcomes, and that impact usually means a larger budget.* Cousineau and Girard (chapter 10) indicate that the presence of a public sector union in a municipality tends to increase government expenditures by about 6 percent. Kiewiet (chapter 6) notes that the oversupply hypothesis leads to the prediction that elasticities for bureaucratic production should be less than minus one and that the empirical findings tend to confirm the prediction. Kiewiet also reports a consensus in the literature to the effect that the U.S. Congress engages in little monitoring of bureaucratic behavior, a pattern consistent with the model's assumption that politicians are not strongly motivated to control bureaucrats. Likewise, in parliamentary systems, cabinet members are primarily concerned with defending their department's budget. As one of them candidly admitted, "Ministers are judged by how much money they can spend and how well they can extract money from the system for their projects" (Chrétien, 1986, 72). Unfortunately, we do not have much reliable evidence to confirm or disconfirm Niskanen's assertion that politicians lack information about a bureau's operations and production costs (Kiewiet, chapter 6). The mere fact that productivity is extremely difficult to measure in the public sector (Cousineau and Girard, chapter 10) is consistent with this assumption, but we need to know much more on this question.

Finally, *politicians are far from being powerless in budgetary decisions.* Clearly, the idea of a passive sponsor has to be rejected. The evidence that public spending is related to the partisan composition of government (Castles 1982) and is affected by the electoral cycle (Rogoff 1990; Blais and Nadeau, forthcoming) shows that politicians do exert substantial control on budgetary matters. In the same vein, Campbell and Naulls (chapter 4) report that the budget-maximizing strategy was less prevalent under the Reagan adminis-

tration than under the Carter administration. In the United Kingdom, the Conservative government managed to reduce the size of
the civil service by 18 percent (Dunsire, chapter 7). Aucoin (chapter
5) argues that management reforms have changed the bureaucratic
culture in many countries; self-restraint has become a norm directly
competing with the (traditional) budget-maximizing strategy. Last,
Lynn (chapter 3) stresses the fact that the budgetary game is an
interactive one, in which bureaucrats must anticipate other actors'
reactions. Niskanen seems to acknowledge the validity of these
criticisms. In chapter 1, he contends that the discretionary budget
will be spent in ways that serve the interests of the bureaucrats and
the political authorities, through bilateral bargaining.

What do these various pieces of evidence tell us about the overall
usefulness of the budget-maximizing model? Three observations
must be made before we attempt to answer the question. First, as
we pointed out in the introduction, it is crucial to distinguish the
major propositions of the model; some may be more interesting
than others. Second, in many cases the evidence is still ambiguous,
and any judgment on the validity of the model must be tentative.
Third, any general assessment hinges on considerations about
which aspects of the model are deemed the most important.

With these reservations in mind, we can state our own position.
The great appeal of the Niskanen model lies, we believe, in its
capacity to account for the well-established propensity of bureaucrats to seek larger budgets. It does make sense to assume that
bureaucrats attempt to maximize their budgets and to make that
assumption the central proposition of a theory of bureaucratic
behavior. (From our perspective it is irrelevant whether it is the
total budget or the discretionary budget; it could be a mixture of
the two.) Indeed, we have not come across any other proposition
that would seem to apply as widely to the whole bureaucracy. Of
course, the proposition does not hold everywhere and at every
point in time, but the pattern is consistent enough to serve as the
building block of a theory.

The model asserts that the maximizing strategy is driven by
well-conceived interests. As we have seen, the evidence on this is
far from conclusive. The direct benefits associated with increased
budgets seem to be small. It looks more plausible to suppose that

their values as much as their interests induce bureaucrats to seek larger budgets.

Last, the proposition that bureaucrats are all-powerful in their relationship with politicians must be dismissed. This, of course, does not mean that bureaucrats do not have any influence on budgetary outcomes—their influence is still an open question. It should also be pointed out that the model has the advantage of stressing a particular power resource (information), which is of great theoretical interest.

There are two ways to react to these various observations. On the negative side, one can argue that the first central assumption of the model (bureaucrats seek larger budgets) is only partly right: the evidence supports a budget-boosting rather than a budget-maximizing strategy, and the link between that strategy and bureaucratic interests is tenuous. In the same vein, one can point out that the second major assumption (bureaucrats systematically manage to maximize their budgets) is simply dead wrong. From a more positive perspective, one can contend that the first and most basic proposition captures a crucial aspect of bureaucratic behavior and that, even though bureaucrats are not as powerful as the model assumes, they do exert some influence and precisely for the reasons (the information gap) suggested by Niskanen. We conclude that the theory is useful in pointing out an important aspect of bureaucratic behavior and strategy, that it has some serious shortcomings, that it needs to be substantially amended, and that more research needs to be done on many points.

We would like to end with a suggestion on what we believe to be a top research priority. It seems to us that the most important task now is to examine in depth the link, at the microlevel, between budgets and bureaucratic interests, especially with respect to promotions. It appears that bureaucrats' salaries are largely independent of budget increases, mainly because of uniform pay increases across the whole public sector. It is possible, however, that senior bureaucrats who manage to get increased budgets (or to avoid cuts) are more likely to accumulate prestige, to be perceived as dynamic, and consequently, to get promoted. It is also possible that budget minimizers are mainly outsiders (Dunsire, chapter 7) or political appointees with no roots in the bureaucracy, bound to leave as soon as the government that appointed them is replaced. In short, we need to understand precisely when, where, and how the ability to obtain larger budgets contributes to promotions.

The book has assembled many diverse pieces of evidence on the budget-maximizing bureaucrat model. In this conclusion, we have focused on the findings that appear the most central. Obviously, many other observations should be taken into account. We hope that readers will be able, on the basis of the whole array of findings reported and discussed here, to reach their own conclusions on the merits and limits of the model, and that fruitful research avenues will come to their minds.

REFERENCES

Blais, André, and Stéphane Dion. 1990. Are bureaucrats budget maximizers? The Niskanen model and its critics. *Polity* 13:655–75.

Blais, André, and Richard Nadeau. Forthcoming. The budget electoral cycle. *Public Choice*.

Castles, Francis G. 1982. The impact of parties on public expenditure. In *The impact of parties: Politics and policies in democratic capitalist states,* ed. Francis G. Castles. Beverly Hills, Calif.: Sage.

Chrétien, Jean. 1986. *Straight from the hearth.* Toronto: Key Porter.

Johnson, Ronald N., and Gary D. Libecap. 1989. Agency growth, salaries and the protected bureaucrat. *Economic Inquiry* 27.431–51.

Kahneman, Daniel, and Amos Tversky. 1984. Choices, values and frames. *American Psychologist* 39:341–50.

Kamlet, Mark C., and David Mowery. 1983. Budgeting side payments and government growth: 1953–1968. *American Journal of Political Science* 27:636–64.

Leloup, Lance T., and William B. Moreland. 1978. Agency strategies and executive review: The hidden politics of budgeting. *Public Administration Review* 38:232–39.

Peters, B. Guy. 1978. *The politics of bureaucracy: A comparative perspective.* New York: Longman.

Rogoff, Kenneth. 1990. Equilibrium political budget cycles. *American Economic Review* 80:21–36.

Wildavsky, Aaron. 1964. *The politics of the budgetary process.* Boston: Little, Brown.

Notes on Contributors

Peter Aucoin is professor of political science and public administration at Dalhousie University, Halifax. He is the author and editor of ten books on Canadian government and administration, the most recent being *The Centralization-Decentralization Conundrum: Organizational Design and Management in Canadian Government*. In 1990–91 he was director of research for the Canadian Royal Commission on Electoral Reform and Party Financing.

André Blais is a professor in the department of political science and a research fellow with the Centre de recherche et développement en économique at the University of Montreal. He is also associate editor of *Canadian Public Policy*. He is the author of *A Political Sociology of Public Aid to Industry* and articles in the *British Journal of Political Science, Comparative Political Studies, Public Choice, European Journal of Political Research,* and other journals.

Donald E. Blake is professor and head of the Department of Political Science at the University of British Columbia, Vancouver. His areas of interest are public opinion and voting, Canadian politics, and comparative politics. He is coauthor of *Two Political Worlds: Parties and Voting in British Columbia, Grassroots Politicians: Party Activists in British Columbia,* and "The Public Private Sector Cleavage in North America."

Colin Campbell, S.J., is the University Professor in the Isabelle and Henry Martin Chair of Philosophy and Politics at Georgetown

363

University, Washington, D.C., where he is also director of the Graduate Public Policy Program. He is co-founder and co-editor of *Governance* and has published several books including *Managing the Presidency: Carter, Reagan and the Search for Executive Harmony; The Canadian State: A Lobby from Within;* and *Politics and Government in Europe Today.*

Jean-Michel Cousineau is a professor in the Ecole de relations industrielles and a fellow at the Centre de recherche et développement en économique at the University of Montreal. His publications in English include "Imperfect Information and Strike Activity: An Analysis of Canadian Evidence," "The Determinants of Minimum Wage Rates" (coauthor), "The Impact of Foreign Ownerships on Strike Activity" (coauthor), and "The Determinants of Escalator Clause in Collective Agreements" (coauthor).

Stéphane Dion, a specialist in public administration and organization theory, is associate professor, Department of Political Science, University of Montreal. He is currently studying the public/private sector cleavage in attitudes and voting, as well as the policies of governments and political parties toward the public sector, in North America and Europe. His major publications include *La politisation des mairies,* and articles in *Governance, Polity,* and *Comparative Political Studies.*

Andrew Dunsire is emeritus professor of politics at the University of York, England. His areas of interest include bureaumetrics and the applications of control theory to the study of governance. His major publications include *Administration: The Word and the Science; Implementation in a Bureaucracy; Control in a Bureaucracy;* and *Cutback Management in Public Bureaucracies: Popular Theories and Observed outcomes in Whitehall* (coauthor).

Anne-Marie Girard is an economist at the Centre de recherche et développement en économique at the University of Montreal. Her major research interests are health and safety at work, public policy, and trade unions.

D. Roderick Kiewiet is professor of political science at the California Institute of Technology, Pasadena. His major research interests are political economy and American public policy. He is the author of *Macroeconomics and Micropolitics: The Electoral Effects of Economic Issues* and *The Logic of Delegation: Congressional Parties and the Appropriations Process* (coauthor), as well as numerous articles.

Laurence E. Lynn, Jr., is professor of social service administration and of public policy studies at the University of Chicago. He has held senior positions with the federal government and chaired National Academy of Sciences/National Research Council committees on Child Development Research and Public Policy and on National Urban Policy. His most recent book is *Managing Public Policy.*

Donald Naulls is assistant professor of political science at Saint Mary's University, Halifax, Nova Scotia. His research interests include the comparative study of political chief executives, public policy, and empirical theory and methodology. His articles include "Policy Makers and Facilitators: The Boundaries Between Two Bureaucratic Roles" (coauthor) and "Social-Science Training as Related to the Policy Roles of U.S. Career Officials and Appointees: The Decline of Analysis."

William A. Niskanen is chairman of the Cato Institute, a policy institute in Washington, D.C. He previously served in several federal positions, as chief economist of the Ford Motor Company, and as a professor at the University of California at Berkeley and at Los Angeles. His primary research interests are policy analysis and public choice. Major publications include *Bureaucracy and Representative Government* and *Reaganomics: An Insider's Account of the Policies and the People.*

B. Guy Peters is Maurice Falk Professor of American Government and chair of the Department of Political Science at the University of Pittsburgh. He is co-editor of *Governance* and formerly co-chair of the International Political Science Association Research Committee on the Structure and Organization of Government. He is the author of numerous books and articles in public policy and public administration, including *The Politics of Bureaucracy, Comparing Public Bureaucracies,* and *Public Administration: Challenges, Choices, Consequences.*

Robert A. Young is associate professor of political science at the University of Western Ontario. He is also co-director of the Political Economy Research Group in the faculty of Social Science. In the field of Canadian politics, he has written on industrial policy, regional policy, federal-provincial relations, public administration, and U.S.-Canadian trade policy.

Pitt Series in Policy and Institutional Studies
Bert A. Rockman, Editor